COMPLETE
Trimwork
& Carpentry

Meredith® **Books**
Des Moines, Iowa

Stanley Complete Trimwork & Carpentry
Editor: Larry Johnston
Senior Associate Design Director: Tom Wegner
Photo Researcher: Harijs Priekulis
Copy Chief: Terri Fredrickson
Publishing Operations Manager: Karen Schirm
Book Production Managers: Pam Kvitne,
    Marjorie J. Schenkelberg, Rick von Holdt, Mark Weaver
Edit and Design Production Coordinator: Mary Lee Gavin
Contributing Copy Editor: Sharon E. McHaney
Technical Editor, The Stanley Works: Mike Maznio
Contributing Proofreaders: Ellen Bingham,
    Fern Marshall Bradley, Sara Henderson
Contributing Photographer: Scott Little
Indexer: Barbara L. Klein
Editorial Assistant: Renee E. McAtee

Creative Resource Group
Publishing Director: Carl Voss
Writer: Robert Settich
Illustrator: Tom Rosborough
Graphic Designer: Tim Abramowitz

CA Photography
Photographers: Craig Anderson, Dennis Kennedy
Director and Set Builder: Brent Boyd

Holtorf Photography
Photographer: John Holtorf

Meredith® Books
Editor in Chief: Linda Raglan Cunningham
Design Director: Matt Strelecki
Managing Editor: Gregory H. Kayko
Executive Editor: Benjamin W. Allen

Publisher: James D. Blume
Executive Director, Marketing: Jeffrey Myers
Executive Director, New Business Development: Todd M. Davis
Executive Director, Sales: Ken Zagor
Director, Operations: George A. Susral
Director, Production: Douglas M. Johnston
Business Director: Jim Leonard

Vice President and General Manager: Douglas J. Guendel

Meredith Publishing Group
President, Publishing Group: Stephen M. Lacy
Vice President-Publishing Director: Bob Mate

Meredith Corporation
Chairman and Chief Executive Officer: William T. Kerr

In Memoriam: E.T. Meredith III (1933-2003)

Additional Photographs
(Photographers or companies listed may retain copyright © to
    listed photos)
L=Left, R=Right, C=Center, B=Bottom, T=Top
Ferche Millwork: 6BL, 8, 9
Ornamental Mouldings Inc.: 7B (all), 16TL, 17, 18, 19, 20, 21,
    22T (three moldings), 23

All of us at Meredith® Books are dedicated to providing you
with the information and ideas you need to enhance your home
and garden. We welcome your comments and suggestions
about this book. Write to us at:
Meredith Books
1716 Locust St.
Des Moines, IA 50309–3023

If you would like more information on other Stanley products,
call 1-800-STANLEY or visit us at: www.stanleyworks.com
Stanley® and the notched rectangle around the Stanley name
are registered trademarks of The Stanley Works and
subsidiaries.

If you would like to purchase any of our home improvement,
cooking, crafts, gardening, or home decorating and design
books, check wherever quality books are sold. Or visit us at:
meredithbooks.com

Note to the Readers: Due to differing conditions, tools,
and individual skills, Meredith Corporation assumes no
responsibility for any damages, injuries suffered, or losses
incurred as a result of following the information published
in this book. Before beginning any project, review the
instructions carefully, and if any doubts or questions remain,
consult local experts or authorities. Because codes and
regulations vary greatly, you always should check with
authorities to ensure that your project complies with all
applicable local codes and regulations. Always read
and observe all of the safety precautions provided by
manufacturers of any tools, equipment, or supplies,
and follow all accepted safety procedures.

Quick Reference Guide

Here are some pages you may want to refer to while planning or building a project. To find broader subjects, such as building a wall, see the complete table of contents, which begins on the next page.

The complete index begins on page 237.

Metric Conversions

U.S. Units to Metric Equivalents			Metric Units to U.S. Equivalents		
To convert from	Multiply by	To get	To convert from	Multiply by	To get
Inches	25.4	Millimeters	Millimeters	0.0394	Inches
Inches	2.54	Centimeters	Centimeters	0.3937	Inches
Feet	30.48	Centimeters	Centimeters	0.0328	Feet
Feet	0.3048	Meters	Meters	3.2808	Feet
Yards	0.9144	Meters	Meters	1.0936	Yards
Square inches	6.4516	Square centimeters	Square centimeters	0.1550	Square inches
Square feet	0.0929	Square meters	Square meters	10.764	Square feet
Square yards	0.8361	Square meters	Square meters	1.1960	Square yards
Acres	0.4047	Hectares	Hectares	2.4711	Acres
Cubic inches	16.387	Cubic centimeters	Cubic centimeters	0.0610	Cubic inches
Cubic feet	0.0283	Cubic meters	Cubic meters	35.315	Cubic feet
Cubic feet	28.316	Liters	Liters	0.0353	Cubic feet
Cubic yards	0.7646	Cubic meters	Cubic meters	1.308	Cubic yards
Cubic yards	764.55	Liters	Liters	0.0013	Cubic yards

To convert from degrees Fahrenheit (F) to degrees Celsius (C), first subtract 32, then multiply by $\frac{5}{9}$.

To convert from degrees Celsius to degrees Fahrenheit, multiply by $\frac{9}{5}$, then add 32.

CONTENTS

ELEMENTS OF STYLE　　6

PLANNING YOUR REMODELING PROJECT　　24

HANGING DOORS　　36

WINDOWS　　64

WALL-BUILDING BASICS　　84

CUSTOMIZING YOUR WALLS　　110

CUSTOMIZING BASEBOARDS　　128

CROWNING TOUCHES 140

GREAT IDEAS 156
THROUGHOUT THE HOUSE

CHOOSING TOOLS 168

CHOOSING MATERIALS 190

TECHNIQUES AND TIPS 202

FINISHING SECRETS 222

ELEMENTS OF STYLE

Moldings give a room personality. Tacking up some generic moldings makes a room look like millions of others, but installing a few stylish moldings brings it to life.

Most homeowners want to express at least a little about themselves through their homes. For some, a spark of originality is enough. But others want to ignite a bonfire of individuality.

Wherever you are in the spectrum of self-expression, you'll need a starting point of inspiration.

Take a deep breath

Inspiration takes many forms. Seeing wainscoting on a wall may bring memories of sun-drenched summer days at a beach cottage to some people. For others, the warm tones of an Arts and Crafts interior may evoke a feeling of serenity and security. Still others will delight in the visual exuberance of a Victorian home.

The best style for you is the one that feels like home. It should bring a powerful and undeniable emotional response that you may not be able to put into words. Instead of a style other people may like but you ultimately will not, pick the style you feel most comfortable with.

Get out the rule book

After you settle on a general style, you may find yourself studying appealing installations, trying to learn the rules behind the style. But instead of rigid regulations, think of what you learn as general guidelines, and realize that even those are frequently shattered.

For example, some people will advocate a wainscot that's 36 inches tall, but others will recommend soaring it to 60 inches. Which one is correct? Both are. That's why you'll sometimes have to resort to mock-ups or chalk lines snapped onto the wall to help you better visualize the completed installation.

Enjoy the process

Individualizing your house isn't as much a destination as a journey. Along the way, you'll cherish discoveries of things you enjoy and discard notions that don't work for you. Enjoy the exploration, and along the way you'll transform your house into a home.

Inspiration arrives in a variety of styles.

CHAPTER PREVIEW

Classical theme and variations
page 8

Paneled walls
page 10

Arts and Crafts style
page 12

Steeped in tradition
page 14

Wall frames abound in both this room and the adjoining hallway. The proportions vary from jumbo widths to slightly wider than a wall sconce.

Wainscoting and corner blocks
page 16

Combining elements
page 18

No secret— it's Victorian
page 20

Ornate decorative moldings
page 22

CLASSICAL THEME AND VARIATIONS

The classics—in both architecture and music—share many elements of style, vocabulary, and methods of expression. For example, both can state a theme and explore its variations.

In the room shown, classically designed elements combine in rhythmic repetition: fluted casings for doors and windows and as fireplace pilasters. But each one has a different width, a variation on the theme. In a similar way, crown molding tops the walls, door casing, and fireplace surround, but each site presents a different interpretation, providing a unity of design but individuality of expression.

— Frieze board

The frieze board above the doorway provides an opportunity to repeat the dentiled crown molding that surrounds the room. The fluted side jambs repeat the pattern of the windows and fireplace.

There wasn't enough room above the windows to install frieze boards like those over the doors, so the windows are trimmed with bevel casings and back boards. Introducing variety to the trim avoids monotony. See the Molding Gallery starting on page 196 for profile details.

The fluted pilaster of the fireplace surround evokes the timeless appearance of a classical column shaft. Appropriately, the crown molding flares outward to mimic the capital that topped a column. The pilaster rests on a plinth (see large photo)—another classical element.

The classical appeal of this room soars with clear-finished birch woodwork.

PANELED WALLS

The Arts and Crafts headboard and bedside tables in the room shown on the opposite page would suggest that this wall treatment follows that same style. But the furniture could be any style—country or cottage, for example—and the paneled walls would still look right at home.

Some people define the walls as a blended style; others say it's best to forget the name game and appreciate that the walls look great no matter what you call them.

For a quick-change display, perch pictures along the cap rail. For a more permanent placement, hang them above the paneled wall.

Paneled walls—about 6 feet high—painted a serene white transform this nook into a sun-drenched retreat.

ARTS AND CRAFTS STYLE

The Arts and Crafts style, which originated during the late-19th and early-20th centuries, was a reaction to the decorative excesses of the Victorian period. This back-to-basics movement banished florid carving and emphasized straight lines and no-nonsense joinery. Quartersawn white oak, with its distinctive tiger-stripe patterning, replaced exotic woods.

If stained oak is too somber or expensive for your taste, less expensive materials with painted finishes are equally authentic.

Quartersawn white oak and impeccable joinery are two hallmarks of the Arts and Crafts style.

Build your own paneled wall following the step-by-step procedure that starts on page 116. Want to cap it with a plate rail? See the directions beginning on page 124. The plate rail can be a separate project or installed as a custom-length wall shelf. The choice is yours.

For all its simplicity of form, the Arts and Crafts style is a visual treat with pleasing proportions and warm tones. Tranquility and harmony make the room a no-stress zone.

STEEPED IN TRADITION

During the 1920s, home design began to move away from rigid period styles as American cities boomed with houses boasting modern conveniences such as electrical wiring and indoor plumbing. Several companies enticed the home buyer with catalogs filled with standard house designs, making house-hunting an armchair experience.

You can easily transplant the traditional elements of the 1920s into your home. Wide casings, a definite do-it-yourself project, allow individual expression in your choice of moldings along their edges.

Picture-hanger molding is another simple project because the materials are affordable and the skills required are modest.

You don't need to make a whole-house choice between painted casings and natural finishes. But neatness is absolutely essential at the junction. If you paint, pry back the casing at the jamb, paint, then tap back into position.

The painted sunroom embraces furnishings of the Arts and Crafts movement. See pages 50–51 and 82–83 for variations on trimming doors and windows.

The window casing isn't Arts and Crafts, but it blends effortlessly with the Stickley-inspired floor clock from that period. Another lesson from this room: Don't be shy with wall colors; bold is beautiful.

A picture-hanger molding nailed near the ceiling can fulfill its traditional role as well as visually serve as a crown molding. To avoid the tedious task of painting the wall color right up to the ceiling line, see page 123.

WAINSCOTING AND CORNER BLOCKS

Some people shy away from wainscoting and other wall treatments, fearing that they will be too much. But consider that vast expanses of plain drywall can be a virtual stylistic desert. With that view, wall treatments can be as refreshing as an oasis.

Corner blocks are another stylistic problem-solver, as well as being an antidote to miter phobia.

The door casing appears Victorian and the wall treatment Arts and Crafts, but the shared paint color unites the two styles.

Corner blocks—like this bull's-eye—are more than a crutch for the miter-impaired. Corner blocks also provide an opportunity to add style and interest to casing around doors and windows.

Beaded-board wainscoting is surprisingly affordable and easily adds style to a room. Paint accessories, such as these wineglass racks, an identical color to blend them into the installation.

COMBINING ELEMENTS

If your ceilings are high enough for a multi-element crown treatment, including it will achieve an effect that's positively regal. And you won't have to create the combinations from scratch. Get your inspiration from this page or the suggestions for built-up crowns beginning on *page 148.*

To unify the design throughout the room, you'll probably use one or more of the elements in a solo role, as with the rope molding in this room.

And just past the doorway of this room is an attractive built-in niche cabinet. Although this one is deeper than a standard stud bay, you can still replicate it by referring to *pages 126–127.*

This built-up crown treatment includes a rope motif that repeats throughout the room (opposite page) for emphasis and unity.

2¾-inch rope chair rail at bottom of multi-element crown

4-inch beaded casing

4-inch rope baseboard

Will a variety of molding styles work together or fight each other? If you have doubts about compatibility, temporarily tack a short length of each molding into place and study the effect over several days.

A 4-inch baseboard with a rope motif neatly ties together with the rope element of the built-up crown treatment.

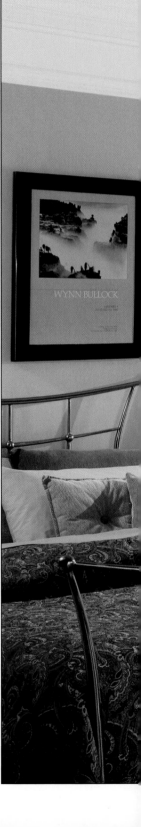

NO SECRET—IT'S VICTORIAN

If there's one guiding principle behind the Victorian style, it's that anything worth doing is worth doing excessively.

Rooms of the period were often decked out in exuberant combinations of colors and patterns that many people today would think positively garish.

So what passes as Victorian today is relatively mild—even with its bold hues, florid wallpaper, and ornate accents. Even though Victorian is nearly no-holds-barred, use a bit of discretion to keep your room from becoming gaudy.

A frieze and crown float freely above a doorway without jambs or casing.

A Victorian-era home? Hardly! This new construction was trimmed with Victorian accents that grace the entranceway with 19th-century charm.

Stair bracket

Cast corbels

5½-inch Victorian baseboard

Carved or cast, corbels play an important supporting role in Victorian installations. Hung singly, as in the photo on the opposite page, a corbel holds a vase or other decorative accent. A pair of corbels can brace shelves and mantels.

A hardworking trio of chair rail, wall frames, and baseboard helps establish the style of this room. The stark contrast between the green walls and white trim makes both more intense. The stair brackets in the photo at right echo the floral themes of the wallpaper. Installing the brackets is no more complicated than spreading adhesive and driving a few brads. Presto! You've added Victorian flair.

ORNATE DECORATIVE MOLDINGS

In vintage homes, carved and cast decoration was a display of wealth. In today's elegant homes, similar motifs belong to those who simply know where to find them. Ornamental Mouldings is one manufacturer (see the "Resource Guide" on *page 236* for contact information).

Study the guide below to acquaint yourself with the design vocabulary of moldings.

In the photo on the *opposite page*, the keystone-shaped pieces at the midpoints of the friezes above the door and wall niche evoke the central locking stone of an archway. A similar piece could help conceal minor pattern or grain mismatches in applications where a single piece of molding is not long enough.

5½-inch Versailles cornice molding

1½-inch Versailles chair rail

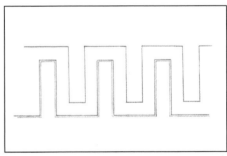

4½-inch Versailles base molding

Bead refers to pearl-shaped elements, used singly or in combination with other forms.

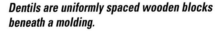

Dentils are uniformly spaced wooden blocks beneath a molding.

Greek key mimics the undulating rectangular lines of ancient Greece in a repeating pattern.

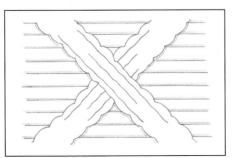

Ribbon and reed represents reeds or stems bound diagonally with ribbon.

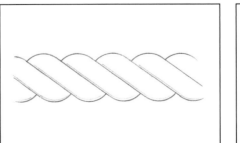

Rope is a raised interwoven pattern that can be used alone or combined with other motifs.

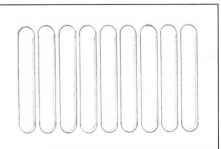

Scallops are repeating curves, sometimes used to adorn a molding edge.

This double wall frame is best installed by painting the wall first and then attaching the molding. For details, see pages 112–113.

PLANNING YOUR REMODELING PROJECT

Almost every home can benefit from a little remodeling. Newer houses, for instance, often have basement space that could be subdivided to provide rooms for separate activities and more efficient storage. Small, warrenlike rooms in older homes can be transformed into larger, more inviting spaces by rearranging or removing a wall or two. In addition, by remodeling you can adapt a home to meet the changing needs of your family or to correct design problems from previous poor planning or construction.

Although remodeling can be as ambitious as creating new living space, simply replacing moldings can transform a room. There's no need to live with the ordinary after you've learned how easy it is to create your own customized look.

What's in this book

This book serves as your guide to home remodeling. Photos of completed jobs may help inspire you to begin your own project. Step-by-step instructions will show you exactly how to bring your project to successful completion.

Along the way, you'll gain valuable information on planning the job, on the tools and materials you'll need, and on the tricks and techniques that can make your work easier and faster. You'll discover the specifics of remodeling: demolition, framing walls, hanging and finishing drywall, installing doors and windows, and upgrading your house with moldings.

The Prestart Checklist for a project lists the tools, materials, and skills involved and gives you an idea of how long the project will take. Each project has step-by-step directions to guide you along. Stanley Pro Tips provide additional advice and information to help you work easier and smarter. "What If" questions address unusual situations you may run into.

Getting started

This chapter will help you translate your remodeling needs and desires into a project plan and show you how to create floor plans and materials lists.

For all but the simplest remodeling projects, a plan is essential for your success.

CHAPTER PREVIEW

Anatomy of walls and ceilings
page 26

Developing a project plan
page 28

Is this wall structural?
page 30

What's in the wall?
page 31

The planning stage of a remodeling project takes time, but it's time well spent. A good plan helps transform your dreams into a reality and helps prevent costly mistakes.

Estimating moldings
page 32

Planning the project sequence
page 34

ANATOMY OF WALLS AND CEILINGS

The projects featured in this book revolve around the construction and modification of interior walls and spaces. They involve basic carpentry skills and techniques. Most houses in this country are stick-framed; that is, their skeletons are built from a framework of relatively small pieces of wood. Typical interior walls are framed with 2×4s. This makes walls about 4½ inches thick (3½ inches of wood covered on both sides by ½-inch-thick drywall). The illustration on the opposite page shows how the assembled pieces form a wall and names the specific parts of the framing.

Terminology

All 2×4s look the same, but as you begin to fasten them together, you'll call them by different names, depending on their position within the wall. The **studs** are the vertical pieces that make up most of a wall's frame. The cavities in between the studs are called **bays** (or stud bays). A horizontal piece at the bottom of the wall is called the **bottom plate.** The studs are nailed to this plate, which is nailed to the floor. At the top of the wall is the **top plate.** Often a doubled 2×4, it

anchors the top ends of the studs as well as ties the wall into the ceiling.

In new construction, the walls are usually built while on the floor, with a single top plate. The second layer, which ties them together, is added after the walls are raised into position. Sometimes **blocking** is added between the studs. Blocking provides a solid spot in the wall for attaching things such as cabinets or handrails. In some situations, blocking is required as a fire-stop where a stud bay extends between floors. This keeps the bay from acting as a chimney for a fire. Without fire-stops, a fire could quickly spread from floor to floor. Blocking and extra studs also are used to catch the edge of the drywall at corners and in places where the stud spacing doesn't work out perfectly.

Openings for doors or windows

An opening in a wall, such as one for a doorway or window, has its own set of terms. The opening itself is called the **rough opening.** The size of the rough opening is specified by the manufacturer of the door or window. Typically it's 1 inch larger than the outside dimensions of whatever is to fill it. Doubled studs stand on both sides of the

opening. One stud of each pair runs from plate to plate, called the **king stud.** The other stud determines the height of the opening. This is the **jack stud,** or **trimmer.** Resting on top of the jack stud is a **header.** Depending on how much weight (load) the wall has to carry, the header may be fairly thick (the weight has to be transferred from over the opening to the jack studs) or it may be quite thin (if the wall doesn't support any weight). Sometimes headers are topped by short pieces of wood known as **cripple studs,** which are used to help support drywall and trim pieces.

Types of walls

A wall that supports the weight of the building above is a **bearing wall** and is said to be **structural** *(page 30).* If a wall merely divides the interior space, it is not structural but simply a **partition wall.**

The framing members in the floor and in the ceiling are called **joists.** Underfoot, a **subfloor** is nailed to the joists. The walls are usually fastened to the subfloor. Overhead, drywall can be attached to the underside of the ceiling joists, or if you prefer, the grid for a dropped ceiling can be attached to them.

FRAMED WITH 2×4S
Skip the skinny sticks

You might be tempted to frame a wall using 2×3s to save money and space, but don't do it. The slight amount of space you'll gain and the few pennies you'll save are not worth the frustration you'll encounter working with 2×3s. These skinny sticks of lumber are notorious for warping and twisting. If you build with warped and twisted wood, there is little chance that the wall will turn out straight and true.

Why 16 inches?

In much residential construction, the wall studs and the floor and ceiling joists are spaced 16 inches on center. (On center, or OC, indicates the distance from the center of one member to the center of the next.) Why 16 inches? Plywood or oriented strand board used to sheathe the outside of the walls and the drywall used to finish the inside all come in sheets 48 inches (4 feet) wide. The 4-foot width spans four studs spaced 16 inches apart, with the edges of the sheet at the middle of the outer studs. Spacing studs and joists 16 inches on center is a nice compromise between strength and economy that allows efficient use of 4×8 sheet stock.

FRAMING TERMINOLOGY

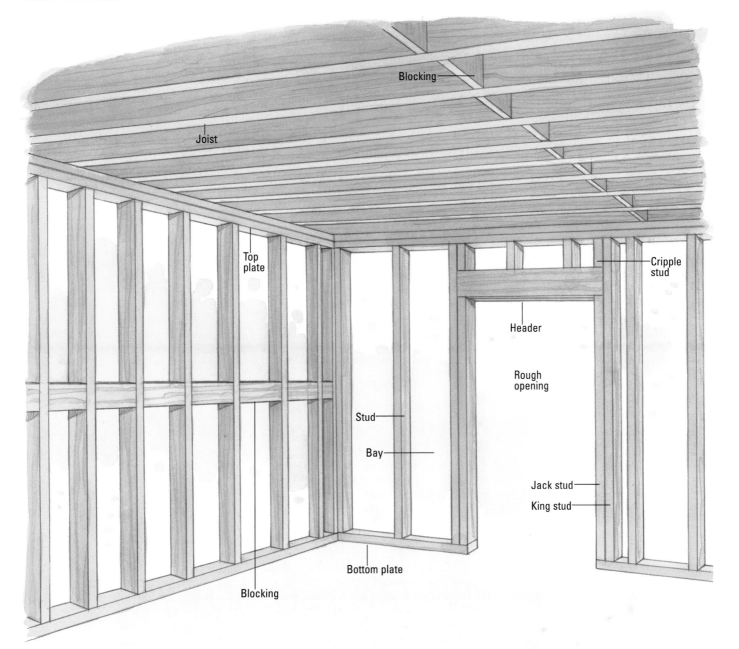

Blocking

Joist

Top plate

Cripple stud

Header

Rough opening

Stud

Bay

Jack stud

King stud

Bottom plate

Blocking

Before planning your interior wall project, learn the names and roles of all the wall-framing components.

DEVELOPING A PROJECT PLAN

Remodeling a house—or even just a room within a house—disrupts daily home life and requires hard work and money. It's well worthwhile to plan the project thoroughly before you begin. A good plan reveals problems before they happen and suggests solutions that might not have occurred to you otherwise.

The first part of developing a remodeling plan is to put together a program. A program is a list of the results you would like to accomplish by remodeling. Be as objective as you can when working on the program. If you start out listing "more closet space," you are likely to be locked into developing a plan for closets. If, however, you list "more storage space," you may discover a better, more workable solution than an additional closet provides.

Once you have your program, draw a floor plan of the existing space and make copies of it using tracing paper overlays. Sketch in ideas that accomplish the goals defined in your program. Draw each idea on a different copy of the floor plan to compare or combine them.

1 Start by drawing a floor plan of the existing space on graph paper. A scale of ¼ inch to 1 foot usually allows plenty of detail without being so big that you need a large piece of paper. Show all the walls, doorways, and windows.

2 Once you have completed your floor plan, make tracing paper overlays to test out possible designs. Avoid erasing—if you make a mistake or if you don't like the way something looks, just make another overlay.

STANLEY® PRO TIP

Create a clear materials list

As you go over your drawings to list the materials you need, a couple of steps make the task easier. First, divide the list into four parts: **lumber** (for 2× material), **trim** (for moldings and 1× material), **sheet stock** (for drywall and plywood), and **miscellaneous** (for fasteners, hardware, doors, windows, and such).

Second, be consistent in the way you list the sizes of the lumber needed. List it as thickness × width × length. Don't worry about adding in the units of measure (feet and inches). For example, a 2×4×8 is an 8-foot 2×4.

When to involve the building inspector

Almost every community has some kind of building code: a set of rules that spell out who can build what in a house and the standards a construction job must meet. Although the requirements can seem a nuisance, building codes are worthwhile—they protect everyone from shoddy work and potentially dangerous construction practices.

Rules vary from community to community. In some areas, for example, anyone can do home remodeling, as long as the job is inspected. In other areas, inspections are required only for jobs costing more than a certain amount. Some areas require contractors to be licensed.

To stay on the right side of the law, the best thing to do is to call your local zoning or code enforcement office. Find out exactly what is allowed in your community and what you

must do to comply. You may even want to set up an appointment to talk with a building inspector about your project.

If you do decide to meet with an inspector, jot down a list of questions to ask ahead of time. Although most inspectors are happy to point you in the right direction, they are busy and will appreciate it if you have thought out what you need to know before meeting. Key questions to ask include:

- Do I need a permit to build the project I have in mind?
- What information will I need to provide to apply for the permit?
- If I need to supply drawings, do they need to be signed by an engineer or architect?
- What inspections will I need?
- How do I arrange for an inspection?
- Is there anything I am forgetting to ask?

3 When you are happy with your new floor plan, make a scale elevation of the new design. An elevation is a view of a wall's face. The ¼-inch-to-1-foot scale works well here.

4 Create an overlay for the elevation drawing. On it show the framing that you will be doing and include the critical dimensions of the new design. If there are problems or special circumstances, note them in the margins.

5 Consult your framing diagram to make a materials list. Keep in mind the bottom plate of a wall runs the length of the wall—even if you plan to include doors. You'll cut the part that runs across the doorway after the wall is in place.

Thinking about light and traffic

Any time you build new walls, whether to divide an open basement into rooms or to rearrange other living spaces, you alter the dynamics within your home. Some changes are obvious; you now have an office instead of a desk tucked away in a corner. Others are much subtler; the basement is now a lot darker because the only window is in the new office.

Subtle changes can be tough to predict and, therefore, hard to plan around. But there are two that you specifically need to consider: how your alterations will affect the light in the space, and how they will affect traffic flow.

As you plan, sit in the space at different times of the day and note how light enters the room. Perhaps your plan to divide a room allows plenty of windows in both new spaces, but are you blocking morning sun from the new breakfast nook? What can you do to keep the alteration from having a negative impact on the space?

Can you add interior windows or a half-wall partition that lets the light continue to penetrate deeply into the space? Filling the top half of the wall with glass blocks is an effective way to create privacy without blocking light.

Traffic is the other issue that deserves serious consideration. Will your proposed change redirect traffic through your house? Will the kitchen suddenly become the preferred thoroughfare to the back door? It may be worth marking off the proposed spaces with tape or even cardboard to try out various arrangements before settling on the final plan.

Adding a wall in the basement can limit sunlight from reaching into the room. A door with glass panels may help the situation.

IS THIS WALL STRUCTURAL?

As you plan a remodeling job, you'll begin to see your house in a new light. Things that appeared permanent before—walls, for example—may not seem that way anymore. You'll soon realize that almost any alteration is possible if you are willing to do the work and bear the expense. Before you get carried away and start knocking down walls, however, you need to understand that there are two kinds of walls in a house: bearing (or structural) and nonbearing (or partition) walls.

Bearing walls help carry the weight of the building and its contents to the ground. **Partition walls** simply divide interior space. It is far easier to remove or relocate a partition wall than it is to do the same to a bearing wall. In many cases you may want to rethink your project before deciding to remove or modify a bearing wall.

How to spot the difference

The next step in planning is to determine whether an interior wall is a bearing wall. This book deals with interior remodeling only, so discussion is limited to interior walls.

If the wall runs parallel to the ceiling and floor joists, it is probably not a bearing wall. Short closet walls, for example, usually are not bearing. If the wall runs perpendicular to the ceiling and floor joists, there is a good chance it is a bearing wall.

How can you tell which way the joists run? Most of the time joists run perpendicular to the roof's ridgeline. If the wall is under an attic, go up and see if the joists cross over the wall. If joists end on top of a wall, it definitely is a bearing wall. If the attic has floorboards, they run across the joists; you'll see the lines of nails where they are fastened to the joists. If your roof is

supported by trusses, the answer is simpler. Trusses have diagonal pieces that run from the attic floor to the rafters. They transfer the weight of the roof to the outside walls, so all the interior walls in the story directly below are probably partition walls.

If you can't check above, check below. Is there a wall directly under the one you want to remove or modify? If there is, they both are probably bearing walls. If there is a basement or crawlspace below the wall you want to change, go there and see if a beam supported by posts or piers is directly under the wall. If so, you can assume the wall above is bearing.

If you still have doubts, hire a carpenter or a structural engineer to help you.

IDENTIFYING A BEARING WALL

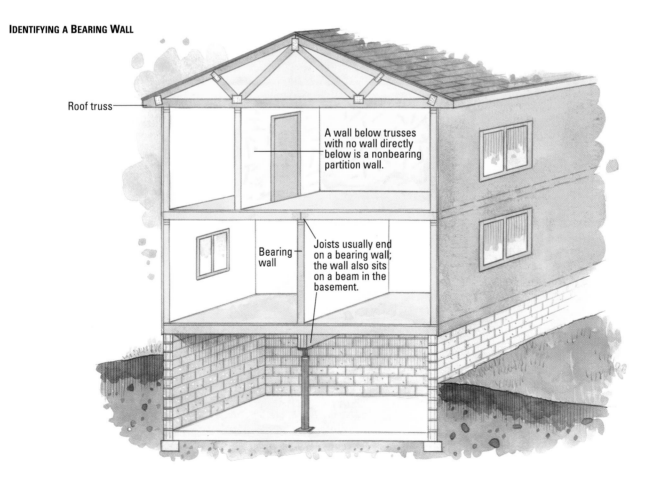

Roof truss

A wall below trusses with no wall directly below is a nonbearing partition wall.

Bearing wall

Joists usually end on a bearing wall; the wall also sits on a beam in the basement.

WHAT'S IN THE WALL?

When you start thinking about modifying existing walls, you need to consider what runs through their bays. The walls in most houses are strung with a network of wires, pipes, and ductwork for the various utility systems. If you decide to move or get rid of a wall, you must deal with the utilities it contains.

At the very least, a wall usually contains some electrical wiring. You'll see evidence of it on the surface in the form of receptacles or switches. Wiring is easier to reroute than other utility systems.

As for plumbing and ductwork, the best way to determine if the wall contains one or the other is to get underneath the house in a basement or crawlspace and see what goes up into the wall. These utilities seldom run horizontally through a wall, so if you don't see anything running up into the wall from underneath, there's probably no plumbing or ductwork in the wall. Note likely utility locations on your plan.

Once you have an idea of what you are up against, call the appropriate trade professionals and explain the situation to them. Tell them what you are doing and ask at what point they want to come and remove, reroute, or add to the system. Most will want you to notify them when the wall is stripped of its covering so they can come and get right to work.

STANLEY PRO TIP

Schedule the pros

If you discover something in a wall that you are unqualified to or don't want to deal with yourself, hire a professional to do the job. If you do hire a plumber or an electrician or a heating, ventilation, and air-conditioning contractor, schedule his or her time before you start demolition. Keep in mind, the tradesperson may have to come twice: first to disconnect and later to reconnect after you frame the new walls.

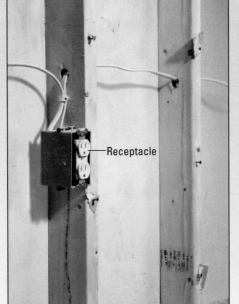

Electrical wiring is found in most walls. Most receptacles are wired in conjunction with receptacles on other walls, so changing the wiring may be more involved than it first appears. Check both sides of a wall and neighboring walls.

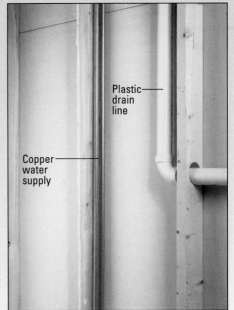

Plumbing can be involved in a wall's modification too. If there is a bathroom or kitchen directly above (and sometimes below) the wall you intend to work on, you will probably find pipes in that wall.

Heating and air-conditioning ductwork is difficult to trace. Often second-floor vent lines and return air lines pass through stud bays but are difficult to spot from underneath because other ducts block them from view.

Drain-waste-vent lines can be trickier to locate than plumbing supply lines; they take less direct routes. Besides being much larger than supply lines, drains and vents often run from the basement through the roof, requiring extensive rerouting.

ESTIMATING MOLDINGS: THE LONG AND SHORT

When you're adding up how much molding to purchase, you need to consider more than the total number of feet needed. You also need to plan how the available lengths will suit your project.

For example, if you're installing crown molding in a room that measures 10 feet, 6 inches by 11 feet, straight addition tells you that you need 43 lineal (also called running) feet of trim. If you purchase 8-foot lengths, you'll need six pieces. But the real problem in this scenario is that every wall will have a scarf joint (see *page 219*).

Scarf joints require extra work, plus there's the risk that a less-than-perfect fit could spoil your project's look. In this example, you'd be wise to shop for 12-foot lengths so you'll have an uninterrupted flow of molding from corner to corner.

The situation gets even more confusing when you deal with hardwood moldings, which are typically sold in random lengths. You may find strips that range from 6 to 16 feet. Check whether your supplier will let you select the pieces or if you're at the mercy of the order picker.

If you do end up with random lengths, it's good installation practice to deal with the longest run of wall first. That way, even if you make a cutting error, you'll still have a strip that's long enough to reuse in another location.

At first glance, standard molding profiles from various lumberyards may look similar, but subtle differences could complicate your installation. To avoid this problem, buy all of one molding profile from a single source. For example, purchase all of your crown molding from supplier A. And if supplier B has a better price on door casings, purchase all of that profile from that source.

If you insist on matching moldings in a vintage house, you may need to have a millwork shop run a custom job for you. This can be pricey, especially if custom cutting knives must be ground. Get quotes from several shops, if possible.

Counting the number of molding pieces

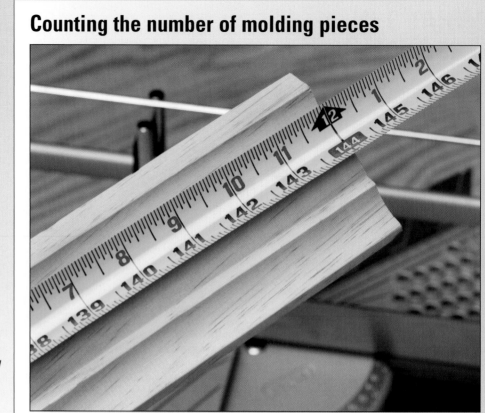

Softwood moldings are often sold in fixed lengths, but various lumber outlets may carry different sizes. One lumberyard may sell 12-footers and another might stock only 8-foot lengths. When sizing up your needs, consider which supplier's inventory is the best match for your project's needs.

Organize your supplies

One of the big challenges in remodeling is keeping all your tools organized. Use plastic storage crates from an office supply store to separate electrical supplies from plumbing tools. This helps you find what you need when you need it. These tough, inexpensive, stackable crates are invaluable.

Drywall—more than just square footage

When you're figuring how much drywall to buy, sketch out each ceiling and wall so as to minimize the number of seams. Generally, you'll minimize the overall number of seams by hanging sheets of drywall horizontally on walls. But if your walls are more than 8 feet high—the width of two drywall sheets—you'll get better results by installing the sheets vertically.

Many home centers stock ½-inch-thick drywall in even-foot lengths starting at 8 feet, so you can choose 10- or 12-foot-long pieces to minimize end-to-end (or butt) seams. That's a real convenience because butt seams require far more skill to finish than the joints between tapered drywall edges.

If you're using various thicknesses of drywall for different parts of the project, that will add another complicating factor. If you feel yourself getting confused, don't hesitate to ask for help at your lumberyard or home center. They deal with drywall every day and have the experience and know-how to give you expert advice.

Don't forget the other supplies you'll need: fasteners (either nails or screws), panel adhesive, drywall tape, joint compound, sanding sheets, and at least one high-quality dust mask. For more details, see "Choosing Tools" on *page 168*.

While you're at it, look over your drywall tools. Even a small nick on the blade of a drywall knife will produce an annoying ridge every time you try to lay down a smooth layer of joint compound.

PRO TIP

Ringshanks fight nail pop

If the walls of your house have vertical rows of domes about the size of a quarter coin, you know exactly what a nail pop is. In extreme cases, the rusty head of the fastener will show through the paint. Ringshank nails, like those in the photo at right, offer superior pullout resistance and are inexpensive insurance that your walls will stay smooth for a long time.

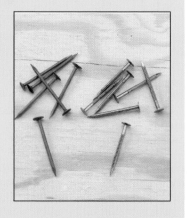

How much waste?

Waste is an unavoidable part of every construction project. And though you can minimize needless waste by careful planning, no amount of forethought will ensure you'll use every inch of every piece of material you buy.

You should generally overbuy materials by about 15 percent. A 25 percent waste allowance may be more realistic for some phases of your project. The waste allowance accounts for materials that may get damaged during handling, unusable offcuts, and good old-fashioned mistakes.

If you don't allow for a reasonable amount of waste, you may find yourself spending more time driving back and forth to the home center than actually working. Besides robbing your project of forward momentum, you'd be wasting time—something that can't be replaced.

PLANNING THE PROJECT SEQUENCE

Novice remodelers often approach a project with more enthusiasm and impatience than planning. In their eagerness to get going, they may throw the elements of a project out of sequence. As a result, it may cost them more time than if they had followed a methodical strategy.

For example, if you install baseboard before you've applied the stain and finish, you're going to spend a lot of uncomfortable hours on your hands and knees. Staining the loose pieces at sawhorse level is more comfortable and efficient.

While the construction of a new home proceeds from the bottom up, remodeling often flows from the top down. For example, you'll complete the ceiling before dealing with the walls, and the walls before dealing with the flooring.

If you get confused, take a few minutes to list all of the components of your remodeling job on a sheet of paper. Initially, write down every step that needs to be accomplished without worrying about the sequence. Next, assign each step a number to achieve an efficient work flow.

STANLEY PRO TIP

Trust notes, not memory

There are few things more frustrating than discovering that you've returned from the home center without one of the key items for your project. Avoid this problem by keeping your shopping list in your wallet.

By updating the list every time you think of something else you need, you'll keep your project moving forward with less movement to and from the home center.

Where do I start?

Although finishing may seem like a final step, do your back a favor by applying stain and varnish before nailing baseboards and other moldings in place.

Expect the unexpected

Home-improvement programming on TV doesn't always seem to follow today's trend toward reality. In a typical half-hour segment, a couple will plan and execute a complete kitchen makeover. This includes all of the shopping for materials, plus visits to a few factories. Speedy workers, they accomplish most of the installation while you watch a few commercials. At the end of the program, they have enough time remaining to prepare a gourmet meal for a few dozen friends.

In the real world, the progress of a remodeling project is often agonizingly slow and is further complicated by unpleasant surprises such as discovering water damage or termites. Seasoned remodelers know that a major project will almost certainly include at least one time-consuming detour. Some people even feel a sense of relief when the surprise reveals itself. To keep up your spirits during a long project, celebrate the accomplishment of milestone steps.

You'll avoid undue stress if you realize that remodeling almost always takes more time than you expect. Keep a loose hold on your project timeline while maintaining a firm grip on your sense of humor.

Document your project

Before closing ceilings and walls, take snapshots to document what's behind the drywall. This way, you'll have a visual record of the location of pipes, ducts, and wiring for future reference. The photos will be handy if you ever need to work on any of those systems and can help you avoid puncturing a pipe or breaking a wire when hanging a picture.

 PRO TIP

Beat the crowds

If you're a weekend remodeler, you know that a trip to the home center on a Saturday morning can take a big bite out of the time you had hoped to devote to your project. Jump-start your work day by buying your materials during the week. Then, come Saturday morning, you can dive straight into the task.

Collecting your ideas

Design professionals keep idea files by clipping photos from magazines, catalogs, and other sources. Adapt this idea by creating a clipping folder for each room of your house.

Clip anything that appeals to you—from a molding detail to a decorative paint treatment. When you're ready to begin your project, flip through the appropriate folder for the inspiration and ideas you have collected.

HANGING DOORS

After the drywall has been hung and finished (and perhaps painted), it's time to hang the doors in their openings. This is when you find out just how good your framing is. Walls and openings that are not plumb and square make hanging doors a challenge, but you'll learn the tricks to overcome that.

Hanging doors was once painstaking work, left to one of the top carpenters on a job. The jamb (door frame) had to be joined and assembled, the hinge jamb and the door had to have mortises cut for the hinges, and the whole thing had to be fitted to the opening. Thanks to prehung doors, the task isn't nearly as tricky now. Although requiring some precision and skill, it is easily within the scope of most do-it-yourselfers.

Many interior remodeling jobs include closet construction. Bypass and bifold doors are convenient space-saving alternatives to swinging doors for closets. They're relatively easy to install because they don't require as many adjustments as a swinging door.

Door construction

Most doors are constructed in one of three ways. The least expensive are hollow-core doors, so named because their inside structure consists of corrugated cardboard. Their exteriors can be flush (flat) plywood or hardboard that's molded to look like wood-panel doors. In the midprice range are solid-core doors, which have a wood-fiber core covered with a veneer of wood or paintable hardboard. Most costly are wood-panel doors, built with solid-wood rails (crosspieces) and stiles (vertical pieces) that surround solid-wood panels.

Reusing doors

If you want to reuse a door that is not prehung, expect a more complicated job. The door may have been salvaged from the remodeling job, or it may be a used door you acquired from another source. So why bother to reuse a door? It's worth it for the same reasons it is worth recycling almost anything: You'll save money over buying a new door, particularly if you want solid-wood, raised-panel construction, and you may be able to match details to other doors and trim in your house.

Prehung doors take the difficulty out of installing doors.

CHAPTER PREVIEW

Preparing the rough opening
page 38

Setting jambs for a cased opening
page 40

Fluted casing
page 46

Installing a prehung door
page 52

Check your work often as you install a door. Keeping the jamb plumb is especially important.

Precut wood shims are a must for hanging doors. They are sold in packages at home centers and hardware stores.

Take your time when hanging a door. Not only does careful craftsmanship look good, but you will also appreciate it every time you open and close the door.

Installing bypass doors
page 56

Hanging an old door in new jambs
page 58

Fitting a new door to an existing opening
page 60

Tuning up an old door
page 62

PREPARING THE ROUGH OPENING

A perfect opening—one with flat, plumb (perfectly vertical) walls on both sides—is the key to hanging a door successfully. But you'll rarely see a perfect opening. Instead, you'll usually discover one—or both—walls out of plumb, creating what's called a cross-legged jamb.

If you try to hang a door without correcting the opening, either the top or the bottom of the door will close first. This results in a door that balks at latching, causing unnecessary force every time the door is closed and opened. This condition also puts strain upon the hardware, jambs, trim, and the door itself.

But with a few tricks of the carpentry trade, you can quickly straighten walls and persuade them to be perfectly plumb. Even if you have to settle for a degree or two off of absolutely plumb, you can conduct an easy string test to ensure that the walls are in the same plane.

PRESTART CHECKLIST

☐ **TIME**
About ½ hour per opening

☐ **TOOLS**
4-foot level, hammer, 8-pound sledgehammer, drill bits, power drill/driver

☐ **SKILLS**
Checking for plumb, driving nails and screws

☐ **PREP**
Wall should be framed and drywall applied to both sides

☐ **MATERIALS**
Nylon mason's line, 6d finishing nails, 3-inch screws

1 Hold the edge of a level against the face of the wall to check it for plumb. On the bottom of the stud, mark the direction it needs to move in order to make it plumb. Repeat the process on the other side of the opening.

2 If it's necessary to align the wall, remove the baseboard. Then place a scrap 2×4 along the bottom of the wall, and whack it with a sledgehammer until the wall moves into alignment.

A cross-legged opening

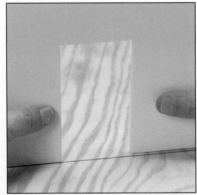

This model shows the problem of a cross-legged opening, with the wall twisted out of alignment. The solution described above should produce a wall that's both flat and plumb. But if you have to compromise between flat and absolutely plumb, flat is more important.

WHAT IF...
**You have
lath and plaster walls?**

Hitting the base of a lath-and-plaster wall with a sledgehammer can cause damage. You can break the keys—the plaster that oozed between the lath strips at installation—and loosen the plaster. Surface cracks are another risk.
You can minimize the risk of damage by applying steady pressure instead of sudden force. Create a solid anchor point, and place an automotive jack horizontally on the floor. Be sure to direct the pressure against the lower plate of the wall, not merely onto the studs at the opening. Work slowly and carefully.

3 To secure the wall, drill diagonal pilot holes, then drive 3-inch screws through the stud and into the subfloor. Repeat Steps 2 and 3 on the stud on the other side of the opening.

4 Check your work with diagonal strings. Partially drive finishing nails at each corner of the opening and stretch mason's line crossways between them. With the strings flush against the wall, the lines should lightly touch each other at the center of the opening. If the lines show tension against each other, you'll need to nudge one wall or the other to bring both walls into the same plane.

 PRO TIP

A long level promotes accuracy

Always use the longest level that the job permits to get the most accurate results. The extra length spans possible low areas in the wall that could throw off the reading. In addition, the edge of the level acts as a dependable straightedge to identify irregularities in the wall.

WHAT IF...
You don't have a long level?

Improvise and adapt by holding your shorter level against a dependable straightedge. Sight down a length of lumber to find a straight piece, or rip ¾-inch plywood into a 2-inch-wide guide. To keep a plywood straightedge from bowing, gauge from its edges— not its face.

SETTING JAMBS FOR A CASED OPENING

A cased opening derives its name from the casing—the decorative trim—that surrounds the passageway. But before you can install that trim, you need to set the opening's two jamb legs and head. You'll have the best results if you have in place an opening that's been prepared properly. See "Preparing the Rough Opening" on *page 38* for instructions.

A cased opening can function as the finished passageway between two rooms, or it can serve as the initial phase for the installation of bypass or bifold doors.

The width of each jamb part is equal to the thickness of the wall stud plus the wall material on both sides. For a 2×4 wall covered with ½-inch drywall, the standard jamb is slightly oversized at 4⁹⁄₁₆ inches wide. If you use ⅝-inch-thick drywall, buy jamb stock that's 4¾ inches wide.

PRESTART CHECKLIST

☐ **TIME**
About ½ hour per opening

☐ **TOOLS**
2-foot and 6-foot levels, tape measure, 6-inch steel rule, hammer, countersinking drill bit, power drill/driver, nail set, fine-tooth saw

☐ **SKILLS**
Checking for plumb and square, driving nails, accurate measuring

☐ **PREP**
Wall should be framed and drywalled on both sides

☐ **MATERIALS**
Door jamb kit, 8d finishing nails, #6×1½-inch screws, 1×2 strips, tapered shims

1 If you have to cut the jamb legs to length, be sure to trim the end opposite the rabbet. Cut the head to length, then put one of its ends into the rabbet. Drive #6×1½-inch screws through the jamb legs and into the head.

2 With the jamb flat on the floor, tack two 1×2s across the assembly. Check that the distance between the two legs is equal at the head jamb and at the bottom of the legs. Drive a single nail through the 1×2 into the jamb. This keeps the legs parallel but permits pivoting to level the head.

Plumb, level, square, and flat

Sometimes terms are interchanged as if they have the same meaning. But to a carpenter, plumb, level, square, and flat have four distinct meanings.

Plumb describes a vertical line, such as the leg of a doorjamb, or a vertical plane, such as a wall. To determine plumb, use a level held upright or a plumb bob. The reading from these tools points to the earth's center.

Level is a horizontal quality, and it's at a right angle (90 degrees) to plumb. For example, you'd check the head jamb of a door for level.

Square describes lines or planes that are at a right angle to each other. In theory, your house's floors and walls should be square to each other.

Flat means that an entire surface is in the same plane. In practical construction terms, flat is a relative term, describing a surface that's free of visible waves, dips, and twists.

Hang a plumb bob from a length of string, and its tip will point to the center of the earth. The string is a dependable reference line for gauging plumb.

3 Gently lift the jamb assembly into the rough opening, using the 1×2 stretchers to register it against the wall. Recruit a helper, if possible, to steady the jamb while you tackle the next steps.

4 Put a level against the head and put shims under a downhill leg to correct any imperfection. This step is important if you're going to hang bifold or bypass doors in the opening. Installing carpet on the floor will conceal the fact that the jamb doesn't touch. To deal with finished floors, see "What If" on *page 42.*

STANLEY PRO TIP

Know when to use your nail set

The crowned face of a quality hammer permits you to drive fasteners nearly flush. A nail set finishes the task by easily sinking the head.

Many beginners make the mistake of using a nail set when the head of the fastener is too far from the surface of the wood. As a result, the set may slip off of the head and scar the woodwork. Use your hammer to drive the nail nearly flush with the surface—to within ⅛ inch or less. Then you can set the nail with one or two hammer blows, minimizing the chances of scarring the wood.

REFRESHER COURSE
What's a spirit level?

Ever since ancient times, builders have relied upon the self-leveling quality of fluids to establish construction reference lines. Although an aluminum-framed level represents a significant improvement over the ancients' water-filled clay bowl, both instruments work on the same principle.

However, the fluid vials in the modern level wouldn't be much use in cold weather if they were filled with water. Instead, the vials are filled with a nonfreezing fluid, such as an alcohol solution. Spirit is another name for alcohol, and that's how the spirit level got its name.

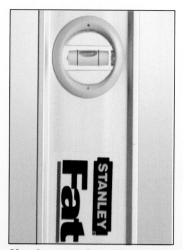

Manufacturers often add dyes to the nonfreezing solution inside the vial of a spirit level to make the bubble more visible.

SETTING JAMBS FOR A CASED OPENING *(continued)*

5 Hold one jamb leg against a stud and check for plumb. If necessary, add shims at the bottom and tack-nail the jamb to the stud using 8d (2½-inch) or longer finishing nails. Tack-nail the same jamb about 6 inches down from the head. Again, add pairs of shims if needed.

6 Using a long level or a straightedge, check that the jamb is straight. Any light that seeps between the level and the wood indicates a gap that you'll fix by shimming. Tack-nail through the jamb and shims into the stud. Finish securing the jamb by driving additional nails no farther than 20 inches apart vertically.

 PRO TIP

Use shims in pairs

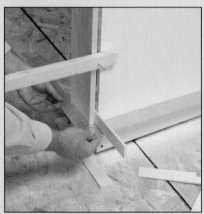

Pairing up tapered shims will help ensure that the jamb stays square to the wall. But to be doubly sure, use a framing square at several locations along each jamb leg.

WHAT IF...
You need to fit the end of both jamb legs flush against a finished floor?

Level up the head jamb as described in Step 4 and carefully measure the amount of adjustment required, if any, on the downhill leg. Transfer this measurement to the uphill leg of the jamb, then trim away that amount by using a mitersaw. Of course, you'll need to remove that leg from the jamb assembly, but that's a simple matter of removing a couple of screws. When you reinstall the assembly, the head should be level when the ends of both legs rest on the finished floor.

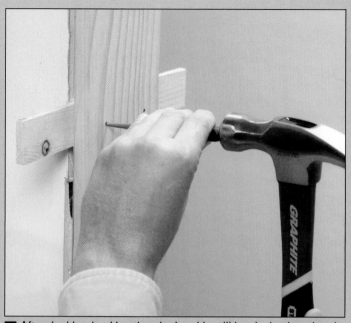

7 After double-checking that the head is still level, plumb and tack-nail the opposite jamb leg. When you're satisfied with the fit of all the parts, finish driving the nails, setting their heads 1/32 inch below the surface of the wood.

8 Although you may be tempted to break off the shims, the impact could spoil your careful alignment work. Instead, saw them off with a fine-tooth saw.

Driving nails into the head

If the cased opening you're building is 36 inches wide or less and will serve as a passageway, it usually isn't necessary to nail the head jamb into place. When the casing is nailed into the edge of the jamb, the assembly essentially becomes a U-shape beam that will resist deflection over that short span.

The rule changes for wider passages and especially if the opening will bear the weight of top-mounted doors, such as bypass or bifold closet doors.

In those cases, you'll need to shim and nail the head jamb to the header, spacing the fasteners no more than 24 inches apart. Toenailing—driving the fasteners at an angle to each other—adds pullout resistance.

INSTALLING DOOR CASING

Casing is the term for the molding that frames a door or window opening. In addition to dressing up the opening, casings cover the gaps between the walls and the jambs and hide the raw edge of the drywall. Before wrapping casing around a window or exterior door, loosely fill the gaps with shreds of fiberglass insulation poked in place with a drywall knife or similar tool.

   The casings usually are the same throughout a room—if not throughout a house—but that isn't a hard rule. In fact, creating a hierarchy of casing details adds visual interest and richness to a room or home. Consider making the casings for exterior doors wider than those for interior doors. Or link the casing size to the size of the opening: Larger openings get larger casings. Use your imagination.

PRESTART CHECKLIST

☐ **TIME**
About 45 minutes to 1 hour per door

☐ **TOOLS**
Tape measure, combination square mitersaw or miter box, hammer, nail set, screwdriver

☐ **SKILLS**
Measuring and laying out, cutting accurate miters, nailing, driving screws

☐ **PREP**
Walls should be finished (and painted, if possible), doors should be hung

☐ **MATERIALS**
Molding; 4d, 6d, or 8d finishing nails (depending on molding thickness); 2-inch trim-head screws

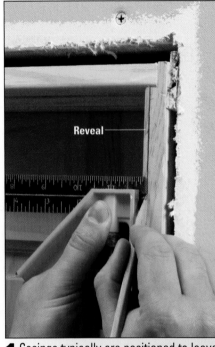

Reveal

1 Casings typically are positioned to leave ⅛ inch of the jamb's edge visible. This is called the reveal. To lay out the reveal, set a combination square to ⅛ inch, put a pencil point in the notch on the edge, and draw a line along the head jamb and both side jambs.

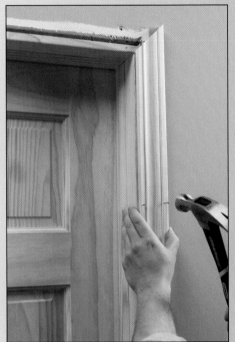

2 Measure from the floor to the head casing reveal on both sides and cut side casings to length. Attach the side casings with five pairs of nails from top to bottom. Allow the nails to protrude in case you have to pull them out to trim the casing or adjust its position when you fit the head casing.

TRIM OPTIONS
Cutting butt joints

Miters are necessary if you want a molding profile to continue seamlessly around a door. But if your casings consist of flat boards, butt joints are traditional—and easier. In a butt joint, the ends of the pieces are cut square and one piece is simply butted up against the other. Most often the head casing sits on top of the side casings, but occasionally the head casing is fitted between the side casings—it's a matter of preference.

   During the Victorian era, corner blocks came into use. The blocks add a decorative element while allowing butt joints when using ornate molded casings. The blocks are slightly wider and thicker than the casing, making them the most forgiving way to frame the corner of a window or door.

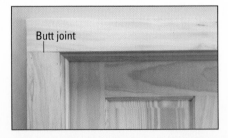

Butt joint

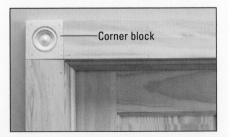

Corner block

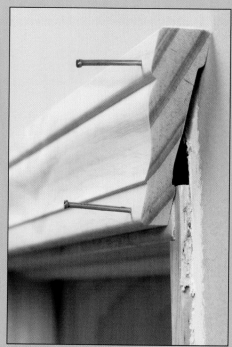

3 Most casings are back-cut; that is, they have a shallow channel (or channels) cut in their backs. This accommodates irregularities in the wall so the molding can fit tightly against the wall and jamb. When you install casing, drive the nails through the solid edges.

Head casing

4 Cut the head casing roughly to length. If the molding is mitered as shown here, start with a piece that's long and carefully trim it to fit. For a butt-joined head casing, cut one end square and hold it in place to mark for an exact cut on the other side.

5 Nail the head casing to the wall and head jamb with three pairs of nails. As insurance against the miters opening, drill holes in the casing, then drive 2-inch trim-head screws through the head casing into the side casings as shown. Set all the nailheads once you are happy with the fit.

STANLEY PRO TIP: **Gauge a casing to eliminate measuring**

When you install mitered casing around a door or window, it's usually easiest to install the left side and then the top and right side. (Left-handers may find it more convenient to reverse that sequence.)

Trying to measure the length of the final jamb can be frustrating because the pieces that are already installed make it difficult to get an accurate measurement to the inside corner of the miter. One approach is to measure to the outside corner of the miter, but there's an even easier way to deal with this situation.

Sidestep the problem by cutting a miter on a length of casing, then invert the casing to mark its length. Of course, the second cut will be a straight crosscut. When you install the casing right side up, you'll have a snug fit at both the top and the bottom.

Special glue for moldings

Add glue to reinforce mitered molding joints. The thin consistency of most glues means that you'll probably have to clean up as much as you apply unless you use a thick-bodied glue specially formulated for moldings. (See *page 187* for more information on specialty adhesives.) These glues hold securely even on the slippery slopes of miters.

No matter what type of adhesive you use, make certain that you clean up all traces of it from the face of the molding. That's because even a microscopic layer of glue can prevent stain from penetrating the wood. Prevent glue from squeezing out by applying it sparingly to the joint.

FLUTED CASING

Fluted casings give a room a decidedly upscale and formal appearance, evoking the Federal or neoclassical style. Despite the stately appearance, the look is relatively easy to achieve, involving a minimum of miter cuts.

The trim pieces are standard molding profiles you can purchase at your local home center. If you have a router with a roundnose bit, craft your own fluted casings. (See *page 50* for fluting details.)

The optional ornamental motif on the frieze board requires no carving skills. You simply glue on the embossed molding (available at many home centers) and then paint the ornamentation.

By the way, the reveal that you set for the casing is related to the width of the plinth block. Obviously, you want the casing centered on top of it. You can let the width of the block determine the reveal, or you can size the block to produce the reveal that you want.

PRESTART CHECKLIST

☐ **TIME**
About 1½ hours per opening

☐ **TOOLS**
Combination square, 6-inch steel rule, mitersaw or miter box, sandpaper and sanding block, hammer

☐ **SKILLS**
Accurate marking and cutting, driving nails

☐ **PREP**
Jambs should be installed

☐ **MATERIALS**
4d and 8d finishing nails, 1-inch brads, glue, painter's caulk, putty

1 Use 8d (2½-inch) finishing nails to attach the plinth blocks at the bottom of the jambs. A plinth block can have a decorative profile (as shown above) or be a basic block. Drilling pilot holes minimizes the risk of splitting. Leaving a scant 1/16 inch between the edge of the block and the jamb is easier than attempting a perfectly flush fit.

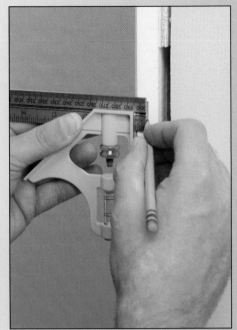

2 Center the casing on top of the plinth block to determine the reveal on the jamb. Set your combination square and draw pencil lines along the inner edges of both jamb legs and the head for the reveal (3/16 inch in this case). You don't have to draw a continuous line—an inch-long mark every 18 inches is sufficient.

WHAT IF...
You need to make your own plinth blocks?

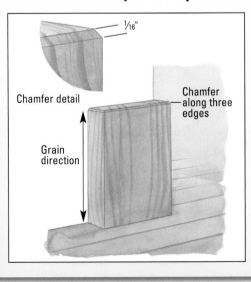

1/16"

Chamfer detail

Chamfer along three edges

Grain direction

Making your own plinth blocks is a fast and easy process. Count the number of blocks you'll need, add a few spares, and set up your shop for mass production.

If you're making the blocks from solid wood, rip the stock to width, then crosscut the individual blocks to finished length. Of course, grain direction isn't a consideration if you are using medium-density fiberboard (MDF).

Rout, plane, or sand a 1/16-inch chamfer along three top edges of the block. This helps prevent chipping of the edges.

3 Use your mitersaw to square-cut one end of each fluted casing—don't trust the factory cut. Rest the end of the casing on the plinth block, roughly align it with the reveal marks on the side jamb, and mark for the top end cut.

4 Starting at the bottom of the jamb, align the casing's edge with the reveal marks, and partially drive 4d (1½-inch) finishing nails through the casing and into the jamb. Work your way upward, nailing only into the jamb, not the wall. When you reach the top, work downward, nailing the outer edge of the casing to the wall with 8d (2½-inch) finishing nails. Make certain you do not pull the jamb out of plumb.

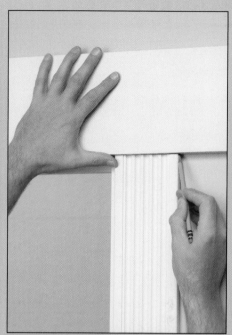

5 Cut the frieze board to width—6 inches wide in this example. Choosing medium-density fiberboard (MDF) for a painted installation is a smart choice because the manufactured product won't warp like solid wood can. Square-cut one end and place it on top of the casings to mark the frieze to the exact outside-to-outside size.

WHAT IF...
There's a hump in the drywall?

Sometimes you'll find a hump in the wall where the edge of a panel meets a door opening. Fortunately, there's an easy fix for this problem before you add trim.

Mark the width of the molding onto the wall, then shave down the offending area. A tool like the Stanley Surform plane is ideal for this task.

Check your progress often to make certain that you don't remove too much material: Replacing a hump with a trough doesn't represent real progress. Hold the casing against the wall in its installed position and verify that it will lay flat when nailed into place.

You can ignore any roughness on the wall that will be covered by the casing. But if the wall shows any scrapes, erase them with drywall sanding screen or sandpaper. Loading the paper into a hand-sanding block or utilizing a pole sander with a universal-joint swiveling head has two distinct benefits. The large surface of these tools helps ensure a flat surface, and it produces faster results than rubbing the wall with a folded sheet of abrasive.

FLUTED CASING *(continued)*

6 Add 1 inch to the length of the frieze and cut a piece of 1/4×1 1/4-inch bullnose trim to this length. If you can't find trim with a bullnose edge, substitute a lattice strip and use sandpaper to slightly round over the edges. A sanding block with 120-grit sandpaper lets you easily carry the bullnose profile around the ends of the trim.

7 With glue and 1-inch brads, fasten the strip to the bottom of the frieze board. Be sure the overhang is even at both ends. The back edges of the strip and frieze board should be flush with each other.

8 Center the frieze assembly above the casings. The ends of the frieze board should be even with the outer edges of the casing. Drive 4d finishing nails through the frieze into the head, aligning the bottom edge of the frieze assembly with the reveal marks. Drive 8d finishing nails into the wall.

WHAT IF...
You're trimming several doors—any timesaving tips?

When you're casing several openings that have relatively complex trim, you can save a considerable amount of time by working on several pieces of trim at the same time. That way, you can efficiently bunch similar steps together.

If you're working with the style of trim described in the demonstration above, for example, it makes sense to install the fluted casings on all of the openings and then make all the frieze board assemblies at one time. That way, you're not wasting your time by gathering tools and putting them away numerous times. To keep yourself organized, simply identify each door with a number written on the drywall;

the number eventually will be hidden by the frieze board. Write a matching number on the back of each frieze board assembly.

If you're lucky enough to be able to recruit a helper, keep that person busy by showing your recruit how to complete a task on the first opening. Then turn him or her loose on all the other doorways. For example, marking the reveal is an easy task you can delegate with confidence.

9 Mark a line ¾ inch from the top edge and the ends of the frieze and install the crown molding. Install the front piece first, then add the returns. For more information on handling crown molding, see *pages 142–147*.

10 The completed installation needs only a bit of painter's caulk to fill in any gaps. Countersink all nails and fill the holes with putty.

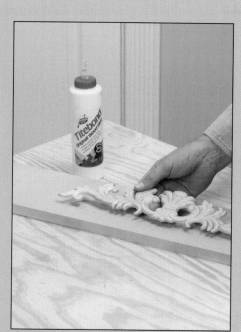

11 To further upgrade the installation, consider an embossed appliqué. For best adhesion, glue the design to the frieze before priming and painting.

WHAT IF...
You want to cover the trough created by the crown molding?

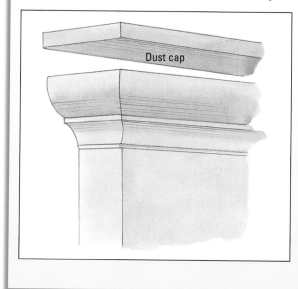

Dust cap

Some people may object to the open trough created by the crown molding at the top of the frieze board, seeing it as a dust-catching location or as an unfinished part of the assembly.

Adding a cap to the assembly is one quick and easy solution. If you're working with painted trim, you can easily make the cap from ½-inch-thick medium-density fiberboard (MDF). If you're working with wood that will receive a natural finish, you'll have to locate solid stock for the cap.

Rip the cap about ½ inch wider than the crown molding's depth; allow for a ½-inch overhang at each end. Rout or

sand a roundover (or create a full bullnose profile) along the cap's front edge and both ends. Do a test assembly to make certain that you like the overhang dimensions.

To install the cap, simply squeeze a few small dots of panel adhesive on the top edges of the crown molding, then lower the cap into place.

TRIM VARIATIONS

Federal fluted

Rip stock to width for the casing sides and rout a ⅛-inch roundover along both front edges. Cut the sides to length. Switch to a roundnose bit and rout the flutes, stopping them about 1 inch from each end. For painted installations—typical with this style—save money by making the casing from medium-density fiberboard (MDF). The material machines smoothly but produces clouds of powdery dust, so protect your lungs with a high-quality dust mask.

Neoclassical variation

There's no need to trash existing colonial casing when you want to make a dramatic entry. Add a bullnose strip, a frieze board (perhaps with a band of half-round molding), and top it with crown molding and a cap. This is similar to the installation that begins on *page 46* but skips the work and expense of the fluted columns.

Arts and Crafts I

Stained quartersawn white oak is the material of choice for this Arts and Crafts door treatment. Although the corner joints look like half laps, they are actually easy-to-make fakes. Butt joints keep assembly simple. If you need an excuse to buy a biscuit joiner, this casing is a good one. Biscuits (#20 recommended) keep the joint segments neatly aligned and minimize tedious sanding to make the surfaces flush.

Arts and Crafts II

The 5/4 stock of the head casing measures about 1¹⁄₁₆ inch thick; that minimizes any minor misalignments with the legs, which measure ¾ inch thick. Quartersawn white oak is the traditional material for Arts and Crafts installations, but the clean architecture of this doorway also would fit the style with a painted finish on inexpensive lumber.

Traditional

A butt-jointed casing gets an upgraded look with either an L-shape wraparound molding or surface-applied strips. Either way, you miter the molding at the corners. If you choose method 2, purchase 1-inch-wide

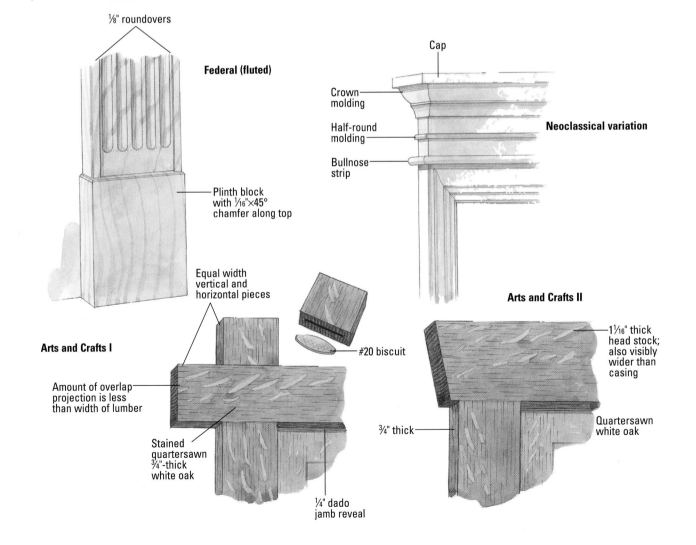

⅛" roundovers

Federal (fluted)

Plinth block with ¹⁄₁₆"×45° chamfer along top

Cap

Crown molding

Half-round molding

Bullnose strip

Neoclassical variation

Equal width vertical and horizontal pieces

#20 biscuit

Arts and Crafts I

Amount of overlap projection is less than width of lumber

Stained quartersawn ¾"-thick white oak

¼" dado jamb reveal

Arts and Crafts II

1¹⁄₁₆" thick head stock; also visibly wider than casing

¾" thick

Quartersawn white oak

lattice strips or rip your own from construction lumber. Any thickness from ⅛ inch to ¼ inch will do. Of course, the thicker the strip, the wider the shadow line it creates. For a clean look, keep the edges of the strips and casings flush.

Rustic

If you like the rustic look, this doorway trim gives you a lot to love. Clear-finished pine shows off the mandatory knotty lumber look, and the pegs evoke the sturdy timber framing of an old hunting lodge. Using faux pegs adds the handcrafted look but lets you skip the backbreaking work. Make a peg by whittling facets onto the end of a piece of ¾-inch dowel with a utility knife. Cut the peg—you want the facets and part of its length to project from the lumber—and glue it into a shallow hole in the head casing. Repeat the whittling and cutting for all the pegs. Slight variations in peg length heighten the rustic look.

Contemporary

This molding profile was considered modern when Sputnik I first traced its path across the sky in 1957. Even though satellite launches are no longer newsworthy, ranch (or clamshell) molding remains a favorite among people who want a contemporary look. Choose this molding in its economical paint-grade version, and you'll pocket some hefty savings compared with its stain-grade counterpart.

Shaker/country

The Shaker sect practiced a no-frills lifestyle that extended into their designs, which were based on function. Although the lines are simple, the appeal is powerful. A peg rail around the top of the room is a seamless extension of the door's head casing. Punctuated with pegs, this rail held chairs between meals. The lower rail featured shorter pegs for storage of tools and other household necessities.

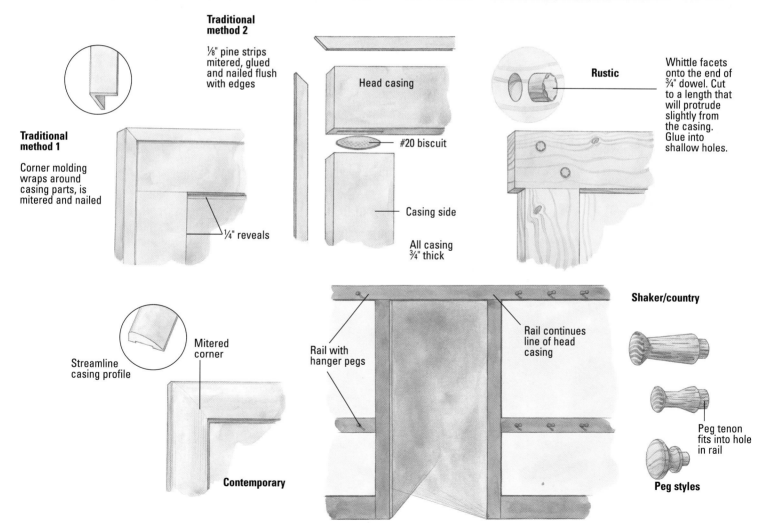

Traditional method 2

⅛" pine strips mitered, glued and nailed flush with edges

Traditional method 1

Corner molding wraps around casing parts, is mitered and nailed

¼" reveals

Head casing

#20 biscuit

Casing side

All casing ¾" thick

Rustic

Whittle facets onto the end of ¾" dowel. Cut to a length that will protrude slightly from the casing. Glue into shallow holes.

Streamline casing profile

Mitered corner

Rail with hanger pegs

Rail continues line of head casing

Contemporary

Shaker/country

Peg tenon fits into hole in rail

Peg styles

INSTALLING A PREHUNG DOOR

The most demanding tasks have already been done when you buy a prehung door unit. Hinge mortises and holes for the lockset and strike are already cut. However, installing a prehung door still calls for careful work to get the best results. Making sure your framing is well-built is one of the most important things you can do to make installing doors easier. A rough opening that is plumb and square is far easier to deal with than one that isn't. Keep double-checking as you build and take the time to fix mistakes as they occur rather than hoping they will be hidden by the next step.

If you are hanging a door in an older house, keep an eye on the big picture. Before setting the nails, step back and look at your work. Even if you have plumbed the door, if the wall or floor is off level or plumb, you may want to align the door frame at least a little bit with its surroundings to make sure it looks right. For example, if the wall leans slightly, match the jamb to the wall. It won't be noticeable as long as the door doesn't lean enough to open and close by itself.

PRESTART CHECKLIST

☐ **TIME**
About 2 hours per door

☐ **TOOLS**
4-foot level, circular saw, layout square, hammer, nail set, utility knife, screwdriver

☐ **SKILLS**
Crosscutting, driving nails, checking for plumb

☐ **PREP**
Doorway should be framed and drywalled on both sides

☐ **MATERIALS**
Prehung door, shims, 8d and 16d finishing nails

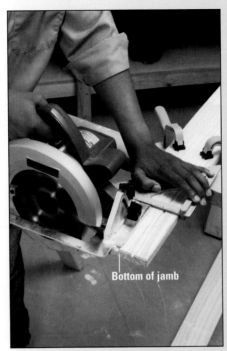
Bottom of jamb

1 Tap out the hinge pins with a screwdriver and hammer. Remove the door. Slip the frame into the doorway and check the head jamb for level. If it isn't, shim under the jamb on the low side. Measure the shimmed space; then remove this amount from the opposite jamb.

2 Check that the jack stud on the hinge side of the opening is plumb. Also check to see if the wall leans. If the jack stud is plumb, nail the jamb directly to it with 16d finishing nails, two below each hinge and two near the center.

WHAT IF...
You are planning to install hardwood flooring or tile?

Prehung doors usually come with a 1¼-inch gap at the bottom of the door. This allows clearance over a carpet and pad about 1 inch thick. If you plan to install hardwood floors, which are ¾ inch thick, shorten the jamb sides by ⅞ inch (¾ inch for the floor plus ⅛ inch to reduce the gap under the door). This allows the flooring to run under the ends of the jambs. If the floor under the doorway isn't level, adjust the jambs as shown in Step 1 above. Tile thicknesses and the thickness of the mastic bed vary, so check these in advance. Allow ¼ inch between tile and the door bottom.

After cutting the jambs to the right length to accommodate hardwood flooring, use spacer blocks to position the jambs in the doorway. Make the spacers from scraps of floor material.

3 If the hinge-side stud is not plumb, nail either the top or bottom, whichever is closer to the center of the opening. Insert shims at the opposite end to plumb the jamb. Below the shims, drive two 16d finishing nails just far enough to hold the shims and jambs in place. Adjust shims if necessary.

4 Before setting nails, check that the hinge jamb is centered across the wall thickness. A typical jamb is slightly wider than the wall thickness to allow for irregularities in the drywall. If adjustment is necessary, pull the nails, protecting the jamb with a scrap under the hammer.

5 Put the door back on its hinges and swing it closed. Insert shims between the jamb and the stud about halfway between the hinges and adjust them until the gap between the door and jamb is equal from top to bottom. Open the door and drive two 16d finishing nails below the shims.

Dealing with doors: Which hand is which?

If you have to order your doors, determine if you want right- or left-handed doors. This can be confusing, in part because locksets and doors use the same terminology but in slightly different ways.

For doors: If the hinges are on the left when you pull the door open, it is a left-handed door, as shown above left. If the hinges are on the right when you pull the door open, it's a right-handed door.

For locksets, the hand is determined from outside the room. If the door swings into the room and the hinges are on the left, the lockset is left-handed, as shown above right. If the door swings out of the room and the hinges are on the left, the lockset is left-hand reverse. If hinges are on the right, the door can be right-hand or right-hand reverse.

The best way to avoid confusion is to show diagrams of what you want to your supplier.

Watch for hidden bumps

When prehung doors are assembled, the hinge screws sometimes poke through the back of the jamb. These little nubs are enough to throw a jamb out of plumb. File them flat before installing the door frame.

INSTALLING A PREHUNG DOOR *(continued)*

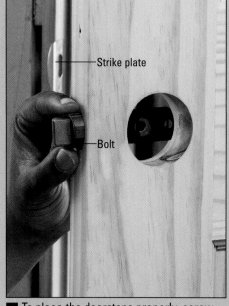

Strike plate

Bolt

A playing card provides the right amount of space between a prefinished door and stop.

6 Nail the strike side of the frame in three places: top, bottom, and middle. Insert shims and adjust so the gap between the door and the jamb is even, top to bottom. Nail the jamb in place with pairs of 16d nails driven through the shims.

7 To place the doorstops properly, screw the strike plate to the jamb, slip the bolt into the door, and screw it in place. You don't need to install the entire lockset at this time.

8 On many prehung units, the doorstops are only temporarily attached, to be mounted permanently after the unit is in place. Pry the stops free. Close the door and hold it tightly against the strike plate. Nail the stops in place while holding them against the door.

WHAT IF...
The jack stud is twisted?

A common problem when installing a prehung door is a twisted jack stud. Even if you carefully select framing lumber and craft the wall frame accurately, studs can move as they adjust to conditions in the house. The result often is a door opening that isn't true. If you attach a door frame to a twisted jack stud, it will look as though the door is standing partially open; actually the entire door frame will be protruding into the room. See *page 38* for more information.

You can force the frame back into the plane of the wall, but you run the risk of damaging the frame. Adding a third shim to each pair of shims that locates the jamb returns the frame to its position without adding stress to the door frame assembly.

A twisted jack stud won't allow a door frame to hang properly in its opening.

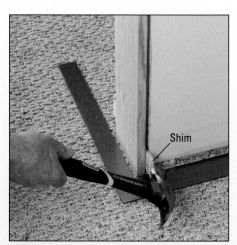

Shim

Adding a third shim to a pair of shims compensates for the twisted jack stud and allows the door frame to assume a proper square position.

Matchbook cover

9 If the door and jamb are to be painted, use a matchbook cover as a spacer between the door and stop as you nail the stop in place. This allows for the thickness of the paint on the various surfaces.

10 When you are satisfied with the fit of the door within the frame, and the frame within the opening, drive 8d finishing nails through the jambs and shims to lock the shims in place. Cut off the shims with a utility knife or handsaw.

11 As a final step, replace two of the screws in each hinge with screws long enough to reach into the jack studs. The door hangs from the jack studs, not just from the jambs.

STANLEY PRO TIP: **There's more than one way to plumb a door**

To install door frames efficiently, you need a long level. A 4-foot model is adequate, but a 6-foot level is the best to use. If you don't want to invest in either of these tools, you can use a plumb bob to check whether the jambs are plumb or not. To use this method, secure the hinge-side jamb to the jack stud, as shown on *page 53*. Drive a 16d finishing nail partially into the jamb near the top (the stop will eventually cover the hole). Hang a plumb bob from the nail so it dangles almost to the floor. Adjust the shims until the gap between the jamb and the string is equal from top to bottom. Pin the shims in place with 8d finishing nails.

Plumb bob

Hang a plumb bob along a door jamb for an easy way to plumb the jamb. This simple tool eliminates the need for a long level when installing doors.

Adjust the shims behind the jamb until the distance from the jamb to the string is equal all along the length of the jamb. Add pairs of shims if necessary to compensate for a warped jamb.

INSTALLING BYPASS DOORS

Bypass doors, the most popular choice for closets, need no room to swing open. However, they allow access to only one side of a closet at a time. Hardware kits are available for openings of 4, 5, 6, and 8 feet. To accommodate other size openings, simply cut the standard tracks with a hacksaw.

The kits are designed to work with standard, 1⅜-inch-thick interior doors. Thicker doors may interfere with each other as they open and close. Thinner doors may have a wide gap between them. The combined width of the doors should equal the width of the opening plus at least 1 inch. This provides ½ inch of overlap between the two doors.

Although some minor variations exist between bypass door kits from different manufacturers, they are all easy to install. Just be sure to check the manufacturer's directions carefully before starting.

PRESTART CHECKLIST

☐ **TIME**
About 1 hour for a pair of doors

☐ **TOOLS**
Power drill/driver, level, tape measure

☐ **SKILLS**
Leveling the track, locating and installing hardware

☐ **PREP**
Opening should be complete with wooden jambs or drywall hung and finished; casings can be installed later

☐ **MATERIALS**
Bypass door hardware kit, doors, shims

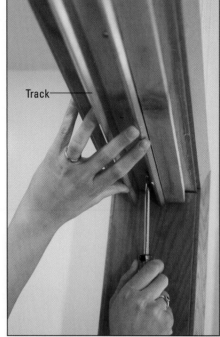

Track

1 The location of the track depends on how you plan to trim the opening. Consult the manufacturer's instructions. Screw the track to the top of the door opening. Check to make sure the track is level; shim if necessary.

2 Attach the hangers to the tops of the doors. The hardware kit specifies the exact locations. Tip the doors to hook the hangers onto the track. After the doors are hanging, install the center guide on the floor to keep the doors in line.

TRIM THE OPENING

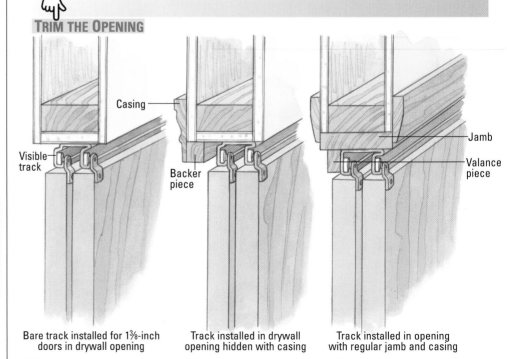

Casing

Visible track

Backer piece

Jamb

Valance piece

Bare track installed for 1⅜-inch doors in drywall opening

Track installed in drywall opening hidden with casing

Track installed in opening with regular jamb and casing

With bypass doors, you have options for finishing the opening. For utility applications, simply hang the doors as is (left). For a more finished look, add trim to the header (middle and right).

INSTALLING BIFOLD DOORS

You can easily install bifold doors in almost any opening in your home. Common applications include closets, privacy doors, or doors to control heat and airflow between rooms. Their chief advantages include ease of installation and a minimum of swing space required. However, they take up more space in the door opening than do swinging doors.

Commonly available with plastic, metal, or wooden doors, bifold door kits come in a variety of styles, including louvered, paneled, and smooth. The kits fit most standard-width openings, although the maximum width of a single door is 24 inches. Units can be combined to cover openings up to 16 feet wide. Wooden doors can be trimmed for a better fit; plastic doors cannot be trimmed. (Keep in mind, if you trim a wooden door kit, each door must be trimmed equally.) Two heights are available—one to fit standard 6-foot, 8-inch openings, the other for 8-foot floor-to-ceiling applications.

PRESTART CHECKLIST

☐ **TIME**
About 1 hour for a pair of doors

☐ **TOOLS**
Power drill/driver, level, tape measure

☐ **SKILLS**
Leveling the track, locating and installing hardware

☐ **PREP**
The opening should be complete with wooden jambs or drywall hung and finished; casings can be installed later

☐ **MATERIALS**
Bifold door hardware kit, doors, shims

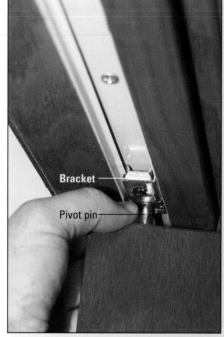
Bracket
Pivot pin

1 Bifold doors require a track similar to that used by bypass doors. Screw the track to the top of the opening. The doors pivot on pins protruding from their top and bottom. These pins engage brackets attached to the floor or jamb and the track.

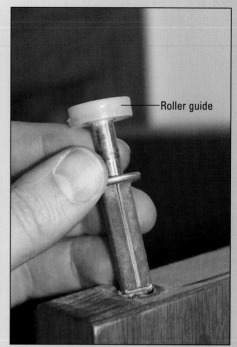
Roller guide

2 Attach the roller or pin guide to the free end of the doors. This guide rides in the track and keeps the doors in alignment.

BIFOLD DOOR TRIM OPTIONS

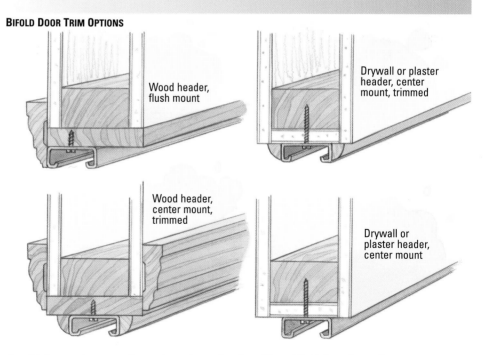

Wood header, flush mount

Drywall or plaster header, center mount, trimmed

Wood header, center mount, trimmed

Drywall or plaster header, center mount

As with bypass doors, you have trim options when installing a bifold door, depending on the look you want.

HANGING AN OLD DOOR IN NEW JAMBS

To reuse an old door, purchase a door frame, often called a jamb kit, at a lumberyard or home center. The kit includes three pieces of 9/16-inch-thick lumber 4⅝ inches wide. The two side jambs have a groove, called a dado, or a ledge, called a rabbet, across the top to receive the head jamb. See *pages 40–43* for additional jamb details.

The first step is to make the door fit the opening or vice versa. The door should be about 2¼ inches narrower than the rough opening and 1 inch shorter than the distance from the header to the finished floor. If you have to cut a door a significant amount in width, trim from both edges to keep the stiles symmetrical. With hollow-core doors, try not to cut beyond the solid edges. If you have to cut into the hollow area, save the solid edges and glue them back into the door to reinforce it.

PRESTART CHECKLIST

☐ **TIME**
About 1 to 3 hours

☐ **TOOLS**
Tape measure, tablesaw, circular saw, layout square, router, chisels, mallet, power drill/driver, plane

☐ **SKILLS**
Measuring and laying out, ripping on a tablesaw, crosscutting with a circular saw, routing hinge mortises, trimming with a chisel, driving screws

☐ **PREP**
Door opening should be framed, used door should be square and flat

☐ **MATERIALS**
Jamb kit, 2½-inch screws, doorstop molding

Head jamb rabbet

1 If the floor will be carpeted, hook the tape measure into the side jamb rabbets or dadoes and measure down a distance 1 5/16 inch more than the height of the door. For a hardwood floor, measure down 7/16 inch more than the height of the door. Cut the jambs to length.

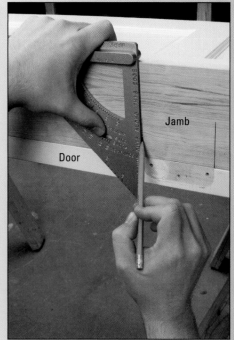

Jamb

Door

2 Hold the hinge jamb along the edge of the door and lay out the hinge locations on the jamb. The top of the door should be just slightly more than 1/16 inch below the edge of the rabbet or dado. Mark the mortise locations with a sharp pencil.

WHAT IF…
The door needs new hinge mortises?

You may want to trim the edge of your used door to eliminate the old hinge mortises. This gives you a chance to start fresh with the placement of the hinges. It also means you don't have to find hinges that match the old mortises.

Locating the new hinges doesn't have to be especially precise as long as the mortises on the door match those on the jamb. Most doors require three hinges (hollow-core doors need only two). Center the middle hinge and locate the top and bottom hinges about 6 inches from the ends of the door.

Door

Scrap 2×4

Cut the mortises in the door first. Clamp some 2×4 scraps on both sides of the door to keep the router from tipping. Square the mortise with a chisel, then transfer the locations to the jamb.

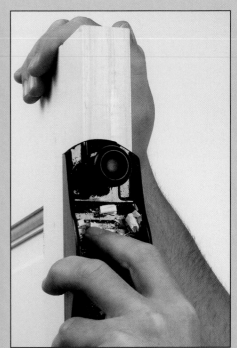

3 Use a utility knife to scribe the hinge leaf outline onto the door edge. Set a ½-inch straight router bit slightly deeper than the hinge leaf thickness. Rout close to the scribe lines. Tune the mortise with a chisel.

4 Cut the head jamb to a length equal to the door width plus the combined rabbet or dado depth plus slightly more than ⅛ inch. Screw the door frame together with 2½-inch screws. Attach the hinges to the jamb and the door.

5 Hang the door as you would a prehung unit. Check its fit in the opening before securing the jamb. Plane the strike-side edge of the door if necessary. Cut the doorstop and install it as shown on *page 54*.

WHAT IF...
You don't have a router?

Edge of jamb

1 You can cut hinge mortises by hand with a chisel. Hold the hinge in place and scribe around it with a utility knife. Mark the depth of the mortise on the edge of the jamb with your knife, using a combination square as a guide. The depth of the mortise must be slightly more than the thickness of the hinge leaf.

2 Sharpen your widest chisel (1–1½ inches is best). Cut down close to the mortise depth all around the perimeter of the mortise.

3 Once you have defined the outline of the mortise, pare away the rest of the material until the mortise is cut to its full depth. Keep the bottom of the mortise as flat as possible so the hinge sits flat.

FITTING A NEW DOOR TO AN EXISTING OPENING

There is no rule that you have to match a new door and trim to what is already in the room. If your existing doors lack style or you simply want a change, you can hang new doors in existing jambs. Sometimes you can reuse hinges and other hardware.

Think twice before deciding to replace the trim, a much bigger job. Swapping doors makes a big visual difference without requiring a lot of labor. Replacing trim makes a more subtle visual difference and requires more time and effort.

Unless your house is very old, you'll have little problem finding doors to fit. The most common door height is 80 inches, although most models also are available at 78 inches tall. Commonly available interior door widths are 24, 28, 30, 32, and 36 inches. Doors are sometimes specified in feet and inches: a 2-6 door is 30 inches wide.

PRESTART CHECKLIST

☐ **TIME**
About 1½ to 2 hours to hang a new door

☐ **TOOLS**
Tape measure, block plane, square, router, chisels, power drill/driver, 2⅛-inch hole saw, 1-inch spade bit

☐ **SKILLS**
Measuring and laying out, planing, cutting mortises, drilling

☐ **PREP**
Remove old door, acquire new hardware if necessary

☐ **MATERIALS**
New door, new hardware (if needed), shims, matchbooks

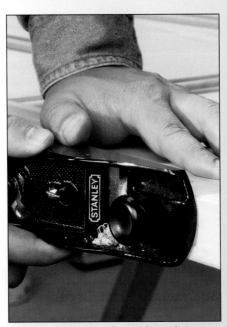

1 Measure the opening and purchase a door that fits. If you have to trim the door, take an equal amount off each side. Plane a slight bevel (about 5 degrees) in the direction of swing on the strike side of the door to ease opening and closing.

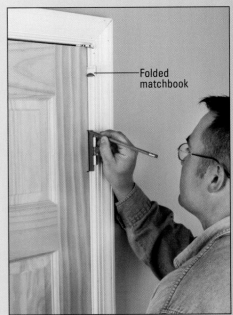

Folded matchbook

2 Check the door's fit. Ideally the gap should be slightly more than 1/16 inch at the top and along each side and about 3/8 inch at the bottom. Spacers made from folded matchbooks (four thicknesses equals about 1/16 inch) and shims at the bottom will help you maintain the spacing. Mark the mortise locations for the hinges on the door and cut the mortises.

STANLEY PRO TIP: **Mortising jigs**

If you have more than one or two doors to hang, consider buying a hinge-mortising jig. These templates guide a router to cut perfect mortises for hinges. The simplest (and least expensive) of the several available models cut one mortise at a time, leaving the placement of the matching mortise up to you. The more complex jigs come with several templates and will position the mortises on both the jamb and the edge of the door. Buy hinges with rounded corners for router-cut mortises. Square-corner hinges work with mortises cut with a chisel.

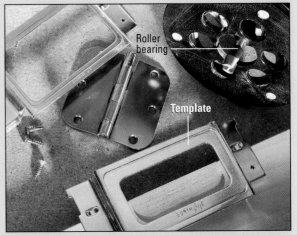

Roller bearing

Template

Most hinge-mortising jigs work with a router equipped with a template guide. The guide could be a roller bearing on the bit, as shown here, or a metal collar attached to the router's base that surrounds the bit and runs along the mortise template.

3 Hang the door. New locksets come with a template to help you locate where to drill holes. If you are reusing a lockset, extend a line across the face of the door with your square, making sure it is centered on the strike plate. Measure the lockset to determine the distance the hole should be from the edge of the door. Drill a 2⅛-inch hole through the door with a hole saw.

4 For the bolt, drill a 1-inch hole through the edge of the door with a spade bit. Make sure the bolt hole is centered from front to back and aligned with the center of the strike plate.

5 Insert the bolt into the hole in the door's edge. Align the bolt plate with the edges of the door and trace around it with your utility knife. Remove the bolt and remove the wood inside the outline to create a mortise for the plate. When finished, the plate should be slightly below the surface.

WHAT IF...
There are no hinge mortises in the opening?

Some houses have openings with jambs and casings but no door. These might be found, for example, between a kitchen and dining room or between a den and a hallway. If you decide to add a door, you'll need to cut mortises in the jambs to hang the door and to install doorstops.

If your opening is finished only with drywall, you may be able to treat it similarly to a rough opening and install a prehung door. If the rough opening was framed to a standard size and ½-inch drywall was used, check to see if the opening is square. If it is, you can nail the door frame directly against the drywall opening. Otherwise you'll need to remove the corner bead and the drywall from the jamb and header faces to make room for shims.

1 Check carefully for nails, then lay out the hinge mortises on the jamb. Rout close to the layout lines. Finish the mortises with a sharp chisel. Hold the door in the opening with shims and transfer the marks.

2 After the door is hung and the lockset installed, rub a little lipstick on the bolt to mark the jamb for the strike plate. Using a spade bit, drill a 1-inch hole for the bolt; mortise the strike plate into the jamb with a chisel.

Hole saw

TUNING UP AN OLD DOOR

As a house ages, parts often shift from their original positions. This inevitable settling can add a bit of charm to a structure, but it also can cause problems. This is especially true of doors, which are particularly sensitive to subtle shifts in their frames. Because you're in a remodeling mood, you may as well tune up any doors that are misbehaving.

Depending on the age of your house, this tune-up could be as simple as tightening a few screws, or it could mean planing down a few high spots before applying a new coat of paint.

If you live in a cold climate and need to plane a sticky door, it is best to wait until the most humid part of the summer to do it. Doors swell up when it is humid, so if you plane just enough to allow the door to close in the summer, you know it will work when it shrinks in the dry winter weather.

Note: If you plane the edge of a door, paint or apply finish to that edge as soon as possible to slow moisture absorption.

Tighten the screws: To fix a loose or sticking door, first tighten the hinge screws. Over time, screws slowly work loose, causing a door to sag slightly in its opening.

Use longer screws: If the screws won't tighten but simply turn in their holes, the holes are stripped. Remove the old screws and replace them with longer ones.

PRESTART CHECKLIST

☐ **TIME**
15 to 30 minutes per door

☐ **TOOLS**
Screwdriver, plane, utility knife, power drill/driver, straightedge, circular saw

☐ **SKILLS**
Driving screws, planing, cutting with a circular saw

☐ **MATERIALS**
2½-inch screws, dry lubricant

STANLEY PRO TIP: **Use steel for strength, brass for good looks**

Carpenters often install doors with brass hardware and brass hinges. Brass hardware is popular because it's attractive, even as it ages. Unfortunately brass screws are not very strong. They hold well enough, but you can easily damage the slots or twist the heads right off when you drive them. To get around these problems, purchase a few steel screws that are the same size as your brass ones. Drive the steel screws in first to cut the threads in the wood. Then replace the steel screws with the brass ones.

No matter what kind of screws you are driving, they will go in easier if lubricated with a little wax. Don't use soap—it attracts moisture, which causes corrosion.

Plane to fit: If the door still sticks, check the edge to see where it is rubbing. Wear marks often indicate where the door is contacting the jamb. Plane down the high spots.

Adding clearance: If the door rubs the floor (or carpet), it needs to be cut. Remove the door and place it on a pair of sawhorses padded with towels or carpet scraps. Using a metal straightedge and a utility knife, deeply scribe a cut line across the door to reduce splintering. Cut with a circular saw.

A touch of lubricant: As you rehang the door, squirt a little dry lubricant, such as graphite, into the hinges and onto the hinge pins to eliminate squeaks and groans from the hinges.

Cutting a hollow-core door

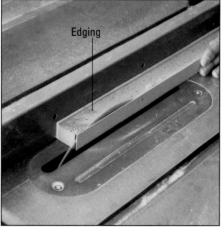

1 Hollow-core doors have solid edges for attaching hardware and to allow slight trimming. If you cut down past the edge, you will expose the door's hollow core. Fortunately, this doesn't make the door unusable.

2 If you need to cut down a hollow-core door significantly (past the edging), save the edging that you cut off. On a tablesaw, cut the facings off the edging to make it the right thickness to be reinserted in the door.

3 Glue and clamp the edging between the two door faces. When the glue dries, the door will be ready to use.

WINDOWS

Windows are easy to overlook. Or perhaps more correctly, most people look right through windows without seeing them. But when good windows go bad, they can be a nuisance that's nearly impossible to ignore, such as when the sash cords of an old double-hung window finally break, and you're forced to prop open the sash with a stick. Or when you realize that the whistling of the winter wind through the sash is the sound of your heating dollars literally going out the window.

Replacement windows
New generations of replacement windows can be custom-made to fit existing openings and are designed for easy installation. As you review the step-by-step procedure, you'll find that the job is well within the ability of a moderately skilled do-it-yourselfer. If you simply want to restore double-hung windows to operating order, follow the instructions for replacing sash cords.

Trimwork for a window
Even if your windows themselves are in great shape, take a good look at the millwork that's framing them. You could be looking at what happened when a penny-pinching contractor hired a trim carpenter who was in a hurry.

There's no need for you to tolerate a dated look or sloppy workmanship. Installing window trim is something you can do in a variety of styles. If you like the rich look of Victorian casing, you'll discover it's easy to install because corner blocks eliminate miter cuts.

If miters are no problem for you, check out the technique of crafting picture-frame trim for your window (see *pages 78–79*).

A gallery of trim variations *(pages 82–83)* shows you other great looks that you can achieve.

Tricks of the trade
If you've shied away from window trimwork because you thought you couldn't achieve the precision necessary, you're in for a surprise. You'll see that laying out and installing several kinds of window treatments doesn't even require a tape measure. By using the pieces of trim themselves to gauge the layout, you'll get great results with much less work than you ever imagined.

Repair or replace problem windows and make them look great with stylish new trim.

CHAPTER PREVIEW

Installing replacement windows
page 66

Replacing sash cords
page 72

Trimming out a window
page 73

Picture-frame window molding
page 78

Washing windows is no longer a dreaded chore when you replace a double-hung window with a tilt-in unit.

Arts and Crafts window trim
page 80

Trim variations
page 82

INSTALLING REPLACEMENT WINDOWS

Until recently, installing replacement double-hung windows involved major surgery to both the inside and outside of your house. But today's replacement windows feature many models that install completely from the inside, making the process safer, easier, and faster.

In addition, you'll find that many manufacturers custom-build replacements to your exact needs instead of restricting you to a limited selection of stock sizes. Surprisingly, custom sizes are priced competitively with standard units.

As you window shop, you'll discover that sash has evolved far beyond framed glass—you can choose from double glazing, low-E glass, argon-filled, and other features. You can select wood or vinyl with a variety of divided-light options for just the appearance you want.

But perhaps the best part of replacement is the fact that you can finally throw away the sticks that prop open your windows.

PRESTART CHECKLIST

☐ **TIME**
About 1 to 1½ hours to install the first window (after you understand the procedure, you'll install subsequent windows considerably faster)

☐ **TOOLS**
Stiff putty knife, utility knife, hammer, levels, pliers, screwdriver, folding rule

☐ **SKILLS**
Hammering, using a level

☐ **PREP**
Acquire materials, clear work area around window

☐ **MATERIALS**
Window kit, brads, touch-up paint or clear finish, painter's caulk or tinted putty

1 After you've selected a window supplier, follow that manufacturer's measuring instructions to ensure a proper fit. Measure at several locations both horizontally and vertically and record the smallest dimension each way. A folding rule with a brass extension makes precise work of interior measuring.

DISCARD

Don't trash the sashes

Put your old window sashes and weights at the end of your driveway with a sign marked "free" and watch how quickly they disappear. Some people will refinish and recycle them as operating sashes in their homes. Those who enjoy gardening can revamp them as cold frames to give tender plants a head start in the spring. Creative types may replace the glass with a mirror to make an interior decorating accent.

Remember, one person's sash is another person's treasure.

2 After your new windows arrive, gently work a stiff putty knife between the interior stop molding and the jamb. As you pry the stops free, take care not to dent the moldings because you'll reinstall them later. Pull the nails through the back of the stops (see *page 87*) to avoid damage and save these pieces.

3 Cut the cords from the front sash; the weights will drop into the pocket in the wall. Then lift out the front sash. If your window has chains, use metal snips or bolt cutters. Discard the old sashes.

4 Remove the side and top parting stops, which are the strips in the jamb in front of the upper sash. Use a utility knife to cut between the stop and jamb to break the grip of the paint. Because you'll discard these stops, don't worry about damaging them. Grab a stop with pliers and wiggle it out of its channel. Repeat with each stop.

5 Cut the cords and remove the upper sash. Remove the screw to open the door in the jamb that provides access to the weight pocket. Retrieve the weights so you can insulate the cavity. Replace the access door. If your jambs lack an access panel, leave the weights in place.

SAFETY FIRST
Be wary of springs

Exercise caution if your present windows have spring-loaded balances that support the sash. Releasing them suddenly can put parts into high-speed motion, posing a risk of injury. Carefully study the mechanism to develop a safe disconnection strategy.

WHAT IF...
Your parting stop channel is narrower than the replacement strip?

Parting stop channels are usually ½ inch wide, so that's the size furnished for the new head-jamb stop. But a few older windows have parting stops and channels that are ⅜ inch wide. If that's the size you have, you may have to plane or rip the replacement stops to the narrower size.

It's worth checking the size of the parting stop before you order the windows. That way, if you have ⅜-inch stops, you can ask whether the window manufacturer can furnish that size for you.

INSTALLING REPLACEMENT WINDOWS *(continued)*

6 Remove the pulley assemblies. Some screw in, others press in, and a particularly nasty type has nails driven through the hubs on the cavity side of the jamb. If necessary, resort to a jigsaw to cut away a piece of jamb. Fill the cavities with insulation and cover the holes with duct tape.

7 Check that the side jambs are straight and plumb and that the head jamb and sill are straight and level. These checks will also prove that the assembly is square. If necessary, shim to correct any problems.

8 Following the manufacturer's instructions, position the jamb liner clips on the side jambs. Fasten them with ¾- to 1-inch galvanized roofing nails.

STANLEY PRO TIP: **Insulating around replacement windows**

Fill the old weight cavities with cellulose insulation or pieces of fiberglass insulation. Make sure you don't pack the insulation too tightly—compacted insulation can lose much of its R-value.

Beware of spray-can foam insulation that expands as it cures; it can potentially push jambs out of alignment and wreak additional havoc. Although there are nonexpanding foam formulations, fiberglass and cellulose are easy to use and have no unpredictable risks.

If you remove the casing around a window, insulate the narrow openings around the jambs. Push in strips of fiberglass with the blade of a putty knife, using a light touch to prevent compacting the insulation.

9 Put a foam gasket at the top of each vinyl jamb liner. When you position the liner, make sure that the blind stop leaf (at the exterior vertical edge of the liner) overlaps the blind stop of the existing jamb.

10 Press the jamb liner firmly to engage it to the clips. If you need to remove the liners for any reason, follow the manufacturer's suggestions to avoid damaging either the liners themselves or the jamb members.

11 Position the new head jamb parting stop so that its weatherstripping faces the exterior of your house. Press the stop into the channel and fasten it with 1-inch brads. Drilling tiny pilot holes minimizes the chance of splitting the tiny stop.

Check for concealed damage

After you've removed the old sash, take a few minutes to carefully inspect the existing window jambs and sills before moving ahead with the installation.

If you see any evidence of insect infestation, such as mud tunnels or burrows in the wood, call a pest control specialist immediately for a thorough inspection and evaluation of the problem.

Probing the wood with the tip of a knife will quickly reveal punky wood, evidence of past water damage. Although sometimes called dry rot, the deteriorating wood fibers are usually the result of water infiltration.

Be sure to correct any problems before installing the new sash.

Giving the old wood a coat of paint also will prolong the life of your windows.

Another style of replacement window

You can purchase a style of replacement window that has the side and head jamb assembled at the factory. Installation is a simple matter of tilting the unit into the prepared opening and driving a couple of screws through each side jamb. Be careful not to overtighten the screws or you could bow the side jambs. Simply drive each screw until it touches the jamb. Check your work with a straightedge to ensure that jambs aren't bowed.

INSTALLING REPLACEMENT WINDOWS *(continued)*

12 Snap a vinyl sash stop into the jamb liner track that's nearest to the interior of your house. Repeat on the other side. These stops keep the lower sash from banging against the head jamb.

13 Stick a flat screwdriver into one of the tracks, then pull the locking terminal downward until it's about 9 inches above the sill. Rotate the driver toward the interior of the house to lock the terminal. Slowly release pressure until you're sure the terminal is engaged. Repeat for each track.

14 Hold the upper sash so that its left end is lower than the right, and put the left cam pivot into the rear track of the left jamb liner. Make sure the cam is above the locking terminal. Lower the right cam pivot into the right rear track. Level the window and rotate its top end into the opening.

Get right to the finish

If your window sashes are made from bare or primed wood, apply a finish promptly. Otherwise, the wood could start absorbing moisture or suffer damage from dirty hands. Don't overlook the bottoms, especially on the lower sash where there's a high risk of contact with water.

The minimum finishing schedule for paint should include at least one coat of high-quality primer followed by two coats of the topcoat.

If you select a clear finish for the interior wood, the water resistance of the formulation is important. Water resistance helps protect the wood from damage due to accidental contact with rain as well as condensation.

Don't paint or varnish the edges of the sash—the thickness of the film could make your windows difficult to operate. If you want to apply a finish to the edges of the sash, choose an oil finish (see *pages 226–227*) that won't build a film thickness.

15 Press in on the jamb liner, compressing it enough to work the upper edges of the sash into their grooves. Work alternately between the two sides to avoid twisting the sash. Lower the window to engage the cam pins with the locking terminals, then raise the sash.

16 Installing the lower sash follows the same general procedure as the upper one but is considerably easier because you're working with the inner set of tracks.

17 Replace the interior stop molding by nailing it into place and touching up the paint or clear finish.

18 Check the installation by tilting the sash inward to remove the manufacturer's stickers and any stray fingerprints on the glass.

REPLACING SASH CORDS

Many older homes have double-hung windows supported by sash cords. When these cords break, the windows do not open and close properly.

Replacing the cords isn't a difficult job. In fact, once you've fixed one window, you'll have the confidence to take on all the broken cords in your house.

The main component of the repair is ordinary cotton sash cord. Don't be tempted to purchase nylon cord: It's much more expensive, it stretches, and it's harder to knot securely. The only practical alternative to cotton sash cord is sash chain, which some hardware stores still stock in several colors. Although expensive, it's extremely durable. Some people object to the appearance of sash chain and the sound it makes.

While you are at it, replace the cords on both sashes in a frame, because it's easy preventive maintenance. Besides, with the lower window removed, you're more than halfway to accessing the upper sash.

STANLEY PRO TIP

Fish for a cord

If you have difficulty pushing the sash cord into the weight box, tie a length of string to the end of the cord and cinch a nut onto the end of the string. Drop the nut over the pulley and use the string to pull through the sash cord.

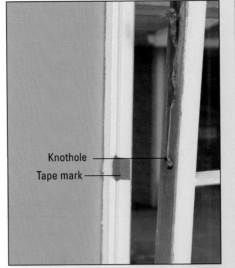

Knothole
Tape mark

1 Cut the sash cords and the weights will fall to the bottom of the pocket. Slice through the paint between the interior stop molding and the window jamb with a utility knife. Pry the stop molding with a stiff putty knife between the molding and the jamb. When you remove the sash, place a piece of tape onto the jamb to mark the knothole position when the window is closed.

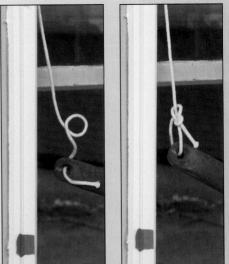

2 Remove the parting stop—the vertical molding between the sash channels. Locate the weight pocket access door in each jamb and open it. Make sure that the pulleys rotate smoothly. Thread the sash cord over the pulley and down into the weight pocket. Tie the cord to the weight with a bowline knot and put the weight back into the pocket.

Spring clamp

3 Pull down on the sash cord to raise the weight. When it gets to the top, clip a spring clamp onto the cord to hold the weight in the up position. Cut the cord about 4 inches below the masking tape on the jamb.

4 Tie a figure-eight knot at the end of the cord and stuff it into the hole in the side of the sash. For added security, you can drive a screw through the knot into the sash. Replace the moldings and touch up the finish if necessary.

TRIMMING OUT A WINDOW

Installing window trim is not as complicated as it looks. The moldings themselves prescribe the layout, and an orderly installation sequence helps ensure success. The reveal around the window jamb is the only measurement required—you don't even need a tape measure for this project.

Whether you're trimming out a new opening or upgrading the appearance of an existing window, the step-by-step procedure strips away the mysteries and guides you to a great-looking installation.

PRESTART CHECKLIST

☐ **TIME**
About 1 hour per window

☐ **TOOLS**
Hammer, mallet, nail set, combination square, utility knife

☐ **SKILLS**
Checking for plumb, driving nails

☐ **PREP**
Window should be installed and old trim removed; wall should be painted

☐ **MATERIALS**
A set of moldings, water-resistant glue, 3d (1¼-inch) and 8d (2½-inch) finishing nails

1 Set your combination square to mark a ¼-inch reveal around the interior edges of the side and top window jambs. The reveal doesn't need to be a continuous line; a few marks will show where to position the casing.

2 At the top corners, draw lines across the jamb onto the wall indicating the inner edge of the jamb sides and head. These marks indicate the ends of the casing and the position of the corner blocks.

Hiring a contractor

If you prefer to have a professional replace the windows in your house, obtain bids from at least two contractors. Ask for names of previous customers as references. Ask those customers specific questions about the contractor's reliability and performance. If you can, arrange to look at the jobs so you can assess the quality of workmanship and make sure it meets your standards.

Also ask the contractor for proof of insurance. A contractor should have liability insurance to cover damage that might be done to your property and workman's compensation insurance. Without workman's compensation coverage, an installer or one of his or her employees who is injured while working at your house could sue *you*—and collect.

Find out if the contractor is licensed in your area. The fact that a contractor is licensed is evidence that the business is legitimate, but is not a guarantee of competence. Often it simply means that he or she has paid paid a fee to a local government agency.

Check the specifications of the windows the contractor will supply. Make sure they are of the quality and style you want.

Ask questions about all the details of the job, from obtaining permits through disposal of the old windows. When the job is completed, get lien waivers as proof that the contractor has paid workers and suppliers for all labor and materials used on the job.

Be wary of a contractor who asks for a large down payment, especially in cash.

TRIMMING OUT A WINDOW *(continued)*

3 At the left side of the window, align a piece of casing with the reveal marks and make pencil lines on the wall along its outer edge at about the bottom of the window frame. (For photographic clarity, these marks are much darker than the faint lines you'll make.)

4 Roll the casing outward onto its edge and align its inner edge with the pencil mark you just made. Draw another pencil mark at the outer edge.

5 When you repeat Steps 3 and 4 at the right side of the window, the outer marks farthest away indicate the overall length of the stool, the horizontal piece at the bottom of the window often mistakenly called the sill. After you square up the left end of this molding at the mitersaw, mark the right end and cut to length.

Window shopping

To find windows that will work well in your home, take time to do some window homework. In addition to matters of style, you should also consider how well a window will perform.

Look for the Energy Star sticker on each window you're considering. The label lists efficiency ratings in several categories:

■ U-factor is the rate of heat loss: the lower the number, the better the insulation.

■ SHGC (solar heat gain coefficient) runs on a scale from 0 to 1. A low number means less heat. In a warm-climate zone, low solar gain can reduce cooling costs.

■ VT (visible transmission) is also on a scale of 0 to 1; a higher number means more visibility.

■ AL stands for air leakage, measuring how much air escapes the weatherstripping. The lower the leakage, the better the window contains heated or cooled air.

The Energy Star label lists the window's performance in key areas. Your climate zone guides the relative importance of each category. For example, are you more concerned with heating costs or cooling costs?

Don't overlook style and convenience while shopping. Grilles between panes provide a divided-light look without the inconvenience of washing tiny frames. Tilt-in windows also make for easy cleaning.

Stool

6 Center the stool side to side and mark the inner edges of the jambs onto it with a utility knife. Set it aside for the moment.

7 Hold the head of your combination square flush against the edge of the jamb and wall, then slide the rule until its end lightly touches the lower sash. Lock this depth marking by turning the nut.

8 Transfer the depth marking to the stool, gauging from the back of the stool toward the front. Also draw a line extending the jamb marks you made in Step 6. Mark a bold X in the waste area to avoid mistakes. Use a fine-tooth handsaw to cut along the inner edges of the lines.

SQUARE THE STOCK

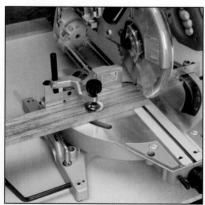

When you begin working with a piece of molding, always square up one end with a mitersaw before cutting the other end to length. The initial cut removes any dings or dents at the end of the molding and establishes a reliably square end.

WHAT IF...
You want to put returns on the stool and apron?

Returns are a mark of high-quality workmanship and add just a few minutes of work to each window. Many do-it-yourselfers appreciate the upgraded look and see those few ticks of the clock as a worthy investment.

Why do so many professional finish carpenters omit returns? It's simple economics. Multiply a few minutes by the number of windows in a house and it adds up to hours of extra labor costs that a client or contractor may not be willing to pay for.

To learn how to make returns, see *page 214.*

TRIMMING OUT A WINDOW *(continued)*

9 After a test fitting, apply glue to the underside of the stool and drive 8d finishing nails through the stool into the sill to secure it.

10 Temporarily hold a piece of casing against the wall and jamb and rest its square-cut end against the stool to ensure that the stool is square to the wall. Tap the stool with a mallet to adjust its position.

11 Gauge the length of the apron by holding it against the inner pair of marks you made earlier. (The apron is the piece that goes under the stool.) Cut it to length, run a bead of glue along its upper edge, and nail it into place.

Casing vs. apron

You'll sometimes purchase a packaged kit of millwork that contains all of the trim parts for a single window. If you examine the parts carefully, you may notice that one piece looks like casing from the front but doesn't have the relief cut on the back.

The lack of the relief cut enables you to simply square-cut the apron to length. If you use casing for the apron, you'll have to create a return to hide the grooved back.

The relief cut (sometimes also called a backing-out cut, or back cut) reduces the tendency of wide moldings to cup. As another advantage, relieved moldings can bridge over irregularities in walls, producing a closer fit at the edges.

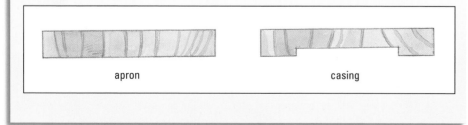

apron   casing

Goof-proof guard

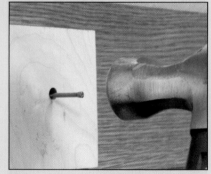

Make a hammering shield from a 3×6-inch piece of ⅛-inch hardboard. Drill a ¼-inch hole 1½ inches from the end and use the shield to prevent a stray hammer blow from marring your moldings. Make your last hammer strike a sharp blow to countersink the nail slightly below the surface of the shield.

12 Square-cut the end of the casing and rest that end on the stool. Gauge the cutline at the upper end at the mark you made on the jamb in Step 2. Repeat for the other side casing.

13 After cutting the side casings to length, align the edge of the casings with the reveal marks on the edge of the jamb and nail it in place. Use 3d (1¼-inch) finishing nails along the jamb side and 8d (2½-inch) finishing nails along the outer edge to penetrate the drywall.

14 Put a corner block on top of the left casing, and align its right edge with the vertical mark you made earlier. The corner of the block should meet the corner of the jamb. Nail only the left block into position.(If you're left-handed, install the right block first.)

15 Gauge the length of the top casing by butting a square-cut end against the left block and marking the cutline at the right end.

16 Nail the top casing into position and install the top right block. Finally, cut the stop molding to length and nail it to each side of the jamb.

PICTURE-FRAME WINDOW MOLDING

Picture-frame molding is often the first choice around casement, awning, and hopper windows. To adapt this approach to double-hung windows, you'll need to add a filler strip on top of the slanted sill. (See "What If" on the *opposite page* to learn how to add a filler strip.)

You can select virtually any molding profile for the picture-frame treatment, but if you team the technique with a simple millwork, you'll achieve a clean, modern look with crisp lines.

Although you can create this look by nailing individual strips to the jamb and wall, you'll probably find that it's faster and more accurate to build the frame on a flat work surface, such as a piece of plywood supported by sawhorses. When you glue the joints, put a strip of waxed paper under the wood to prevent it from accidentally bonding to the worktable.

PRESTART CHECKLIST

☐ **TIME**
About 30 minutes per window

☐ **TOOLS**
Hammer, mitersaw, combination square, clamps, power drill/driver

☐ **SKILLS**
Sawing, hammering, driving screws

☐ **PREP**
Acquire materials, clear work area around window

☐ **MATERIALS**
Moldings, 4d (1½-inch) and 8d (2½-inch) finishing nails, 1½-inch trim screws, painter's caulk or tinted putty to fill holes

1 Set your combination square and mark the desired reveal—³⁄₁₆ inch in this example—along all four edges of the window jamb. A short mark at each corner and the midpoint of each jamb is sufficient.

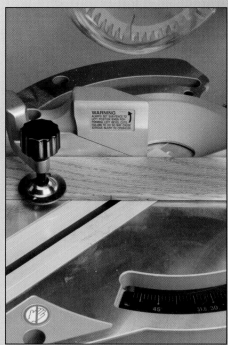

2 Measure and cut the four casings. (See "Cutting Miter Joints" on *pages 206–207* for tips on achieving dependably accurate results.)

What kind of windows accept picture-frame casing?

As a matter of tradition, most double-hung windows have a stool and apron treatment, but you can easily adapt them to picture-frame casing.

Windows that open by tilting or swiveling are naturals for the picture-frame treatment. This hopper window tilts inward, pivoting at the bottom of the sash. Its cousin, the awning window, cranks outward on pivots near the top of the sash. Casement windows usually have picture-frame casing. Sliding windows can go either way—some have stools and others are picture-framed.

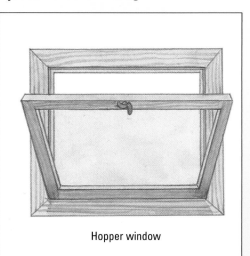

Hopper window

The hopper window tilts inward, opening at the top. See other window styles on pages 80–81.

3 Brush a thin coat of glue on a pair of miters and rub the pieces against each other until the glue starts to grab.

4 Clamp the joint to your worktable and drill a pilot hole for a trim screw. These nearly headless fasteners are virtually invisible, especially if you drive them through the top and bottom casings.

5 Align the edges of the completed assembly with the reveal marks, and nail it into position. If you aren't using a pneumatic nailer, start a few nails into the molding before jockeying it into place.

WHAT IF...
You want to picture-frame a double-hung window?

Instead of installing a stool as on *pages 74–76*, create a stool strip that's tapered to match up with the window's sill. This isn't nearly as difficult as it sounds.

Measure the distance from the wall's surface to the lower sash with a combination square, and rip a board to that width. Next use an adjustable bevel gauge to match the slope of the sill so you can measure it with a protractor. A typical angle is about 14 degrees.

Tilt your tablesaw's blade to that setting and adjust the rip fence so the strip's narrowest width will be about ½ inch. Rip the strip, cut it to length, and test the fit. You'll want to allow the thickness of a business card between the edge of the strip and the window to prevent binding. Glue and nail the strip to the windowsill.

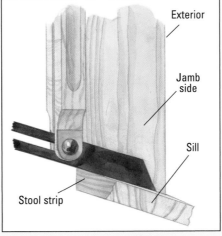

An adjustable bevel gauge helps you accurately match the sill's angle. Tilt your tablesaw to this setting.

When you rip the tapered stool strip, be sure to use the blade guard (it was removed here for photographic clarity). Feed the stock past the blade with a pushstick.

ARTS AND CRAFTS WINDOW TRIM

One of the secrets behind Arts and Crafts window framing is making the head casing slightly thicker than the sides. This creates two beneficial features: a shadow line that adds interest to the construction, and a reveal that conceals eventual wood movement. Alignment and construction are made easy by using concealed biscuits to join the head casing with the side casings.

If you make side casings from standard ¾-inch-thick lumber, make the top casing from a board 1¹⁄₁₆ inch thick. This thicker lumber is called 5/4 (five-quarter) stock.

To add a subtle detail to this installation, plane or rout a chamfer along the vertical edges of the side casings and along both the edges and ends of the head casing. Limit the chamfer to about ⅛ inch in width.

The chamfer gives the stock a finished look, makes blunt edges, which are less likely to chip or splinter, and helps the finish adhere better.

1 Butt the bottom end of a side casing against the window stool, and mark its top cut line at the reveal for the head casing.

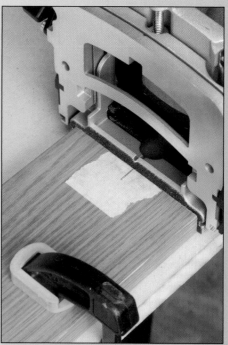

2 Clamp the side casing face up on your workbench, and use a biscuit joiner to cut a biscuit slot centered in the width of its top end. For details on biscuit joinery, see *page 212*. Install both side casings.

PRESTART CHECKLIST

☐ **TIME**
About 1 hour per window

☐ **TOOLS**
Hammer, nail set, combination square, utility knife, biscuit joiner

☐ **SKILLS**
Checking for plumb, driving nails and screws

☐ **PREP**
Window should be installed and old trim removed; wall should be painted

☐ **MATERIALS**
A set of moldings, water-resistant glue, 3d (1¼-inch) and 8d (2½-inch) finishing nails, biscuits

Four more window styles

Sliding window

3 Cut the head casing 1 inch longer than the outside-to-outside measurement of the side casings, then center it on top of the side casings. Transfer the center marks from the side casings to the head casings, then cut biscuit slots at these locations.

4 Glue the biscuits into the side casings and head casing. Nail the head casing in place.

Double-hung window

Fixed sash

Awning window

Casement window

TRIM VARIATIONS

Federal fluted

The flutes on purchased moldings run the full length of the trim. But if you make your own casings, you can add subtle touches that give your installation a true custom look. Rip the stock to width and rout ⅛-inch roundovers along the front edges. Crosscut the lumber to the lengths you need, then rout stopped flutes with a roundnose bit. Stop each flute about 1 inch from each end of the casing. Experiment on scrap stock to set the spacing between flutes, or copy the profile of commercial molding. Painted and clear finishes are appropriate.

Arts and Crafts I

Half-lap corners that run past each other are a recurrent Arts and Crafts design motif. It's a joinery method used in authentic picture frames and furniture. Fortunately, you get the half-lap look without actually going through the trouble of cutting the joint. Simply butt the head casing on top of the side casings, or add a biscuit to maintain the alignment. Adding the top piece with another biscuit joint will give the appearance of complex joinery. If you have a router, cut chamfers on the ends of the head casing and top pieces before assembly.

Arts and Crafts II

This window treatment is definitely Arts and Crafts, using quartersawn white oak in two thicknesses. Make the side casings from ¾-inch-thick stock and the head casing from 5/4 lumber. (Hardwood 5/4 lumber measures approximately 1¹⁄₁₆ inch thick.) Cut angles on the ends of the board to suit your personal taste. Cut a cardboard sample and tape it in place to verify the angle and width of the head casing before cutting your lumber. An angle of about 15 degrees from vertical is a good starting point.

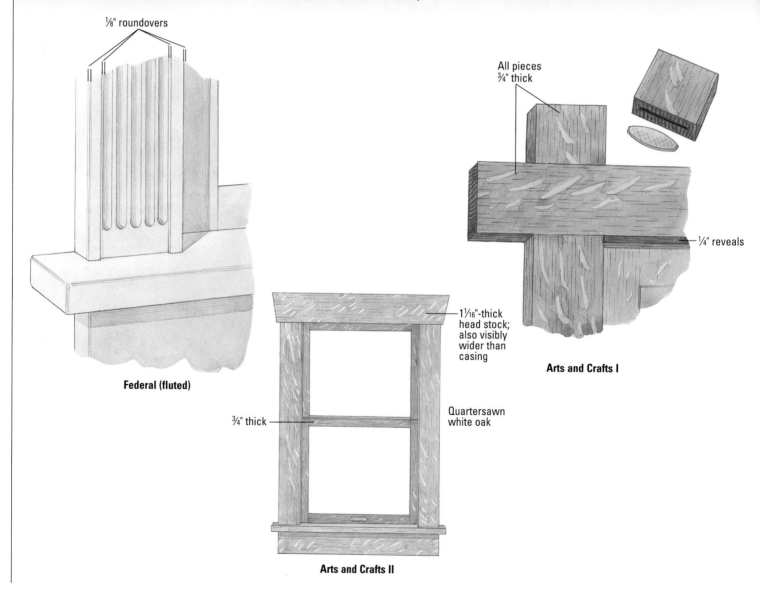

⅛" roundovers

Federal (fluted)

All pieces ¾" thick

¼" reveals

1¹⁄₁₆"-thick head stock; also visibly wider than casing

¾" thick

Quartersawn white oak

Arts and Crafts I

Arts and Crafts II

Traditional

This type of door and window trim was popular in the 1920s, although its clean lines allow it to blend with many contemporary looks. In the past, carpenters made the side and head casings from solid lumber ¾ inch thick and wrapped the edges with an L-shape corner molding that was mitered at the corners. You can do that or create the same look with a simpler and less expensive method. If you're painting the trimwork, make the casings from medium-density fiberboard (MDF). A biscuit at each corner maintains flush joints. Rip pine strips ⅛ inch thick and 1 inch wide or purchase lattice strips. Miter the corners, then nail the strips to the face of the casing so the outer edges are flush with the casing's outer edges.

Contemporary

Some people call this molding profile contemporary or streamline; others call it clamshell because its end view resembles a clam. Still others call it ranch because of its widespread installation in millions of ranch-style homes during the suburban building boom of the 1950s and 1960s.

When the molding has a natural finish, it can evoke a nostalgic retro look. But painted, the profile looks cleanly contemporary.

Cottage/country/modern

Here's a clean-cut installation that's simple enough for a hideaway in the woods or sleek enough for an urban loft. As with any tailored look, neat workmanship is mandatory, and a couple of coats of interior white enamel are a must. For a country accent, finish your trim with a color that complements your furnishings.

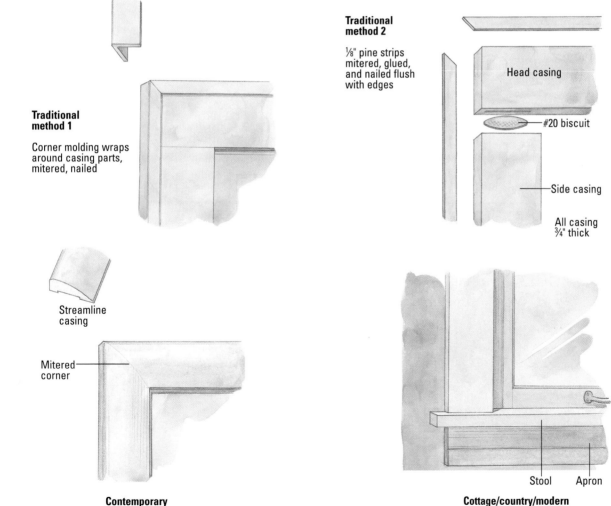

Traditional method 1

Corner molding wraps around casing parts, mitered, nailed

Traditional method 2

⅛" pine strips mitered, glued, and nailed flush with edges

Head casing

#20 biscuit

Side casing

All casing ¾" thick

Streamline casing

Mitered corner

Contemporary

Stool   Apron

Cottage/country/modern

WALL-BUILDING BASICS

Sometimes a remodeling project involves removing a wall to open up a larger area. Other times it may mean adding a wall to redefine a space or create new living areas. Some projects combine partial demolition and new construction.

But before you start swinging a sledgehammer, understand that demolition does not mean destruction. Demolition is carefully planned removal that can involve special techniques to salvage moldings and other components for reuse. In addition, demolition involves planning to protect adjoining surfaces from damage. In short, smart demolition prevents unintentional destruction.

Despite the mess and heavy work that go with demolition, many people enjoy it.

Progress is immediately evident and smashing things has a genuine therapeutic value.

Build walls from wood or metal

Framing new walls can also be a relatively speedy process. When you choose traditional wood studs, you'll generally find that it's easiest to build the wall flat and then raise it into position. Selecting metal studs means you'll probably install the top and bottom plates first, adding the studs between them to frame the wall into place.

As you build, check often that your work is plumb and flat. Investing a few minutes in inspection will make drywalling easier.

After you've added utilities to the wall, you'll be ready to insulate. On exterior walls, you'll need the thermal and vapor barrier properties of insulation. In interior walls, insulation can deaden noise from gurgling drains or a cranked-up sound system.

Drywall covers the structure

Drywalling is another step that shows initial progress rapidly. When you work methodically, you'll hang sheets of drywall efficiently, covering large areas with surprising speed. After that, joint taping and sanding can consume several days, but much of that is simply waiting for each coat of joint compound to dry. After you sand the final coat, your new wall is ready for primer and paint.

If the framing is straight and square, the rest of the job will move ahead with ease.

CHAPTER PREVIEW

Removing and saving moldings
page 86

Removing drywall and plaster
pages 88–89

Preparing the work site
page 90

Framing a wall and a doorway
pages 92–97

With the top plate in place, you can build the wall on the ground and raise it into place.

Adding blocking in advance to a wall frame makes it easy to attach elements such as chair molding or wall cabinets.

Framing is one of the more exciting parts of remodeling. The pieces go together quickly and progress is noticeable.

Framing with metal
page 98

Insulating a wall
page 100

Hanging drywall
page 101

Finishing drywall
page 106

REMOVING AND SAVING MOLDINGS

The first pieces to come off a wall are the last pieces to be reinstalled—the moldings and other pieces of trim. It can be worthwhile to remove them carefully for reuse, especially when dealing with the ornate woodwork found in older homes. Matching new replacements to old woodwork can be expensive.

The challenge is to remove the moldings without damaging them or anything else that will remain. Work slowly and methodically, prying the pieces loose from the nails that hold them.

Nails present two problems. First, if the molding has been painted, the nails are probably concealed. Second, even if you know where the nails are, you won't be able to get at them because their heads are set beneath the surface of the molding. There are two solutions: You can pry the molding away from the wall and pull out the nails from the back or cut them off, or you can drive the nails through the molding. Don't try to back the nails out; their heads likely will chip the face of the molding as they are driven out.

PRESTART CHECKLIST

☐ **TIME**
About 10 to 15 minutes per piece of molding, depending on length

☐ **TOOLS**
Putty knife, 3-inch drywall knife, flat bar, hammer, nail set, end nips, file

☐ **SKILLS**
Prying, driving nails, cutting nails, filing

1 Beginning at one end of a piece of molding, gently work a putty knife between the molding and the wall. You may have to tap the putty knife gently with a hammer to force it between the wall and molding.

2 As the molding loosens, work in a 3-inch drywall knife from underneath or from the other edge. Continue to pry gently along the length of the molding until you can see the nails that fasten the molding in place.

DRIVE THE NAILS THROUGH

One approach to removing trim is to drive the nails through the molding. This frees the molding and eliminates the problem of what to do with the nails protruding from a piece you want to save. This method also eliminates the possibility of damaging or breaking the molding while you pry on it. The drawback is that you can easily split moldings—especially narrow ones—by driving the nails through. And in some cases, if the trim is a hardwood, such as oak, it can be difficult to drive the nails farther in.

First locate the nails. On woodwork that has been stained or coated with a clear finish, look for telltale spots of filler. On painted moldings, you may have to first pry them away from the wall as described above. Once you find the nails, drive them through the molding with a hammer and a nail set. Use a small-diameter nail set to avoid enlarging the hole.

Scrap plywood

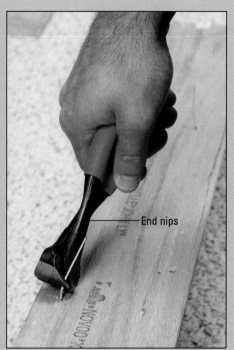

End nips

3 As the gap widens, slip a flat bar behind the molding. Work along the length, gently prying the piece away from its home. Back up the bar with a scrap of ¼-inch plywood to avoid damaging the wall or floor.

4 Free one end of the molding, then work along the rest of the piece, prying where each nail is located.

5 Grasp the nail with end nips at the back of the molding and pull the nail sideways, being careful not to dent the edges of the molding.

Dealing with stubborn nails

The small heads of most finishing nails pull easily through the back of molding, but sometimes, especially with older nails in hardwood molding, you can't pull nails without causing damage. In that case, clip off the nails with end nips and file away any protruding part of the nail until it is flush with the back of the molding.

WHAT IF…
The paint acts like glue?

Paint can act like glue, sticking moldings to walls and to other moldings, especially in a room that has numerous coats of paint. The parts that are stuck can easily break off, particularly if they are older wood, which can be quite brittle. Paint often disguises the seams between moldings, making it difficult to see which parts of a molding are separate pieces of wood. If you have this problem, gently loosen and remove the excess paint with a paint scraper before you attempt to remove the moldings. Use your utility knife to cut through paint seams. Work slowly and carefully to avoid slips that can mar the molding.

REMOVING DRYWALL

After the moldings are out of the way, the next step is to remove the drywall or plaster from the wall. Before you start smashing the wall with a hammer, find out if there are any pipes, ducts, or wiring inside the walls *(see page 31)*.

This is a messy job, so work carefully to avoid creating excessive debris and dust. Remove drywall in large pieces. Start near the top of the wall and work down, prying the drywall free of its fasteners as you go. Drywall is inexpensive, so don't try to save it for reuse. Construction adhesive residue on studs can be a problem, but a heavy-duty paint scraper and chisel may remove enough of it to allow you to hang drywall. Construction adhesive remover should soften troublesome residue spots. Provide plenty of ventilation and give the remover recommended time to do its job. Be sure to wear a dust mask rated for fine dust, not just nuisance dust. A fine-dust mask has two straps and is thicker than a nuisance-dust mask.

PRESTART CHECKLIST

☐ **TIME**
About 1 to 2 hours per sheet (32 square feet) of drywall from start to final cleanup

☐ **TOOLS**
Hammer, flat bar, end nips, utility knife, power drill/driver (for removing drywall screws), reciprocating saw (for removing parts of walls), handsaw

☐ **SKILLS**
Prying, pulling nails, removing screws, cutting with a reciprocating saw

☐ **PREP**
Isolate the work site to contain the mess; determine what utilities may be contained within the wall

1 **Shut off power at the service panel** and remove coverplates from the wall boxes. If you're ending drywall removal at a wall or ceiling corner, slice through the joint compound and tape with a utility knife. A saw cut along a stud forms the boundary of a partial removal job.

2 Punch a line of hammer holes high along the stud bays to create handholds for removal. Work carefully to ensure you don't damage concealed plumbing lines, heat ducts, or wiring.

3 Grip the drywall and pull down, ripping the material in manageable chunks. To avoid excessive handling, drop the pieces directly into a disposal container instead of onto the floor.

4 Clean up the studs by yanking nails or backing out screws. To make sure you find every fastener, slide a putty knife or the edge of your hammerhead along the stud. Even if you're completely removing the wall, fastener removal makes the studs safer to handle.

REMOVING PLASTER

The walls of many older houses are covered with plaster rather than drywall. Plaster is applied as a wet paste over a series of thin wood strips called lath, which are attached to the wall studs. The plaster is squeezed between these thin pieces, oozing into the wall cavities. When the plaster dries, this ooze, called keys, holds the plaster to the wall.

More recently, installed plaster uses an expanded metal mesh rather than wood lath. Use tin snips to cut through the metal mesh. The most difficult aspect of removing plaster is avoiding damage to adjacent areas.

Before you begin removing plaster, **turn off any nearby circuits at the electrical service panel.** Remove all receptacle and switch coverplates. Wear a dust mask rated for fine dust (see *opposite page*).

PRESTART CHECKLIST

☐ **TIME**
About 1 to 2 hours per 8-foot section of wall

☐ **TOOLS**
Hammer, pry bar, power drill/driver (for attaching reinforcing 1×2s), handsaw, reciprocating saw (for removing parts of walls)

☐ **SKILLS**
Prying, pulling nails, cutting with a reciprocating saw and handsaw

☐ **PREP**
Isolate the work site to contain the mess; determine what utilities may be contained within the wall

☐ **MATERIALS**
1×2s to reinforce surrounding plaster, if necessary

1 Plaster is a tough wall surface, but too much pounding and vibration can jar it loose in places you don't want to remove. To avoid problems, attach 1×2s in the corners of walls and the ceiling adjacent to the wall you are removing.

2 If you remove only part of a wall, stop at a stud. You can't cut through lath in the middle of a bay without destroying the plaster. To find the end stud, drill ⅛-inch-diameter holes every inch through the waste section of plaster until the drill hits a stud. Attach a reinforcing 1×2 along the stud.

3 Knock the plaster off the wall with a hammer. It is easier to shovel up the loose debris before the lath is mixed in. If lath strips continue past the end stud, cut them flush to the side of the end stud with a handsaw or reciprocating saw.

4 As you remove the lath with a flat pry bar, some of the lath nails will stay in the studs; others will come away with the lath. Either way, it's best to remove the nails as you go and pile the lath neatly for disposal.

PREPARING THE WORK SITE

The job of putting up a new wall ranges from simple to complex, depending on where the wall will be located. The determining factor is whether the wall runs parallel to the ceiling joists or whether it cuts across them. Walls are usually attached to the joists above, so a wall that goes across the joists is easier to build. This is because the top plate can be nailed through the ceiling to the joists.

Building a wall that runs parallel to the joists is somewhat more involved. Unless you are lucky and your wall falls directly under a joist, you'll have to open up the ceiling to install blocking to attach the top plate. In fact, if moving the wall an inch or two would place it under a joist, consider doing so.

If you are attaching a top plate through a plaster ceiling into joists, predrill the plate and attach it with 3-inch wood screws.

PRESTART CHECKLIST

☐ **TIME**
About 1 hour for a simple wall that's perpendicular to the joists

☐ **TOOLS**
Tape measure, chalk line, hammer, circular saw, power drill/driver, utility knife, layout square

☐ **SKILLS**
Measuring, snapping a chalk line, hammering, crosscutting

☐ **PREP**
Complete remodeling plans

☐ **MATERIALS**
2×4 for top plate, 16d nails

1 Start by locating the ends of the new wall on the ceiling according to the dimensions you worked out on your plan. With a helper, snap a chalk line between the two points.

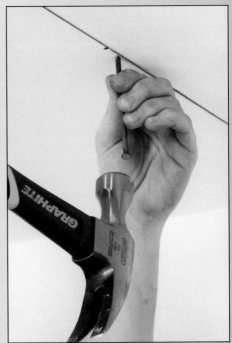

2 Locate the joists by tapping the ceiling with your knuckles. Joists sound and feel solid; the space between them sounds hollow. Drive an 8d nail through the ceiling to double-check. If it punches through easily, you've missed the joist; move over an inch and try again.

WHAT IF...
You don't have a helper?

To snap a chalk line when working alone, drive a nail at one end of your layout. Hook the end of the line on the nail and stretch it tightly at the other end of the layout. Snap the chalk line as usual.

To attach a plate, hold it centered on the layout line. Drive a 3-inch screw through the plate into the joists. (It is easier to hold the plate steady when screwing than when hammering.) Nail the rest of the connections.

3 Once you know where all the joists are, cut a 2×4 to the proper length for the top plate. Measure and transfer the joist locations onto the plate with a tape measure and layout square.

Joist location

4 Starting a nail at each joist location is easy while the plate is still on the floor. Substitute 3-inch drywall screws if you'll be hammering into a plaster ceiling or if you simply dislike the effort of overhead nailing.

5 With a helper, hold the top plate in place along the chalk line and nail it in place right through the ceiling. If the plate isn't quite straight, nail part of it, then push the offending end into line.

Running a wall parallel to the joists

1 Use a handsaw or reciprocating saw to cut away the ceiling flush to the inside faces of the joists where the wall will attach. (For cutting plaster, see *page 89.)* Snap a chalk line along the center of each joist, then use a utility knife to cut away a ¾-inch-wide strip of drywall. This will expose surfaces on the joists for attaching the new drywall.

2 Cut blocking to fit snugly between the joists. Use four toenails to attach each block with its wide face down. Use a ⅛-inch-diameter bit to predrill the ends of the blocks for the toenails.

3 Nail the blocking in place between the joists. Space the pieces 16 inches on center to provide support for the new drywall as well as convenient nailing for crown molding.

FRAMING A WALL

One way to frame a wall is to install the top and bottom plates, then toenail the studs to the plates. But if you have enough space, it's easier to put the pieces together on the floor. This method allows you to nail through the bottom and top plates directly into the bottom and top of the studs, which is much easier than toenailing, especially toenailing over your head. Then you can tip the wall up and move it into position.

To build on the floor, begin by measuring and cutting all the studs to length. Then put the bottom and top plates against each other to mark them for the positions of the studs. Last put the studs between the plates and nail the assembly together.

PRESTART CHECKLIST

☐ **TIME**
About 1 hour for an 8×8-foot wall

☐ **TOOLS**
Tape measure, layout square, circular saw, hammer, chalk line, plumb bob

☐ **SKILLS**
Measuring and marking, crosscutting, driving nails

☐ **PREP**
Install top plate first

☐ **MATERIALS**
2×4s (four for the first 4 feet of wall, three for every 4 feet thereafter, plus top and bottom plates), 16d nails

Build the wall

1 Measure from the underside of the ceiling plate to the floor to determine the wall height. Check in several places and use the smallest dimension as the height.

2 Cut the plates and the studs to length. The length of the studs should be 3 inches less than the wall height you just determined. This allows for the thickness of two 2×4 plates (1½ inches each).

WHAT IF...
There isn't enough room to build flat?

If you are working in tight quarters, you'll have to build the wall in place. Start by laying out the plates as described above. Attach the wall top plate to the plate already attached to the ceiling *(pages 90–91).* Use a plumb bob to locate the bottom plate *(page 94).* Anchor it to the floor. Cut the studs to fit in between the plates. Toenail them in place top and bottom. Predrilling makes nailing easier.

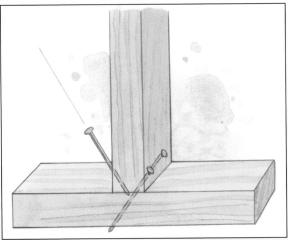

Toenails are driven into the face of a stud at an angle such that they come out the end of the stud and enter an adjoining piece of lumber. Usually three nails are adequate, one driven from one side and two from the other.

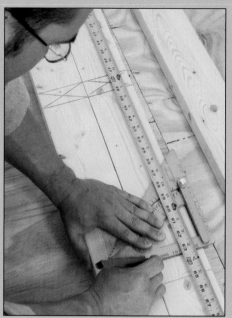

3 Hold the plates side by side to mark the spacing for the studs. The first stud will be offset by ¾ inch; then make a mark every 16 inches to indicate the centers of the studs. Measure ¾ inch on both sides of each mark and draw lines to show where the sides of the studs will be.

4 Place the studs on edge in between the plates. If any studs are not perfectly flat, turn them so that any slight gap is at the bottom. Hold them in position one by one and nail them in place through the plates. Make sure the edges of the studs are flush with the edges of the plates.

5 Blocking may be added to the wall to provide a solid nailing surface for moldings or cabinets. If needed, nail blocking between the studs. Position the blocking with the wide face out. Toenail one side of each block. Here the pieces are positioned to support a chair-rail molding.

SPACING FOR THE STUDS

Laying out the positions of the studs in a wall is a crucial step in construction. Get it right and installing drywall is easy; make a mistake and you'll have problems.

The most common spacing is 16 inches on center (OC). This means the distance from the center of one stud to the center of the next is 16 inches. The space between studs that are 16 inches OC is 14½ inches. The first and last studs in a wall are exceptions to the rule. The first stud is shifted over ¾ inch as its centerline corresponds with the end of the wall, so its side is flush with the ends of the plates. This makes the space between the first and second studs 13¾ inches.

The last stud in the wall may or may not be spaced evenly. Its position depends on the length of the wall. Thus the spacing between it and the second-to-last stud can be anything from a couple of inches to the standard 14½ inches. Whatever you do, don't adjust the spacing of all the studs to avoid having a single odd space. If you do, the edges of your drywall sheets won't line up with the studs.

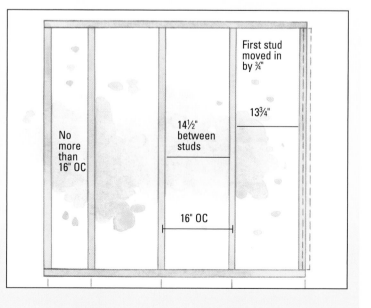

Set the wall into place

Once a wall is framed, put it in place as quickly as possible to free up the floor space. Before lifting the wall, double-check to make sure its height matches or is less than the distance from the floor to the underside of the plate that's attached to the ceiling.

Use a plumb bob and a chalk line to locate the position of the bottom plate on the floor. Lift up the wall and slide it into position, then nail it in place. Whenever you need to attach a new wall to a plaster wall or ceiling, drill pilot holes and use 3-inch-long drywall screws instead of nails to avoid breaking the plaster.

It's a good idea to have a helper for this part of the job. Otherwise, if the wall is long, you could strain your back or rack the wall. Even if the wall is short enough to raise and move yourself, it's easier to mark for plumb and hold the wall in position for nailing if you have a helper.

—Plumb bob

1 Dangle a plumb bob from the end and side of the ceiling plate to transfer the wall location to the floor. If you are working alone, hang the plumb bob from a nail in the plate. Repeat at the other end. This job is quicker with two people: One holds the string, the other marks the spot.

2 Snap a chalk line between the two marks you located with the plumb bob. This line indicates where the side of the bottom plate will go.

WHAT IF…
You are anchoring walls to concrete floors?

Setting up a wall on a concrete floor presents a bigger challenge than merely nailing into a wood subfloor. Fortunately, there are plenty of solutions.

■ If the floor is less than four years old, drive specially hardened masonry nails through the bottom plate into the concrete. One-half inch of penetration prevents shifting, so drive 2-inch nails through lumber that measures 1½ inches thick.

■ A powder-actuated tool uses an explosive charge to drive fasteners. Exercise extreme care and follow all of the manufacturer's instructions.

■ Specialty masonry bits and screws designed for concrete fastening (Tapcon is one manufacturer) are suited for many applications.

■ Drill a hole into the concrete, then you can tap in a lead or plastic plug that accepts a threaded fastener.

■ Construction adhesive reduces the number of mechanical fasteners required, but don't rely on the adhesive alone.

Masonry nails work well to anchor the plate to a slab if the concrete is not too old. Be sure to **wear safety goggles** when hammering nails into concrete because pieces of concrete will fly.

Construction adhesive adds holding power when teamed with mechanical fasteners. Cut the nozzle to produce a ½-inch bead, then lay down a generous amount. A tube that's more than a year old starts to lose strength, so buy fresh adhesive.

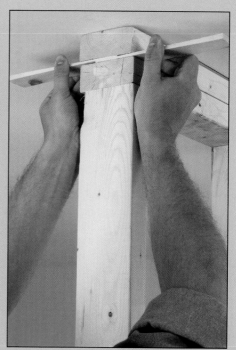

3 Position the wall so the bottom plate is about a foot away from the chalk line. Lift the wall by the top plate and tip it up until it is vertical. Slide it into position under the ceiling plate.

4 Anchor the wall by nailing up through the top plate into the ceiling plate. Make sure the edges of the two plates are flush. To protect a plaster ceiling, install the plate with 2½-inch drywall screws. Check the wall for plumb with a carpenter's level, then nail the bottom plate to the floor.

5 If there is a little space between the top plate and the ceiling plate, slip a pair of shims in between the two before nailing. Drive the nails through the shims to keep them from slipping out.

Framing a corner

If your new wall turns a corner, frame it with four studs or with three studs and blocking as shown here. This creates a sturdy corner that provides a 1-inch-wide nailing surface for inside-corner drywall as well as solid nailing for drywall on the outside corner.

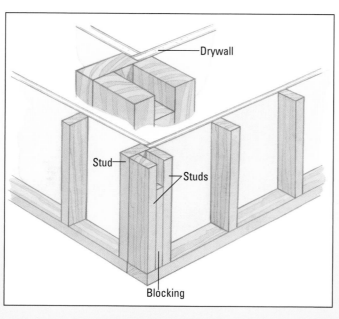

Drywall

Stud

Studs

Blocking

Plumb with a chalk line

If you don't have a plumb bob in your toolbox, use a chalk line instead. The case on most models comes to a point for just this purpose.

FRAMING A DOORWAY

Framing a doorway is similar to framing a solid wall, with a few added elements (see "Anatomy of Walls and Ceilings," *pages 26–27*). Like the rest of the wall, it is easier to make a rough opening for a doorway while the wall is flat on the floor, if you have the room. Select the straightest studs you can find for framing doorways; this will avoid problems later.

When you build the wall, the bottom plate runs across the bottom of the doorway. This keeps the entire wall in one plane as you install it. To make it easier to remove the bottom plate under the door, cut most of the way through it in the correct places with a circular saw. Do this before installing the studs, which later won't leave you room to make the cuts with a power saw. After the wall is anchored securely, you can finish the cuts easily with a handsaw and remove the plate from the door opening.

PRESTART CHECKLIST

☐ **TIME**
About 1 hour

☐ **TOOLS**
Tape measure, layout square, circular saw, handsaw, hammer, level

☐ **SKILLS**
Measuring and marking, crosscutting, driving nails

☐ **PREP**
Determine the size of the rough opening

☐ **MATERIALS**
2×4s, 16d, 10d, 8d nails

Top side of bottom plate

1 Lay out the positions of the jack and king studs on the two plates. Set a circular saw to make a cut 1⅛ inches deep. Cut across the bottom plate to establish the width of the rough opening. Make the cuts on the waste side of the lines marking the sides of the jack studs.

2 The king studs run from plate to plate. Nail them in place as you would regular studs. Cut the jack studs to a length equal to the rough opening height minus 1½ inches to allow for the bottom plate. Nail the jack studs to the bottom plate with 16d nails and to the sides of the king studs with 10d nails.

ROUGH OPENING
Leaving room for more work

A space made in a wall for a door or a window is called a rough opening. For a door, the rough opening is usually 2 inches wider and taller than the size of the door itself, not including the jambs. This allows space for the jambs plus a little extra for shimming the assembly should the opening not be exactly plumb.

A typical residential door is 32 inches wide and 80 inches tall, so the rough opening will be 34 inches wide and 82 inches tall. Rather than rely on these dimensions, however, purchase (or at least measure) the door you will be installing before framing the opening. If you are in doubt about how big to make the opening, add an extra ¼ inch just in case. You can always use shims to make a too-small door fit, but a door that is too big for its opening is a nuisance to cut down. Doors are

available in many sizes, so if a 32-inch door doesn't work for you, ask your supplier what else is available.

Cripple

3 For a header in a nonbearing wall, face-nail two 2×4s with 10d nails and drive 16d nails through the studs. In a bearing wall, make the header from a pair of wider boards with a piece of ½-inch plywood in the middle (2×10s are usually adequate, but check your local building code).

4 Nail one cripple to each king stud with 10d nails to hold the header firmly down on the jack studs. Attach them to the top plate with 16d nails. The infill cripples continue the 16-inch on center (OC) spacing of the wall studs regardless of where the door is located. Space the infill cripples accordingly. Attach them with 16d nails through the top plate and 8d toenails into the header. Make sure the sides of the door opening are plumb. Tip the wall into place as described on *pages 94–95*.

Removing the bottom plate

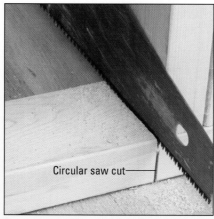

Circular saw cut

After the wall is anchored in place, remove the length of bottom plate that crosses the doorway. Use a handsaw to finish the cuts you made in Step 1. Be careful not to cut into the floor on either side of the doorway.

To avoid damaging a finished floor, make saw cuts (see Step 1) on the underside of the bottom plate instead of the top. This is a little trickier because you have to extend the layout cuts around the plate, cut exactly to the line, and nail the stud exactly in the right spot.

STANLEY PRO TIP

Need an extra set of hands?

When you are trying to tap a wall into position and also make it plumb, it can be awkward to hold a level at the same time. Clamp a level to the side of one of the studs for hands-free viewing.

FRAMING WITH METAL

Wood is the traditional material for framing houses. In commercial construction, steel framing is the norm, largely because steel studs are inherently fire-resistant. Steel framing, however, is gradually catching on with home remodelers. It has some real advantages over wood: It is lightweight, inexpensive, and strong. In addition, it won't rot, shrink, or warp. Steel framing is ideal for framing walls in a basement, where moisture can be a problem.

Walls framed with steel are built in place, one piece at a time. The primary fastener is a sheet-metal screw; the primary tools are a power drill/driver and metal snips.

PRESTART CHECKLIST

☐ **TIME**
About 1 to 2 hours for a 12-foot wall

☐ **TOOLS**
Tape measure, chalk line, plumb bob, power drill/driver, metal snips

☐ **SKILLS**
Measuring and laying out, power-driving screws, cutting sheet metal

☐ **PREP**
Planning where walls are to go

☐ **MATERIALS**
Metal track and studs (four studs for the first 4 feet of wall, three studs for every 4 feet thereafter), pan-head sheet-metal screws

SAFETY FIRST
Protect your eyes

It's always smart to wear safety goggles or safety glasses whenever you drive fasteners, but it is especially so when driving fasteners into concrete, which easily chips and flies when drilled.

1 Lay out both sides of the wall on the floor with chalk lines. For a concrete floor, predrill ⅛-inch holes and attach the track with concrete screws. Use pan-head sheet-metal screws for a wooden floor (see "Fastening metal framing," *opposite, below).*

2 Transfer the layout from the floor to the ceiling with a plumb bob. If your wall runs parallel to the joists, install blocking to provide an anchor point (see "Pro Tip," *opposite, below).* Screw the track to the joists with pan-head sheet-metal screws.

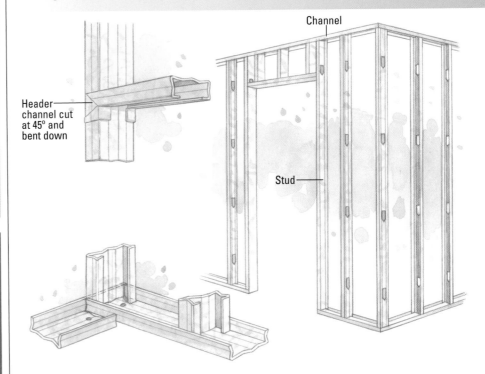

Header channel cut at 45° and bent down

Channel

Stud

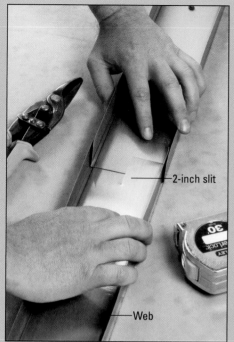

3 To splice two lengths of track together, cut a 2-inch slit in the center of one piece's web. Compress the flanges and slide it into the adjoining piece. For corners, remove the flange from one of the pieces and overlap the webs as shown in the illustration (*opposite, below*).

4 Lay out the stud locations on the top and bottom tracks. Cut the studs to length and stand them in the tracks. Friction will hold them in place while you check them for plumb. Fasten them with short pan-head sheet-metal screws.

5 Make doorway headers from lengths of track. Cut the flanges at 45 degrees and bend down the web to form a right angle. The bent part should be about 1½ to 2 inches long. Attach the header with a single screw driven through each of the four resulting tabs.

Fastening metal framing

Metal framing relies on various kinds of screws. You'll want to stock some of each. One type of screw is a **pan-head sheet-metal screw.** For attaching metal pieces together, use screws that are ½ inch long. These same screws can be used for attaching the track to a wooden floor and to the ceiling joists. If the ceiling is already covered with drywall, you'll have to use 1¼-inch-long screws to reach through the drywall into the joists. For attaching drywall to metal studs, 1¼-inch **drywall screws** are in order; for attaching trim, use 1½-inch (or longer) **trim-head screws.** Trim-head screws have small diameter heads that countersink neatly. The resulting holes are easy to fill. Finally, if you have to fasten metal track to a concrete floor, use **powder-actuated fasteners** or **concrete screws.** The powder-actuated fasteners are fired from a nail gun you can rent. Get a #3 load with a ½- or ⅝-inch pin.

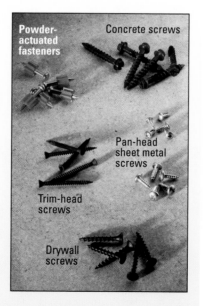

Powder-actuated fasteners

Concrete screws

Pan-head sheet metal screws

Trim-head screws

Drywall screws

Add plywood blocking

If you will be hanging cabinets or trim on a wall that's framed with metal studs, install pieces of ¾-inch plywood between the studs to drive screws into. Likewise you can insert 2×4s into headers and studs at door openings for attachment of doorjambs.

INSULATING A WALL

In exterior walls, kraft-faced fiberglass insulation helps control temperature and humidity inside the structure. But insulation also has a role in interior walls. Woven between 2×4 studs on 2×6 plates, unfaced fiberglass helps deaden sound between rooms. Staggered studs 8 inches on center provide standard 16-inch spacing on each side of the wall, as shown *below right*.

One of the worst aspects of installing fiberglass insulation is that loose particles can be extremely irritating. Protective clothing is one line of defense: long pants and sleeves, collar and cuffs buttoned. Choose a dust mask especially designed to filter fiberglass particles. Thin leather gloves block irritants while still permitting you to handle tools easily. As soon as you've finished installation, take a shower, using cool water at first to close your pores so the fibers don't penetrate your skin. Wash work clothes in a separate washer load, using hot water and an extended wash cycle.

Another way to avoid discomfort is to select insulation that's designed to minimize itching. One product utilizes curled fibers that are less likely to irritate, and another type sheathes the insulation in a plastic sleeve.

PRESTART CHECKLIST

☐ **TIME**
½ to 1 hour for an 8-foot wall

☐ **TOOLS**
Scissors, staple gun

☐ **SKILLS**
Stapling, cutting thick material

☐ **PREP**
For fiberglass insulation, wall should be framed; utilities installed

☐ **MATERIALS**
Fiberglass insulation, ¼-inch staples

Fiberglass rolls and batts

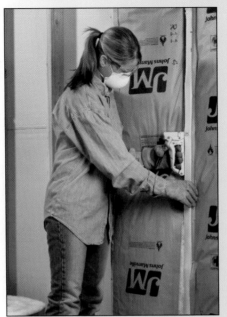

Fiberglass insulation comes sized to fit between studs that are either 16 or 24 inches on center. You can buy it in rolls or in batts that are precut to the length of stud bays. For sound control, the paper facing is not necessary but provides a convenient flap for stapling.

Facing in the right direction

If you are installing fiberglass insulation in outside walls, pay attention to the paper facing. The facing is a vapor retarder, meant to slow the migration of water vapor through the wall. If warm, moist air from inside a house travels through the wall, it will condense when it hits the cold sheathing on the outside. If the sheathing is damp from condensation, it eventually wets the insulation, decreasing its effectiveness. Damp sheathing also is prone to rot. If the outside air is warm and the inside air is cool, the process works in reverse, causing condensation on the drywall. If you live in a climate where you heat in the winter, place the paper toward the inside of the house. If you live where air-conditioning is used more often than heat, face the paper barrier to the outside of the wall.

Adding soundproofing

Weave a continuous roll of fiberglass insulation between staggered studs, using insulation designed for 2×4 walls. Weave loosely to fill the cavity but tightly enough so you won't have to compress the insulation when you install drywall. When you reach the end of the wall, cut off the insulation. Weave additional lengths of insulation in the same manner on top of each other until the wall is filled.

HANGING DRYWALL

You can attach drywall to the framing with nails or screws. Nailing is the faster method, but nails sometimes pop loose later, creating small bumps on the wall surface. (Nail pops occur when studs dry, forcing nails out a little, or if the drywall wasn't nailed tightly to begin with.) Screws cost a bit more in time and money, but they rarely produce pops. Screws must be used when working with steel studs.

Another option is to hold the drywall in place with construction adhesive. This allows you to use fewer nails or screws, reducing the time needed to fill fastener dimples. Adhesive also makes a stiffer wall and reduces nail pops.

You must also decide whether to attach the rectangular sheets horizontally or vertically. Most drywall installers prefer to run the sheets horizontally, which makes a stronger wall, especially over steel studs. In addition it places long joints about 4 feet up from the floor, a convenient height for finishing. Stagger the vertical seams if you can—doing so makes the wall stronger.

PRESTART CHECKLIST

☐ **TIME**
About 15 to 30 minutes per sheet of drywall, depending on the complexity of the shape

☐ **TOOLS**
Tape measure, chalk line, power drill/driver or hammer, drywall T-square, utility knife, jab saw, Surform plane

☐ **SKILLS**
Measuring and laying out, driving screws or nails, cutting with a utility knife

☐ **PREP**
Framing completed; utilities in place

☐ **MATERIALS**
Drywall sheets, 1⅝-inch drywall nails or screws

Hanging horizontal pieces

1 Screw a 2×2 ledger about 52 inches below the ceiling. Place the drywall on the ledger. Make sure the sheet ends on the middle of a stud; if it doesn't, cut it. Mark the stud locations and snap chalk lines. Then push up the sheet tight against the ceiling and fasten it.

2 Cut the bottom piece about 1 inch narrower than the space below the top sheet. With the uncut edge up, pry the sheet tight to the edge of the upper piece and fasten. When installed later, baseboard will hide the gap and the cut edge.

DRYWALL APPLICATION

No blocking needed here

In general, make as few seams as possible. For example, if you are working on 9-foot walls, use 9-foot sheets hung vertically to avoid having a seam 1 foot from the floor (which would occur with two 4-foot-wide sheets hung horizontally). Joints between horizontal drywall sheets do not require blocking if the studs are not more than 16 inches on center as shown above.

Cutting drywall

Front of sheet

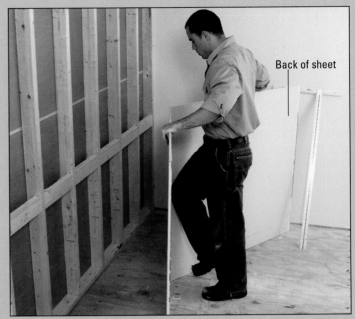

Back of sheet

1 Mark the piece about ¼ inch smaller than the space it needs to fit. Use a utility knife to cut through the outside face of the drywall and into the gypsum. Make two or three passes to deepen the cut; you do not need to cut through the sheet.

2 To complete the cut, bump the back of the sheet at the cut line with your knee as you hold the sheet. This will snap the gypsum so you can fold back the sheet. Slice the back paper along the fold line with a utility knife.

Fastening drywall

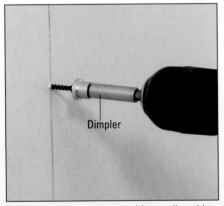

Dimpler

Screws: Use a screw gun with an adjustable clutch or a regular drill with a dimpler attachment. Both the clutch and the dimpler are designed to drive screws so they sink just below the surface without breaking the paper. Space the screws 12 inches apart.

Nails: Double-nail to prevent nail pops. Space ringshank drywall nails 12 inches apart, with a second set about 2 inches from the first. Along the edges use single nails 8 inches apart. When a nail is flush to the surface, hit it one more time to create a slight depression, but don't break the paper surface.

Glue: Apply a bead of drywall mastic to each stud. Drive nails or screws into the sheet to hold it in place while the adhesive sets up. You can space the fasteners 18 to 24 inches apart as long as the drywall is held firmly against the studs.

Making cutouts

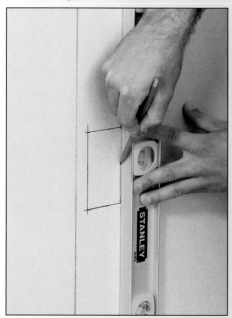

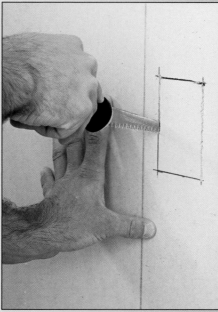

1 Make cutouts to fit drywall around electrical boxes and other obstacles in the wall. Start by measuring and carefully laying out the positions of the cutouts on the face of the sheet.

2 Use a jab saw to make the cutout. To make starting the cut a little easier, drill holes in the corners.

3 If you need to trim the opening a little bit to make it fit, use a Surform plane. Drywall is hard on edge tools, so make sure to have one plane or rasp for drywall work and another for shaping wood.

What's in the wall

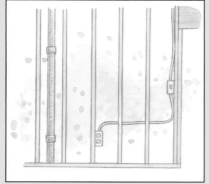

Before closing in the walls, make a diagram noting where the studs fall and the location of anything in the wall, such as wires and pipes. Take a photograph or two as a supplement to the drawings. File them for future reference.

WHAT IF...
You have to cut drywall around a window or doorway?

If the wall you are covering includes a door or window opening, run the drywall right over the opening and cut it out after the drywall is fastened in place. If the sheet ends over the opening (as shown *above*), cut the drywall with a handsaw, guiding the saw against the framing. It doesn't matter if the cuts are ragged or a little uneven because they will be covered by trim or corner bead.

If the drywall runs completely over the top of the doorway, use a handsaw to cut along the jack studs until you reach the bottom of the header on both sides. Snap a chalk line to mark the bottom of the header and cut along the line with your utility knife. Snap back the waste piece and cut the back paper free.

Applying corner bead

After all the drywall is up, the next step is to apply corner bead. The bead serves two purposes: It protects the corner from impacts, and it provides a guide for your knife as you apply joint compound to the corner. You won't need bead in corners that will receive molding because the molding provides protection and joint compound won't be used on those corners.

There are two styles of bead: standard, which makes a crisp, square corner; and rounded, which makes a soft, smooth corner. Both are available in white vinyl and galvanized steel. Both materials work well, so choose based on price and availability.

For an arched passageway or other curve, apply flexible bead. It is similar to standard corner bead but cuts across the flanges at regular intervals, allowing it to bend around a curve.

Whichever type of bead you use, it is better to attach the flanges with drywall nails than with screws, which tend to make the bead pucker. Use nails that penetrate studs or other framing at least ¾ inch.

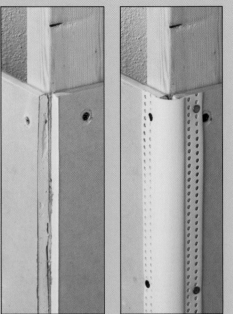

Standard corner bead: Lap one sheet of drywall over the edge of the other *(left)*. Nail the bead in place through the holes in the flanges every 6 to 8 inches. Be careful to keep the flanges flat as you attach them.

Rounded corner bead: This style of corner bead is available in different radii, including some that call for overlapping drywall edges. In most cases though, you'll need to attach the drywall even with the edges of the stud *(left)*. Then nail the bead every 6 to 8 inches.

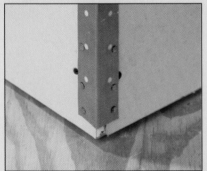

STANLEY PRO TIP

Cut corner bead short

Cut corner bead about ¼ inch short of the corner's height. This makes it easier to put the bead in place. Hold the bead tight to the ceiling as you nail it in place. The baseboard will cover the gap. Drive an extra nail or two at the bottom to reinforce the corner against inevitable kicks and bumps.

WHAT IF…
You have to run drywall up against a post or other surface?

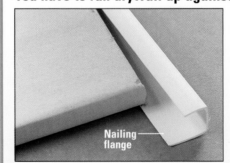

Nailing flange

When a raw drywall edge meets a dissimilar surface, such as wood, it is nearly impossible to get a clean fit. Two products create a crisp edge in this situation: J-bead is nailed into the wall before the drywall is installed. Prepaint it because it remains visible when the job is finished. (Spray paint works well.) J-bead is particularly useful where condensation might wick into the drywall. It encases the drywall, isolating it from the abutting material. L-bead is nailed to the face of the drywall. It is covered with joint compound (as corner bead is) after installation and painted with the rest of the wall. This bead does not extend over the back of the sheet.

Hanging drywall on a ceiling

Drywall
T square

Deadman
brace

1 For a ceiling, all edges of the drywall should be supported by framing, so you must add blocking between the joists. A 2×3 or a 2×4 attached with its wider side facing down makes a good target for fasteners.

2 Snap chalk lines or draw the location of the joists on the sheets before you hoist them into position. Use ⅝-inch drywall if the joists are more than 16 inches OC. Many drywall T-squares have holes in their blades to ease marking. If yours doesn't, drill some on 16-inch (or as needed) centers.

3 Make a pair of deadman braces from 2×4s to help hold the sheets against the ceiling as you work. The length of the legs should be 1 inch more than the floor-to-ceiling height. This allows the braces to be wedged into position.

Using long sheets

Drywall comes in 4×9-, 4×10-, and 4×12-foot pieces, as well as the standard 4×8 sheet. The larger sizes can make your project easier. For example, if you have a room that is 12 feet wide, use 12-foot sheets for two walls and the ceiling to avoid butt (end-to-end) joints, which are more difficult to tape and mud.

Before you decide to use long sheets, make sure you will be able to maneuver them through your home and into the work area.

It's a good idea to have two helpers on hand when you install long sheets. The sheets are awkward and heavy, and they may break under their own weight if not properly supported, especially when being raised to a ceiling.

Fixing a cracked plaster ceiling with drywall

Adding a layer of ⅜-inch drywall is an excellent way to restore a cracked or discolored plaster ceiling. Poke nails through the old ceiling until you locate all the joists (work carefully, there may be pipes or wires present), then snap lines along their length. Apply construction adhesive to the back of the sheet. Use about half a tube of adhesive per sheet, applying it in S-shape beads about 1 foot apart. Fasten with 2½-inch drywall screws into the joists.

Rent a drywall lift—you'll be amazed at how easy it makes the job of drywalling a ceiling, even with 12-foot pieces.

FINISHING DRYWALL

Finishing drywall involves spreading joint compound over the screw or nail holes and joints in the wall to create a smooth, flawless surface. Tape is embedded in the compound over the joints to prevent cracks. The tools and techniques are simple, but creating a smooth surface requires lots of practice. A pro can finish a wall with three coats, but beginners sometimes need to apply more. You'll need three drywall knives: a 6-inch-wide knife for the first coat, a 10-inch for the second coat, and a 12-inch for the final coat or coats. The three knives allow you to feather out the joint—making it gradually thinner toward the edges so it blends in with the wall surface when painted.

The joint compound used to finish drywall joints is commonly called mud. Use ready-mixed joint compound that comes in 5-gallon buckets. Lesser quantities are available for small jobs. Keep the bucket covered at all times so the mud won't dry out. Stir in any water that pools on the surface.

1 Load some joint compound into a mud pan using a 6-inch drywall knife. Start filling the screw or nail dimples with a sweeping motion. Scrape the mud off so the dimple around the screw is filled flush to the surface. Closely spaced dimples can be filled or scraped in one motion.

2 Use fiberglass mesh tape on joints where two tapered edges come together. This self-adhesive mesh costs a little more than paper tape, but it is easier to use and it prevents air bubbles. Start at one end and stick the tape in place evenly across the joint along its length.

PRESTART CHECKLIST

☐ **TIME**
For an 8×8-foot wall, about 1½ hours for the first coat, 45 minutes for each subsequent coat

☐ **TOOLS**
Mud pan; 6-inch, 10-inch, and 12-inch drywall knives; sanding block or sponge

☐ **SKILLS**
Spreading and smoothing joint compound

☐ **PREP**
Check over wall to make sure all fasteners are sunk below surface

☐ **MATERIALS**
Joint compound, fiberglass mesh tape, paper tape (for corners), abrasives

Sponging to smooth a surface

After you apply the final coat of mud and it dries, the final step is to smooth the surface. You have two choices: sponging or sanding. Each method has its advantage. Sponging avoids creating dust, but sanding does a better job of making the joint flat.

To sponge, you'll need a bucket of water and a big sponge. Even better is a sponge made especially for smoothing drywall; it has a coarse mesh on one side that removes excess mud and a plain sponge on the opposite side for refining the surface. Wet the sponge and scrub the wall surface. Rinse the sponge frequently to get rid of the mud that builds up on its surface.

Scrape off the ridges and lumps, then sponge the wall smooth. Be careful not to scrub too hard on the paper areas—you can actually wear away the paper and create a rough spot.

3 Cover the tape with a coat of joint compound applied with a 6-inch drywall knife. Scrape off the mud so the mesh pattern is revealed. Resist the temptation to apply a thick coat—thick applications are hard to keep flat and they crack as they dry.

4 There is no need to sand between the first and second coats. Just scrape away the ridges and blobs with your knife after each coat has dried for 24 hours.

5 Apply the second coat with a 10-inch knife. After the coat dries, scrape the high spots and apply the third coat with a 12-inch knife. Feather out the edges of the mud as thinly and smoothly as possible.

Sanding a wall smooth

For an especially smooth, flat joint, you can't beat hand sanding. This method creates lots of dust, but the results are worth it. Be sure to seal off your work area with plastic sheeting and wear a dust mask to avoid breathing the dust. You might be tempted to use a power sander, but don't. Power sanders fray drywall paper and blast large amounts of dust into the air.

For small jobs, a sanding block with regular sandpaper works well. For larger jobs, invest in a sanding screen (a screen mesh impregnated with abrasive) and a holder. Some holders attach to a shop-vacuum hose, which helps contain dust during sanding.

Scrape the high spots, then scrub down the wall with a sanding screen. Safety gear is in order, including goggles, dust mask, and ear protectors (because of vacuum noise).

Use a pole sander

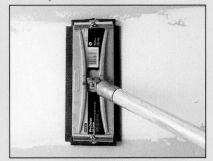

The universal pole sander extends your reach and allows you to work efficiently by making long strokes. Its name comes from the universal joint that attaches the pole to a sanding pad. This joint ensures that the pad is always flat on the wall. The pad is sized for a half sheet of sandpaper or a standard sanding screen and has clamps to hold the paper or screen in place.

Finishing butt joints

The long edges of drywall sheets are tapered. Two tapered edges together form a depression, which makes it possible to create a flat mud joint. The short edges of drywall sheets are not tapered; they meet at a butt joint.

Butt joints are more challenging to finish because they require that you build a slight, gradual mound to hide the joint. To make the mound subtle enough to go unnoticed, you must feather the joint compound over a wide area.

The same fiberglass mesh tape and similar techniques for applying mud are used for butt joints and tapered edges.

Mesh tape—

1 Cover the butt joint with fiberglass mesh tape. Use your 6-inch knife to cover the tape with mud.

2 When the first coat of mud is dry, apply the second coat along both sides of the joint using a 6-inch drywall knife.

3 Apply the third coat with a 12-inch drywall knife, feathering the edges out 8 to 10 inches on each side of the joint. You may leave a ridge down the center, but it can be scraped away later.

STANLEY   PRO TIP: **Check the show coat**

A work light held at a raking angle helps reveal ridges, bumps, and depressions as you scrape and sand between coats. But your best—and last—chance to fix finish flaws is after you have applied a primer coat—the show coat—to the walls. At this point the walls are a uniform color and you'll see irregularities you might not have noticed before priming. The most common beginner's mistake is joints that are too thick. If you find joints like this, add another coat of mud and feather it out farther. Sand these joints again, apply primer to any bare mud, and you are ready to apply paint once the primer dries.

SECOND COAT
Try a drywall trowel

If your project includes several butt joints, consider investing in a drywall trowel. It looks like an ordinary mason's trowel, but the blade has a subtle bow that will form a slight mound over a butt joint. Use the trowel for the second coat only, running it once over the center of the joint.

Finishing corners

Covering corner bead at outside corners is easy because the bead itself guides the drywall knife. Run one side of your knife along the bead to produce a smooth, flat joint as the mud covers the nailing flange. As with other joints, apply at least three coats, sanding in between to feather the joint where it meets the drywall. The bead itself isn't hidden in mud. Simply scrape excess mud off the bead, then paint it along with the drywall.

Inside corners are more difficult. They require taping and mudding. The hard part is smoothing the mud on one side of the corner without messing up the mud on the other side.

Resist the temptation to try to get these inside joints perfect on the first, or even second, coat. Accept that there will be ridges you'll need to sand or knock off in the first two coats. To avoid ridges on the third coat, think of it as a filler coat; press hard on the knife so you fill imperfections instead of leaving behind a thick layer of joint compound. Remember there's no law against going over the joints a fourth time if necessary for a smooth finish.

Finishing inside corners

1 Apply mud to both sides of the corner. Fold a length of paper tape in half (it is precreased) and press it into the mud with a 6-inch knife. Don't use mesh tape for corners; it's not strong enough.

2 Bed the tape in the mud by drawing down the knife along both sides of the corner. Repeat this process to apply additional coats of mud. Sand to smooth the final surface.

OUTSIDE CORNERS
Let the bead be your guide

For outside corners, mud the flanges of the corner bead. Apply several coats, sanding the final coat for a smooth surface.

WHAT IF...
There are bubbles under the paper tape?

If there are bubbles under the tape, the tape doesn't stick to the mud, or it wrinkles, peel it off and apply more mud underneath. This is one time when applying a little too much mud is not a problem.

STANLEY PRO TIP

Consider using a corner knife

One way to achieve straight, smooth inside corners is to use a corner knife. First embed and cover the tape in mud using a 6-inch knife, but don't attempt to smooth the joint. Next hold the corner knife at the top of the joint, angling it slightly away from the wall, and pull it down to near the floor. Do this in one even stroke. The corner knife leaves ridges on both sides of the joint. When dry, scrape off the ridges before you apply a second coat.

CUSTOMIZING YOUR WALLS

Blank walls lack character. They're plain, lifeless, and so downright expressionless that they take away any hint of warmth or homeyness.

Wall treatments help define functional areas, lend character to a room, and can even make spaces appear larger by giving the visitor's eye a variety of interesting paths to follow. Walls that show style and beauty add value to your home too.

Choose your style

There are a variety of wall treatments that will boost the architectural interest of your home. Maybe your home is a vintage structure ready for another element in its established style. Or maybe your home's personality is a bit timeworn and ready for a makeover. Or it may be that your house is searching for an identity.

A beaded wainscot will resuscitate a nearly lifeless family room. You can give your living room a vigorous boost with an Arts and Crafts paneled wall. Maybe you'll show your sense of style by adding classic framed panels to your dining room.

Small jobs, big dividends

Not every wall treatment requires a truckload of molding and a boatload of time to make a lasting impression.

Prefinish some strips of molding and you can run a chair rail around your kitchen in an afternoon. In one more afternoon, you can add a picture molding to a bedroom, creating a vintage look. In addition, you'll be able to change picture arrangements almost instantly and without driving a single nail into the wall.

A plate rail can display fine china, photos, or other artwork. Install the rail all the way around the room or limit it to a simple shelf unit.

Built-ins add charm

Carpenters in the past probably enjoyed exercising their ingenuity by creating built-in shelves and decorative niches. Fortunately, you don't need to serve an apprenticeship before you craft a simple shelf unit and insert it into unused space between studs in your wall. For an even easier project, purchase a ready-made niche. It's a simple way to add character to your home.

Trim serves practical and decorative purposes and puts your finish carpentry skills on display.

CHAPTER PREVIEW

Making and installing wall frames
page 112

Installing wainscoting
page 114

Paneled walls
page 116

Wall and shelf variations
page 120

Quartersawn white oak is traditionally the material incorporated into Arts and Crafts baseboards, wall panels, and plate rails.

Installing chair rail and picture-hanger molding
page 122

Plate rail
page 124

Built-in cabinet
page 126

MAKING AND INSTALLING WALL FRAMES

Wall frames are a traditional design element commonly found in Georgian and neoclassical settings. The molding chosen for this installation is appropriate to those styles. However, both wall frames can be right at home in virtually any style setting—even a house that's decidedly modern.

The frames are a purely decorative element that breaks up expanses of wall. In doing so, the frames add architectural interest everywhere they are used. Some popular locations include an entry, a hallway, a stairway, a living room, and a dining room. You can give the area inside a frame a distinctive treatment by choosing a different paint color from the rest of the wall and even choosing a third shade for the frame itself. If you do this, save yourself a lot of work by painting the walls before installing the frames. Prepaint the frames too. Wallpaper or stenciled motifs are other possible treatments for the field inside the frame.

PRESTART CHECKLIST

☐ **TIME**
About 1 hour for a single wall frame; time per frame decreases when you're making and installing a batch

☐ **TOOLS**
Mitersaw, 2-foot level, hammer, nail set

☐ **SKILLS**
Mitering, driving and countersinking nails, checking for level

☐ **PREP**
Plan the size of the frames

☐ **MATERIALS**
Molding for frames, ¾-inch plywood for assembly jig and gauge block, glue, #6×1¼-inch flathead screws for construction of jig, construction adhesive, finishing nails, painter's caulk

Building wall frames

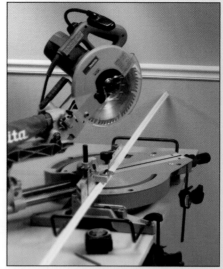

1 Cut the miter joints for your wall frames, utilizing a stopblock setup to ensure uniform lengths. Some saws have an accessory for this purpose, but you can get accurate results by bolting your saw to a sturdy table and adjusting its distance from a wall.

2 Create a corner assembly jig by screwing a square of plywood to a plywood baseboard large enough to fully support your frames. Check the accuracy of the corner with a framing square. Clamp this setup to your worktable, and assemble the frames with glue and countersunk finishing nails. Place each frame on a flat surface until the glue dries.

Designing wall frames

Although you don't have to combine frames with a chair rail, frames that are located low on the wall (below the 36-inch height typical for a chair rail) usually have a longer horizontal element. Frames above the 36-inch mark are almost always vertical. Although this installation shows a rectangular frame, those installed near a staircase may be triangular, or you can intersperse rectangular and square frames. There are no absolute rules for the proportions of the frame, but utilizing the Golden Rectangle is a good starting point. (See the *opposite page*.)

Here's an example for a typical wall frame. The installation site has a 3-inch-high baseboard and a chair rail with its bottom edge set 36 inches above the floor. Assume that you want the frame 5 inches above the baseboard and 3 inches below the chair rail

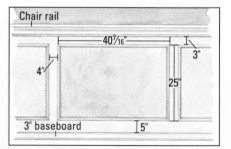

to visually center it in the space. This produces a vertical frame size of 25 inches. Multiply that by 1.618 for a Golden Rectangle, and the length is 40.45 inches, or approximately 40⁷⁄₁₆ inches. If you're running a number of frames along a wall, the space between them should be about the same as the top and bottom spacing. In this case, 4 inches is a good compromise between the top and bottom spacing.

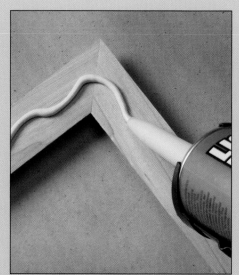

3 Squeeze a tiny bead of panel adhesive onto the rear face of the frame. Make this bead as small as possible so you don't have to clean up messy squeezeout. If you know your walls are relatively flat, you may substitute dots of adhesive, placing one near each corner and no farther than 12 inches apart around the perimeter of the frame.

4 With the help of a plywood gauge block resting on the floor, position the frame on the wall. After you check the frame for level, nail it into position. Nails into studs offer the most security, but even nails driven at an angle into drywall will hold the frame until the adhesive takes over. A pneumatic brad nailer, shown *above*, makes nailing easier and minimizes the risk of splitting moldings.

5 Fill any gaps between the wall and the edges of the frame with painter's caulk. If you cut the nozzle at a taper, you'll have better control and an accurate bead. If necessary, touch up the paint.

The Golden Rectangle

Ever since ancient times, the ratio known as the Golden Section has exerted a powerful attraction for artists, architects, and mathematicians. The design of the Parthenon in Athens is based on the Golden Section, and the ratio has influenced design and proportions of an untold number of paintings, sculptures, and buildings.

The ratio 1:1.618, or about 5:8, is a good working approximation of the Golden Section. But it's helpful to know how to construct your own Golden Rectangle, which is the name of the figure whose sides have lengths that reflect the Golden Section.

This is the construction method employed by the famous Euclid of Alexandria in approximately 300 B.C. Starting with any measurement (we'll call it CD), construct a square with sides of that length. This is ABCD in the example. Divide one side in half (midpoint E), and draw a line (EB) from that

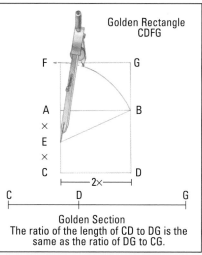

Golden Rectangle CDFG

Golden Section
The ratio of the length of CD to DG is the same as the ratio of DG to CG.

point to the opposite corner. With E as the pivot, swing an arc from B to locate point F. Extending vertical lines from the square and a line FG completes the Golden Rectangle. To salute the ancient mathematician, you can say, "Here's looking at Euclid."

Window dictates frame size

When a window appears above a wall frame, that frame's length should equal the outside-to-outside dimension of the casing. Frames on either side of the window can vary from that size.

INSTALLING WAINSCOTING

A traditional wall treatment that lends a quiet air of quality and warmth to a room, wainscot paneling also makes an extremely durable wall because it resists dents and scuffs better than drywall.

Wainscoting includes any type of wooden paneling applied to the bottom portion of a wall. The tongue-and-groove, beaded-board wainscoting in this project is one of the most popular styles. Beaded board is available in various widths and in thicknesses from ¼ inch to ¾ inch. This project uses ¼-inch-thick boards under ½-inch-thick baseboard to match the thickness of ¾-inch-thick door and window casing.

PRESTART CHECKLIST

☐ **TIME**
About 6 hours for an 8-foot section of wainscoting

☐ **TOOLS**
Tape measure, chalk line, chop saw or miter box, hammer, nail set, circular saw, jigsaw, block plane

☐ **SKILLS**
Measuring and laying out, crosscutting, driving finish nails

☐ **PREP**
Empty room of all furnishings

☐ **MATERIALS**
¼-inch-thick beaded tongue-and-groove boards, ½×4-inch baseboard, cap molding, 8d and 4d finishing nails, construction adhesive, wood glue

1 This project uses a ½-inch cap rail. Snap a level chalk line ½ inch below the height you select for the cap rail. Cut ¼-inch-thick beaded tongue-and-groove boards ¼ inch shorter than the height. Position the tops of the boards along the chalk line to leave a gap at the floor.

2 Apply a bead of construction adhesive to the back of each board. Insert the tongue of each board into the groove of the board before. To snug the board without damaging the groove, put the tongue of a 1-foot scrap of tongue-and-groove board into the groove of the piece you are installing. Then tap on the groove side of the scrap with your hammer.

WHAT IF...
You have to turn an outside corner?

1 If your wainscoting wraps around an outside corner, put the last piece in place without adhesive. Mark with a sharp pencil the location of the corner along the back of the piece. Using a tablesaw or handheld power saw, cut to the pencil line but don't cut away the line. The idea is to allow the last piece to extend very slightly past the corner, thereby creating a tight joint with the next piece.

2 Use a tablesaw or block plane to remove the tongue from the piece that turns the corner. Put construction adhesive on the piece and attach it with the planed face flush to the face of the adjacent piece.

3 **Turn off power to the room at the circuit box.** Disconnect the receptacle or switch. Use a jigsaw to cut boards to fit around the box. Insert a box extender to move electrical outlet and switch boxes out ¼ inch. Reconnect the switch or receptacle and replace the cover plate before turning the power back on.

4 Put the second-to-last piece before a corner in place without adhesive. Measure from the base of the tongue to the wall at top and bottom. If the measurements differ, transfer them to the top and bottom of the last piece to lay out a tapered cut. Make the cut with a saber saw.

5 Because of the tongue, the last two pieces at a corner must be snapped in place together. Put adhesive on the wall. Fit the last two pieces together. Bend them a bit at the joint and fit the second-to-last tongue into place. Press at the joint to snap the last two pieces into place.

6 Before installing the first piece that turns an inside corner, shave the tongue off with a block plane. Install the piece with the planed edge toward the corner.

7 Attach ½×4-inch baseboard over the bottom of the wainscoting by driving two 8d finishing nails into each stud.

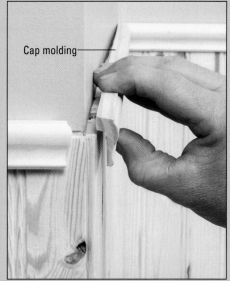

Cap molding

8 Attach a cap molding along the top of the wainscot to cover the top edge of the paneling. At the corner, use yellow carpenter's glue and 4d nails driven at a slight angle toward the wall to ensure they don't come through the face of the top molding.

PANELED WALLS

If you enjoy the allure of Arts and Crafts woodwork, you'll find a lot to like in this project. In fact, this basic design is the springboard for several installations. If you prefer the baseboard alone, check out the version on *page 138*. If you want to top this wall with a plate rail, turn to *page 124*.

The spacing of the stiles is a matter of personal taste. You may choose a dimension that's slightly larger or smaller than the 16-inch centers shown. However, you risk losing the Arts and Crafts flavor if you spread the stiles too far apart. The 3½-inch stile width also could vary. In this case, you'll be safer narrowing the stiles rather than widening them.

Quartersawn white oak is a traditional material for an Arts and Crafts project, but you can substitute a softwood if you're going to paint the wall components. Whichever finish you choose, you'll save time and trouble by applying the finish before installing the parts to the wall.

PRESTART CHECKLIST

☐ **TIME**
About 1 hour per lineal foot of wall

☐ **TOOLS**
Tape measure, combination square, stud finder, biscuit joiner, tablesaw, mitersaw, level, hammer, deadblow mallet, tin snips, screwdriver, nail set

☐ **SKILLS**
Checking for level; driving nails; using a biscuit joiner, tablesaw, mitersaw

☐ **MATERIALS**
Quartersawn white oak for wall components, pine or other secondary lumber for baseboard spacers, ¾-inch plywood for stile spacers, 8d and 10d finishing nails, 1-inch brads, #20 biscuits for joiner, #6×2-inch roundhead screws, masking tape, stain and finish, panel adhesive and caulking gun, white glue and applicator brush

1 Prepare ¾-inch-thick stock for the baseboard and 5/4 stock (about 1-inch thick) for the rails. Cut these parts to length. Rip ½-inch-wide spacers from pine or any other wood. You need two spacers for each length of baseboard. The thickness of the spacers equals the thickness difference between the baseboard and the rail. Don't attach the spacers to the baseboard yet.

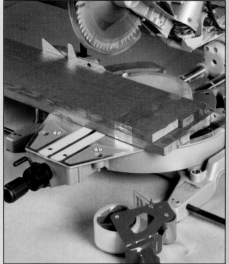

2 Cut the stiles to width and length. Be certain that the end cuts are perfectly square and that all of the stiles are identical in length. Join several stiles into a bundle with packing tape, and cut them all at once. Keep the bundle straight against the fence by using the same number of tape layers for each wrap. For square cuts, always have two tape locations touch the fence. You can also utilize a stopblock setup; see Step 1 on *page 112*.

PANEL ASSEMBLY

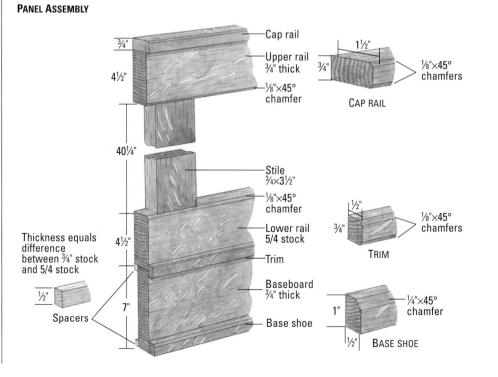

3 Select which face of each stile will face the wall, then mark a centerline near each end. See the Stanley Pro Tip *below* for a quick and easy way to find the center without tedious measuring or dividing fractions. The pencil marks on masking tape assures precision marking.

4 Rip ¾-inch plywood into ¾-inch-wide strips, and crosscut a supply of them. Their length equals the horizontal distance between stiles. Lay out the bottom rail, pine spacers, and stiles. Position the end stile. (If your installation goes around a corner, see "What If" on *page 118*.) Lay in a plywood spacer, then mark the stile's centerline on the rail. Repeat down the length of the rail.

5 Put the top edge of the lower rail against the bottom edge of the top rail; make sure the ends of the two pieces are flush. With a combination square and pencil, transfer each stile location from the lower rail to the upper rail.

Marking the centerline

The linked capital letters C and L are the symbol for centerline. It's standard practice to place the actual mark for the centerline above or below the symbol. The direction of the centerline is parallel to the two edges of the piece of lumber from which the center was determined.

Finding the center

Here's an easy way to find the center of the stile. Set your square to the approximate center of the board and make a short line. Hold the square against the other edge of the board and make another short line. (This procedure works whether you set the square slightly less than half or slightly more.) The center is halfway between those lines; you can easily eyeball the midpoint. Reset your square to the center.

WHAT IF...
You don't have a biscuit joiner?

The biscuit joiner isn't absolutely essential to this project—it simply allows you to reduce the number of nail holes through the components. Your wall layout probably won't permit you to fasten each stile to a stud. But you can still obtain decent holding power by driving finishing nails at opposing angles. This process, called toenailing, will hold the stile until the construction adhesive takes over. Drilling pilot holes minimizes splitting the lumber.

PANELED WALLS (continued)

6 Set up your biscuit joiner with the fence down to register the cut from the upper surface—in this case, the back face of the rails and stiles. Approximately center the cutter in the thickness of the ¾-inch stock. Cut the slots into the edges of the rails and into the ends of the stiles.

7 Combine glue with brads or headless pins to attach the pine spacers flush with the edges on the rear face of the baseboard. (Actually, you can cheat the spacers ¹⁄₁₆ inch or so toward the center of the base to make sure the spacers don't overhang the edges.) The spacers make the baseboard as thick as the rail and also create the effect of a back cut so that the molding bridges irregularities along the wall.

8 Place the upper edge of the baseboard against the bottom edge of the lower rail, with both pieces face up. Also make sure that the ends of the two parts are flush. Make pencil marks onto masking tape about every 12 inches along the joint. After registering your plate joiner against the front face of these parts, cut biscuit slots at each marked location.

WHAT IF...
You have to turn a corner?

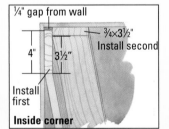

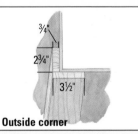

At an inside corner, you want both stiles to appear at the width you've chosen—3½ inches in this example. Instead of trying to make the tips of the edges meet perfectly, cut the first stile 4 inches wide, and install it ¼ inch from the corner. This gap allows you to plumb the stile without scribing it to the wall. Butt the stile on the second wall against the first stile. If the first wall is out of plumb, you'll have to scribe the second stile. See *page 213* for scribing techniques and tips. At an outside corner, you need to rip one stile, reducing its width by its thickness. In this case, a 3½-inch stile that's ¾-inch thick gets ripped to 2¾ inches wide.

WHAT IF...
Your slots don't match?

Although it's certainly desirable to attach the stiles to the upper rail with biscuits, it's not absolutely essential.

Before spreading glue onto all the parts of the assembly, it's a good idea to conduct a dry assembly—meaning without glue—to make certain that the parts will fit. If the biscuit slots are slightly misaligned side to side, you can often spare yourself the trouble of cutting new slots by simply switching to the next smaller size of biscuit. For example, substitute a #10 biscuit instead of the larger #20. You'll sacrifice some joint strength, but strength is not the biscuit's main

role in this wall project. Its primary function is to keep the parts aligned until the panel adhesive dries.

9 When you nail the baseboard to the wall, make sure it's level. (See *pages 130–131* for baseboard installation tips.) Then add the lower rail to the assembly by gluing the biscuits into their slots. If necessary, tap the lower rail with a deadblow mallet to close the joint.

10 Squeeze a bead of panel adhesive onto the back of the first stile, add glue to the bottom biscuit joint, plumb the edge of the stile, and nail it in place. To add the next stile, repeat the construction adhesive and glue and add plywood spacers at the top and bottom between stiles.

11 To hold the top end of the stile against the wall while the glue and construction adhesive set, use a modified biscuit. Drill a 3/16-inch hole through one end of a #20 biscuit and cut 1/2 inch from the other, using tin snips. Insert the clipped end into the slot, but do not glue it. Then drive a roundhead screw through the top of the biscuit into the wall; drive the screw by hand so you don't tear a hole in the drywall.

12 After the adhesive and glue set, remove the modified biscuits and the plywood spacers. Test-fit the upper rail, then glue it to the tops of the stiles with biscuits and to the wall with construction adhesive. For added security, drive nails through the rail into studs.

13 Test-fit the cap rail on top of the upper rail. If your wall is wavy, you'll have to scribe the cap rail to get a tight fit. See the scribing tips and techniques on *page 213*. With your stud finder, locate the wall studs, marking their centers onto pieces of masking tape. Drive nails diagonally through the top of the cap rail into the studs.

14 Attach the 1/2×3/4-inch trim with brads, centering this molding over the joint between the baseboard and the lower rail. Finally, attach the base shoe following the procedure on *pages 138–139*.

WALL AND SHELF VARIATIONS

Arts and Crafts I

This installation requires more planning than versions in which the wall acts as the panel. Although you can rabbet the stiles and rails, the more direct approach is to strip off the ½-inch-thick wallboard and replace it with pieces of oak plywood of identical thickness. Centering the bookmatched pattern within each panel requires a bit of work, but the high-quality look it produces is worth the effort. A close fit between the plywood panels isn't necessary because the rails and stiles disguise any discrepancies.

Arts and Crafts II

Heighten the drama of an Arts and Crafts wall by adding a second row of panels on top of the first. This approach is actually quite economical because you can put short offcuts onto the wall instead of into the trash. Although shown here with the wall in the panel fields, you could install plywood panels. If your budget doesn't permit quartersawn white oak, substitute an inexpensive hardwood, softwood, or even medium-density fiberboard (MDF). All of them look virtually identical under a couple of coats of paint.

Neoclassical shelf

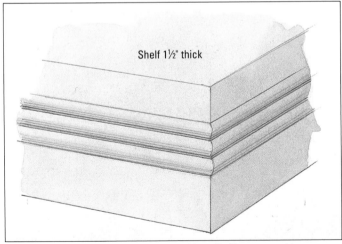

Shelf 1½" thick

Add a touch of elegance to a room with a shelf supported by surprisingly affordable corbels. Whether you need a short shelf or you're planning a mantel for a fireplace surround, you'll find corbels sized and styled to match your project's requirements. For the shelf itself, simply grab a piece of 2× construction lumber (it measures 1½ inches thick) and sand it smooth. Around its midsection, add a mitered belt of decorative molding. The ¾-inch-wide one shown here has three reeds and is sometimes called screen door molding.

Federal/colonial

You can adapt a raised panel installation to a variety of different styles, but when painted white, it's right at home in a Federal or colonial setting. In some vintage homes, all the walls in entire rooms have the paneled treatment. This could be a bit overpowering in a modern home, but a single wall or a wainscot treatment around the room could carry the style without going over the top. If you make the panels from solid wood, be sure to carefully allow for the seasonal expansion and contraction of the lumber. That's why medium-density fiberboard (MDF) is a good material for this installation.

Traditional I

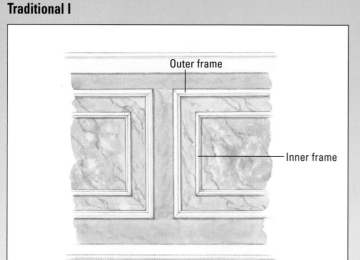

If a single wall frame is a good idea, then doubling the frames is twice as good. To impart depth to the installation, consider using two moldings that are identical (or at least similar) in form but different in scale. Make the inner frame from the smaller molding profile. Wallpaper is one traditional treatment for the panel field but you could also consider faux finishes. Choosing different tones but using the same paint technique for the inner and outer fields is another way to give the installation depth and interest.

Traditional II

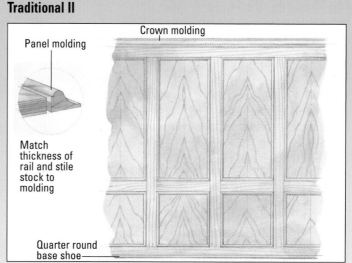

Here's a wall treatment that evokes the feeling of a traditional den or perhaps the clubroom of an exclusive country club. The warmth of a natural finish surrounds you with floor-to-ceiling luxury. Birch is a reasonably priced hardwood that takes a finish well, although it tends to blotch under certain oil stains. A prestain conditioner can tame that problem or you could dye instead. (See chapter 13 starting on *page 222* for finishing tips.) The molding shown is usually employed as a baseboard cap, with its narrow tip upward.

Country/folk

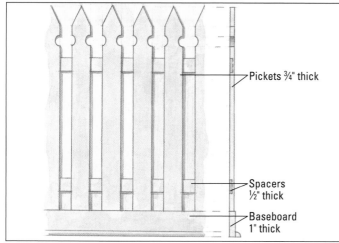

With this wall treatment, almost any indoor room will feel like a sunroom. To add depth to the installation, make the baseboard from lumber 1 inch thick and choose ¾-inch-thick stock for the pickets and ½-inch material for the spacers. You can save time by purchasing ready-made pickets at your home center or craft a custom design of your own. Of course, white is a traditional choice for a picket fence. Paint the wall a soft green before adding the fence and you'll feel like you're lounging in your backyard—but without the mosquitoes.

Modern shelf

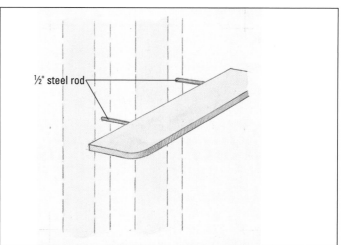

The only thing sleeker than this shelf is the slick invisibility of its mounting. With a stud finder, locate the centerpoints of the studs along the shelf's path, then carefully transfer those marks to the rear edge of the shelf. Drill holes for a ½-inch diameter steel rod into both the shelf and the studs. About 2 inches of penetration at each location will support a medium-duty shelf. Unless your wall is extremely straight, you may need to scribe the rear of the shelf. (See *page 213* for scribing techniques.)

INSTALLING CHAIR RAIL AND PICTURE-HANGER MOLDING

Along with baseboard and crown, you'll find two other moldings installed on walls: chair rail and picture molding. Chair rail, installed 34 to 36 inches above the floor, helps break up the vertical surface of a wall and protects the wall from damage from chair backs and other furniture.

Picture molding breaks up the vertical expanse of a wall when it's installed about 18 inches from the ceiling. But when you place it higher, within a few inches of the ceiling, it also serves as a decorative crown. In older homes, carpenters sometimes nailed it within an inch of the ceiling. Rather than scar a wall with nails or screws, you hook a wire (or wires) over the molding, extend the wire down the wall, and attach the wire to the back of a framed photo or painting.

Both types of molding are installed similarly to crown and baseboard, using coped joints for inside corners and miter joints for outside corners.

Chair rail: Some molding is sold specifically as chair rail, but you can make your own by combining moldings. Here a piece of cap molding is added to an inverted piece of baseboard to create a wide chair rail.

Chair rail is sometimes considerably thicker than door and window trim, so a butt joint would leave an unattractive chunk of wood extending past the casing. Ease the transition with a miter cut that slices away the excess stock. Sand smooth, and touch up the finish.

Solo measuring

Making a measurement along a wall from one side of a room to the other can be a real challenge if you are working alone. Because walls sometimes lean in or out, you should take the measurement right at the height where your molding will run.

It can be difficult to hold your tape measure in exactly the right place. To make the task easier, drive a nail into a stud near one end of a wall, in a spot where the hole will be covered by the molding. Measure from the corner to the nail. Then hook your tape on the nail and measure to the other corner. The sum of these two measurements is the length of the molding run.

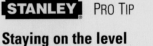
STANLEY PRO TIP

Staying on the level

The key to installing chair rail is to keep it level. Rather than bothering with chalk lines or levels, cut a spacer from a piece of scrap and use it to hold the molding at a constant height above the floor. This works well as long as the floor is reasonably level.

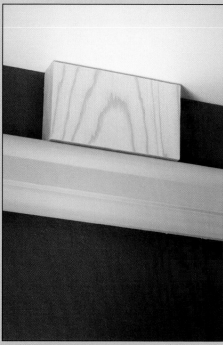

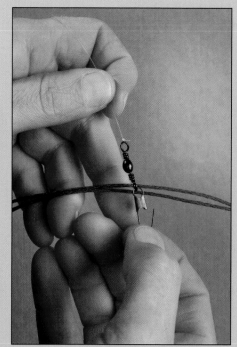

Picture-hanger molding: In a room with standard 8-foot ceilings, a full complement of molding (base, chair, picture, and crown) is overpowering. If you like picture molding, consider applying it to one or two walls only.

Spacer blocks, registered between the ceiling and picture-hanger molding, eliminate tedious measuring. When you're installing trim this close to the ceiling, it's better to run it parallel. Adjusting it to level—unless the ceiling is perfect—would simply emphasize the discrepancy.

For a hanging system that's nearly invisible, choose fishing line instead of wire. Tie a swivel snap (also from the fishing supplies aisle) onto the end of the line. Changing pictures is literally a snap.

Keep your picture level

Install self-adhesive rubber feet to the back of your picture frames and they won't vibrate out of position. Hardware stores usually stock these feet near the casters.

Wrap ceiling color above molding

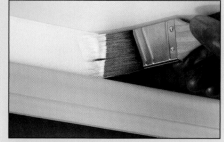

When picture-hanger molding is near the ceiling, carry the ceiling paint down to the trim. This eliminates the need for tedious "cutting in" of the wall color and the creation of a narrow color band. For the molding itself, choose a clear finish, match the wall or ceiling color, or paint it a contrasting tone. The most conservative approach is to match its finish to other moldings in the room.

PLATE RAIL

A plate rail is a traditional way to top an Arts and Crafts wall treatment. For details on the construction of the wall itself, see the procedure that begins on *page 116*. But instead of ending that wall with the cap shown in those instructions, extend it with the ledger and plate rail.

Construction of the plate rail is quite straightforward; feel free to substitute construction methods that suit the tools you have. For example, if you don't have a biscuit jointer, simply make the L-shape assembly with glue alone or with glue reinforced with nails. There's plenty of long-grain to long-grain gluing surface, and the finished joint can actually be stronger than the wood itself.

Referring to the drawing, cut the components for the length of plate rail that you're building. There's a bracket centered over every stile in the wall system, so simply count the stiles and make an equal number of brackets. The molding is easy to make with angled rip cuts on your tablesaw.

PRESTART CHECKLIST

☐ **TIME**
About ½ hour per lineal foot of rail

☐ **TOOLS**
Tape measure, combination square, biscuit joiner, mitersaw, tablesaw, hammer, drill with bits, nail set, clamps

☐ **SKILLS**
Driving nails; clamping; using a biscuit joiner, tablesaw, mitersaw

☐ **PREP**
Wall surface should be painted; apply finish to all plate rail components

☐ **MATERIALS**
Quartersawn white oak for plate rail components, 4d and 10d finishing nails, 1-inch brads, #20 biscuits for joiner, masking tape, stain and finish, panel adhesive and caulking gun, white glue and applicator brush, colored putty for filling holes

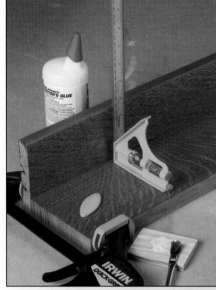

1 Cut biscuit slots into the ledger and plate rail. (For plate joinery tips and techniques, see *page 212*.) Glue and clamp the assembly, and carefully check it for square. Avoid excessive clamping pressure—advance the clamps until you bring the parts firmly together, then stop.

2 After the plate rail/ledger assembly dries, attach it to the top of the upper rail of the wall. Biscuits align the ledger and rail, and construction adhesive on the back of the ledger holds the unit to the wall. For good measure, drive 10d (3-inch) finishing nails through the ledger and into a few of the wall studs.

PLATE RAIL ASSEMBLY

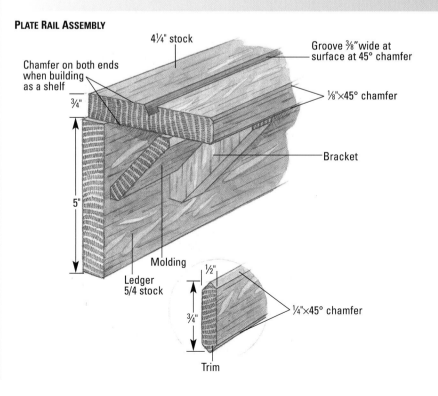

4¼" stock

Groove ⅜"wide at surface at 45° chamfer

Chamfer on both ends when building as a shelf

¾"

⅛"×45° chamfer

Bracket

5"

Molding

Ledger 5/4 stock

½"

¾"

¼"×45° chamfer

Trim

3 Attach the first bracket, carefully centering it above one of the stiles. To avoid splitting the wood, drill diagonal pilot holes through the wood for the 4d (1½-inch) finishing nails. (See *page 210* for countersinking techniques and tips.) Make certain you install the bracket squarely.

4 Mark the location of the next bracket onto a strip of masking tape. Square-cut one end of the molding with your mitersaw and butt it against the first bracket. Mark the cut line on the molding and install it with 4d finishing nails driven through pilot holes. Keep adding brackets and molding strips until you complete the installation. Make certain that the bottom edge of the molding follows a straight line.

5 Center the trim strip over the joint between the upper rail and the ledger. Nail on the trim strip with 1-inch brads to complete the installation. Fill all nail holes with colored putty, following the tips on *page 231*. If there's a gap between the plate rail and wall, fill it with painter's caulk.

WHAT IF...
You want to build a shelf?

To build a plate rail as a shelf, shorten the ledger so that the top overhangs by 1 inch at both ends. For a shelf up to 24 inches long, simply utilize one pair of brackets as shown in the photo. But if the shelf is to be longer, space the brackets so that they are no farther than 16 inches apart.

Interlocking metal connectors from your hardware store provide an invisible means of support. Screw half of the connector to the shelf and its mating part to the back of the ledger.

WHAT IF...
You want to prop photo frames on the rail?

To prevent photo frames from sliding forward on the rail, make some stops from scrap lumber. Rip the lumber so that it fits into the plate groove, then cut it wide enough to provide a solid resting point for your frames. Cut the strips into any convenient length.

For safety, make the rip cuts in lumber that's at least 12 inches long and utilize featherboards and push blocks to keep your fingers away from the blade.

Apply stain and finish so that the strips match your rail system.

BUILT-IN CABINET

Built-in cabinets are one of the architectural features that give character to a vintage house. But even if your home is brand new, you can add style and value by building the cabinet yourself.

A little detective work goes into finding the right location on an interior wall. You need to find the wall's wiring, plumbing, heat ducts, cold-air returns, and other obstructions. If you can get into the attic and basement of your house, look for pipes, wires, and so forth going into the stud bay you're considering.

The cabinet construction is absolutely straightforward—nothing more complicated than butt joints assembled with glue and screws. There's no fancy fitting for the back either. The frame for the front can be butt-jointed or mitered to coordinate with the window and door casings in your home.

PRESTART CHECKLIST

☐ **TIME**
Approximately 4 hours, plus time for the finish to dry

☐ **TOOLS**
Tape measure, stud finder, 2-foot level and torpedo level, drywall saw, combination square, mitersaw, tablesaw, hammer, drill with bits, nail set

☐ **SKILLS**
Driving nails and screws, drilling, using tablesaw and mitersaw

☐ **PREP**
Wall surface should be painted; apply finish to all components of the cabinet

☐ **MATERIALS**
2×4 lumber for blocking, #6×2-inch flathead screws, quartersawn white oak or other lumber for box and optional shelves, shelf pins, masking tape, ¾- and 1¼-inch brads, stain and finish, construction adhesive and caulking gun, woodworking glue and applicator brush, colored putty

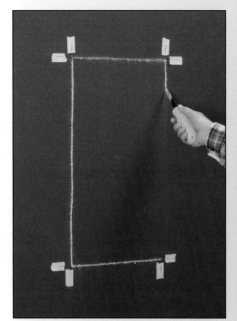

1 After selecting the cabinet's location, locate the studs and mark their edges on masking tape. With a 2-foot level, draw the horizontal lines for the opening. Jab your drywall saw through the drywall and cut the perimeter. Let the edges of the studs guide your saw for the vertical cuts.

2 Cut a piece of 2×4 lumber as blocking to fit between the studs at the bottom of the opening. Drive screws through the drywall to secure the blocking in a level position, then add screws driven through angled pilot holes into the studs. To avoid interference with the cabinet, countersink the screw heads. Blocking at the top of the opening is optional.

CABINET ASSEMBLY

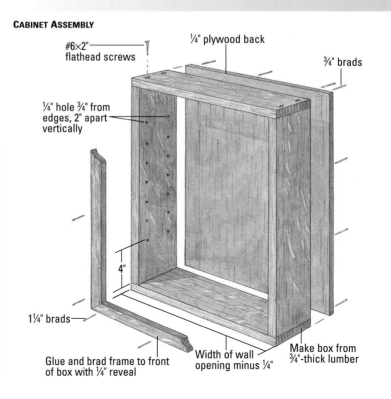

#6×2" flathead screws

¼" plywood back

¾" brads

¼" hole ¾" from edges, 2" apart vertically

4"

1¼" brads

Glue and brad frame to front of box with ¼" reveal

Width of wall opening minus ¼"

Make box from ¾"-thick lumber

3 Referring to the drawing *opposite*, cut the lumber for the sides, top, and bottom of the cabinet. If you drill holes for adjustable shelves, make the lowest holes 4 inches from the bottom of the sides, and the topmost holes 4 inches from the top of those pieces. You'll probably find shelf pins that require ¼-inch holes, but be aware that they're also available in several metric sizes. Screw and glue the box together; double-check for square before attaching the back.

4 Make a face frame for the cabinet, allowing a ¼-inch reveal around the front edges. To build a mitered frame, refer to *pages 206–207*. Attach the face frame to the cabinet with glue and 1¼-inch brads. If you make the frame from stock that's ¾ inch thick, choose 4d (1½-inch) or longer finishing nails.

5 Apply construction adhesive to the back edges of the face frame and to the lower blocking. Slide the cabinet assembly into its hole. Adhesive will hold it securely, or you can drive finishing nails through the vertical stiles of the face frame into the studs. Fill all holes with colored putty.

Prefabricated niche

A prefabricated niche allows you to skip the work of shaping the insert. In addition, you'll find that manufacturers produce these products in flowing and ornate forms that would require an expert carver to duplicate. Plastic and fiberglass are two common materials, but the products have convincing wood texture and appearance. Renovator's Supply is one supplier for these niches (see the "Resource Guide" on *page 236*).

With some niches, you cut out a template that's printed on the shipping box and trace around it between studs at the installation site. Install blocking (see Step 2, opposite) if the directions for your niche suggest it.

Some niches may require that you use a special adhesive, while others recommend ordinary construction adhesive around the perimeter. For extra security, drive finishing nails or trim-head screws, then patch the holes.

CUSTOMIZING BASEBOARDS

If you've ever been involved in a total room makeover or new construction, you already know that the installation of baseboards is a milestone event. And it's not simply because you can see the end of the project. Baseboard installation transforms expanses of drywall into individual walls and the work deck finally looks like a floor.

Despite the important role that baseboards play in setting the character of a room, many people tend to overlook them. Baseboards are low on a wall, but they deserve a high level of attention.

Plinth blocks simplify installation
Blocks at the base of a door casing trace their origins to classical architecture. The casing represents a column and the block is like the plinth—the bottom support element. So it's no surprise that including plinth blocks adds a classic, upscale touch.

Enterprising manufacturers also produce blocks for inside corners that eliminate the need for inside copes and outside miters. But learning to cope is important—in carpentry and in life itself—and it's worth the time you'll invest to learn this skill.

Widen your horizons
Many people think there are only two or three baseboard profiles because that's all they see at the home center. If you fall into that group, visit a specialty millwork yard for an eye-opening experience. You may pay a bit more than at the discount store, but it's definitely money well spent to have moldings you really like. After all, if you're happy with your baseboard choice, you probably won't replace it in this lifetime.

Another option is making your own baseboard, either from solid wood or plywood. With a router and tablesaw, making base shoe moldings is more dusty than it is difficult.

It's no obstacle course
Every room presents its own challenges, whether it's a wavy floor or a protruding heat register. But by meeting these challenges, you'll learn how to turn obstacles into opportunities.

When you get right down to it, you'll discover that the installation of baseboard and base shoe can be a satisfying task that gives the other trimwork in the room a firm visual and stylistic foundation.

Baseboards serve as the visual and stylistic foundation for all the trimwork in a room.

CHAPTER PREVIEW

Installing baseboard
page 130

Plinth blocks
page 132

Shopmade moldings
page 134

Working around obstructions
page 136

Heat registers don't have to look like an awkward afterthought. Careful planning integrates them into the design.

Baseboard styles go far beyond the few samples you'll see at the home center. In this example, a wide baseboard of quartersawn white oak is a simple but effective beginning of an Arts and Crafts wall treatment.

Base shoe molding
page 138

Installing Baseboard

Baseboard covers gaps where the floor and the walls come together. It also protects the wall from errant vacuum cleaners, feet, and furniture. Aesthetically it eases the transition from vertical to horizontal, adding visual appeal to both the wall and floor. Choose baseboard that complements the rest of the trim.

Install baseboard after the walls are painted, hard flooring is installed, the door casings are attached, and any built-in cabinetry is in place. If the room is to be carpeted later, use a wider baseboard or elevate the baseboard with blocks.

If the baseboard will be painted a color different from the walls or will meet a finished floor, prime and paint the baseboard before installing it. Painting or finishing baseboards and shoes before installation also minimizes tiresome time on your knees painting. After installing the baseboard and shoe, fill the nail holes and then apply your final coat of finish.

It's always a great idea to paint the walls before you install moldings. Painting walls is faster and easier without cutting in around the woodwork.

Prestart Checklist

☐ **Time**
About 1½ hours for a room with four walls (including a doorway)

☐ **Tools**
Tape measure, mitersaw or miter box, hammer, nail set, coping saw, block plane, utility knife

☐ **Skills**
Measuring and laying out, cutting pieces to length, coping joints, cutting miters

☐ **Prep**
Walls should be finished and painted, door casings in place

☐ **Materials**
Baseboard molding, 8d finishing nails

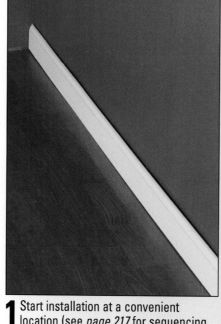

1 Start installation at a convenient location (see *page 217* for sequencing tips). Cut baseboard to reach from corner to corner. For runs longer than 5 feet, cut the pieces about ¹⁄₁₆ inch longer than the measurement. The molding will bow slightly and thus will press tightly into position when nailed in place.

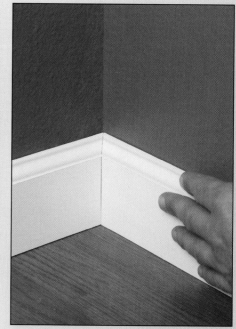

2 Fasten the baseboard with 8d finishing nails driven into the studs and along the bottom plate. Use as many nails as needed to close any gaps between the molding and the wall. Cope the end of the next piece of molding, leaving the other end long for now.

Using multipiece baseboards

While most new houses use a one-piece baseboard, a more traditional approach is to use two or even three pieces of molding to form the baseboard. A multipiece baseboard begins with a piece of baseboard, which is installed first. Cover it with a piece of cap molding, which is small and bends easily to conform to variations in the wall. The final piece is the base shoe. To allow for seasonal movement of a wooden floor, the base shoe is nailed at a slight downward angle into the baseboard—not the floor—with 4d nails. It, too, is quite flexible and disguises gaps between the floor and the underside of the baseboard.

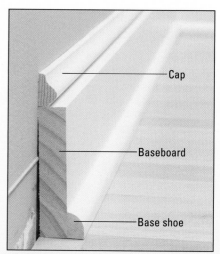

Cap

Baseboard

Base shoe

Multipiece baseboards add a nice touch to the bottom of a wall. Some installations dispense with the cap molding and simply use a baseboard and a base shoe.

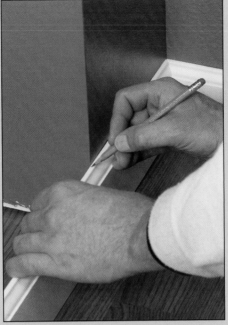

3 After coping the end of the second piece, measure and cut it to length. Again, add about 1/16 inch to the length for a tight fit. If the piece runs into a door casing, use a notched piece of plywood to help mark it for length.

4 Outside corners are mitered. Fit the coped end of the molding first, then mark the miter location with the piece in place. Keep in mind that corners are rarely perfectly square. You may need to adjust the miter angles slightly for a good fit. Make test cuts in scrap.

5 If the joint is open at the front, a stroke or two with a block plane at the back of the joint tightens the fit. Another way to change a miter angle slightly is to place a playing card between the mitersaw fence and molding, as described on *page 207*.

WHAT IF...
You have to splice a molding?

It is neater to install moldings that run the full length of a wall, but that isn't always possible. Moldings are available in lengths up to 16 feet (occasionally you can even find 20-footers), but getting these long lengths home can be a problem. And some walls are longer than even the longest pieces available, so you may have to join two pieces.

The best joint to use when splicing is a scarf joint. You can make a scarf joint by cutting 45-degree angles on the adjoining pieces, which overlap one another. Plan the joint so it falls over a stud for secure nailing. Because the joint occurs at the ends of the pieces, avoid splitting the wood by predrilling the nail holes before driving the nails. See *pages 219–220* for more details.

With a little glue and some judicious sanding, a tight-fitting scarf joint practically disappears, especially if the molding is painted after it is installed.

STANLEY PRO TIP

Nail to a solid base

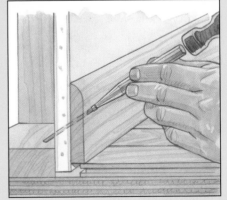

There may be times when you need to drive a nail in a baseboard to eliminate a gap, but a stud isn't where you need it. Drill a hole and drive a 16d finishing nail at a downward angle through the molding to catch the bottom plate.

PLINTH BLOCKS

There are two compelling reasons to consider plinth blocks as a part of your next trim application. First, the blocks provide a solid visual termination point for both vertical and horizontal moldings. Second, when used on a corner, a plinth block eliminates the need for miter or cope cuts on baseboards.

Sizing the plinth block is relatively easy. Its height must be greater than all of the elements that form the baseboard. Precisely how much higher is a matter of aesthetic judgment, but if you need a rule of thumb, allow ½ inch more than the baseboard. The vertical element—usually a casing—should be centered on top of the plinth when the casing is set at the desired reveal on the jamb. (For additional tips, see "Fluted Casing" on *pages 46–49*.) The thickness of the plinth must be greater than the vertical and horizontal elements. A base shoe is usually not considered in the calculation because accommodating its full thickness would usually make the plinth block look too chunky. Nicking the end of the base shoe is the usual solution.

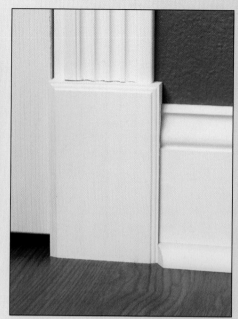

When you install a plinth block against a doorjamb, set it with a reveal of about ¹⁄₁₆ inch. Attempting to get the edges perfectly flush is needless work. If the floor surface is irregular, scribe the bottom of the block so that its edge parallels the plumb surface. You can skip doing this if carpet will cover the floor.

Here you can see how the thickness of the casing and the baseboard elements influence the size of the plinth block. In addition, the block must be wide enough to provide a firm foundation for the door casing. Nicking the end of the base shoe molding makes it visually dive into the plinth block.

Back-cut the block

If you make your own plinth blocks, consider plowing out a back cut while the stock is still a long stick. This is an easy process with a dado head in a tablesaw. The back cut allows the block to bridge over irregularities between the doorjamb and the wall. The casing on top of the block hides the channel.

Baseboard plinth blocks

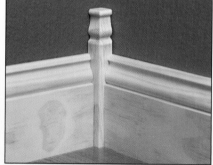

Take a look at inside and outside plinth blocks if you want to eliminate inside coping and outside miter cuts from baseboard installation. The block for inside corners has a square profile to accommodate the thickness of the baseboard. The outside corner block has a rabbet along one corner to register it to the wall. Millworks that manufacture plinths make baseboard in a coordinating height and style.

A sample installation shows how the plinth block simplifies baseboard installation. If you decide to make your own plinth blocks, carefully scale them so they are no larger than necessary to handle the thickness of the baseboard. Otherwise, they take on a chunky, unattractive appearance.

Variations

In "Molding Gallery" on *pages 196–199*, you'll see an assortment of standard baseboard profiles. But even though some of these shapes may be familiar, such as the standard colonial base, you may be surprised that baseboard comes in such a variety of widths. However, you may have to visit a millwork yard instead of a home center to find these special sizes.

You can create a tremendous number of baseboard profiles by combining a flat baseboard with standard molding shapes. Once you break away from the standard narrow moldings, you'll be living large with the vast possibilities and choices of do-it-yourself baseboards. And after you finish a room with tall baseboards, ordinary molding will look downright puny.

The baseboards shown here are adaptable to several styles, so they'll be discussed in terms of options available.

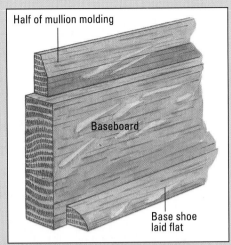

Option 1: The key to this do-it-yourself baseboard is a mullion casing (⅜×2¼-inch) that you rip in half with your tablesaw. If you can't find this molding commercially, it's fairly easy to make your own with a tablesaw. The resulting style works well in an Arts and Crafts room but is equally at ease in a colonial room. In fact, it would be hard to find a style in which this installation didn't fit.

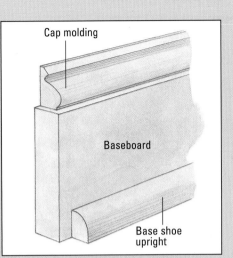

Option 2: This combination of moldings coordinates well with the neoclassical style, especially if you utilize the same molding for the creation of wall frames. The look also blends with colonial or traditional room treatments. You'll find this style of base cap in a variety of different sizes in a well-stocked millwork facility.

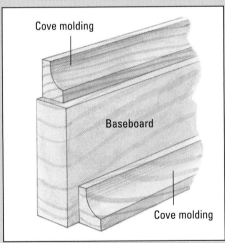

Option 3: This is another look that fits into almost any room, from neoclassical to modern. Of course, it will have a different feel depending on whether you give it a natural finish or paint it. Before you commit to any particular height of baseboard, create several samples to survey the effect.

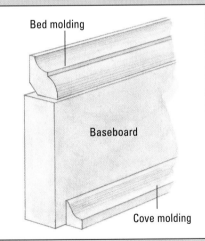

Option 4: This baseboard features a small bed molding inverted from its usual orientation. (Bed moldings are usually employed between wall and ceiling.) This styling is an effective complement in nearly any room that has a crown molding installation. Note the choice of a base shoe with a curved profile to coordinate with the shape of the bed molding.

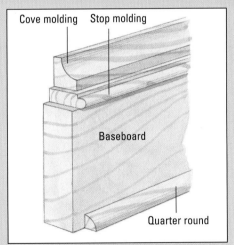

Option 5: There's no rule that limits the number of moldings you can combine. In this installation, the top of the baseboard has a stop (WM 953) that's inverted from its ordinary installation position. You may need to rip the stop to get the amount of projection you want. The cove at the top makes as smooth a transition to the wall as the quarter round does at the floor.

SHOPMADE MOLDINGS

Making your own moldings isn't difficult, and it's a process that produces plenty of benefits. For example, you may be able to mill your trim moldings from the same lumber that you chose for a wide solid baseboard. That will give you a match of grain and color that's simply not available with lumberyard moldings. In addition, you can make moldings thicker or wider than those available ready-made. And not least, there's the possibility of saving money.

Utilizing plywood for wide baseboards and casings is one example. There are several easy methods to hide the edges of plywood by utilizing iron-on strips or solid wood banding. The 8-foot length of a plywood sheet dictates the maximum length of the molding you can make, but that's more than sufficient for door and window casings. If you use plywood baseboards, beware of outside mitered corners because they can be a bit fragile. In that event, consider a hardwood plinth block as shown on *page 132.*

Iron-on edge banding is relatively inexpensive and very quick to install. Its standard width easily spans the edge of ¾-inch plywood. Set an ordinary household iron at a high enough setting to melt the adhesive; "cotton" is usually about right. Keep the iron moving so you don't scorch the wood. Follow up the iron with a 2×4 block, applying pressure to the strip while the adhesive cools and grabs. If you make a mistake, reheat the strip to reposition it. Sand the edges flush with the plywood.

If you have a tablesaw, you can rip ⅛-inch-thick strips of solid hardwood edge banding to cover the raw edges of plywood. Make certain that your strips are slightly wider than the plywood itself; you can trim off the excess after gluing. Apply glue sparingly to minimize messy squeezeout. Apply strips of masking tape every few inches to hold the strip while the glue sets. If possible, let the glue dry overnight before machining the joint.

Rip moldings from wider stock

For safety, you should always form a molding profile along the edge of a wider board, then cut it free at the tablesaw. Use your blade guard (the one above was removed for photographic clarity). Also use featherboards and push sticks to keep your fingers away from the blade.

Trim edge banding easily

Simplify the task of cutting edge banding flush with the plywood surface with the setup shown at *right.* Make your plywood fence high enough to stabilize the stock you're trimming. It's a good idea to rout all the waste except a tiny nub; then remove that with a final hand sanding. Be careful about sanding the surface of plywood with too much energy, because the face veneer is usually only 1/32-inch thick.

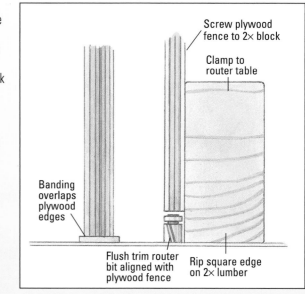

Screw plywood fence to 2× block

Clamp to router table

Banding overlaps plywood edges

Flush trim router bit aligned with plywood fence

Rip square edge on 2× lumber

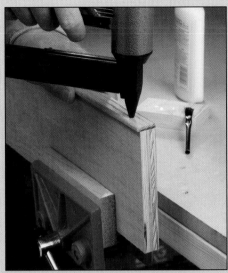

Routing a profile onto the edge of the banding adds a decorative feature while subtracting the unattractive appearance of the edge plies. Using glue plus brads means that you won't have to wait for the adhesive to dry. If you have a headless pinner, this is an ideal application for it because the tiny fasteners provide adequate holding power but are nearly invisible.

If you make wide moldings from solid lumber, consider adding a back cut that bridges over irregularities in the wall. You can mimic the double cut often found in commercial millwork (as in the example on the *left*) or make a single wide channel like the one in the sample on the *right*. The wider cut requires extra time at the tablesaw, but may reduce problems during installation.

Poplar is a good choice for painted baseboards because it combines durability and stability, and it has a relatively low cost for a hardwood. Coating the back of wide boards with a high-quality primer slows down the seasonal absorption and release of moisture from the wood, which reduces its tendency to warp or cup. This process is called back priming. Wood that's back primed can have paint or a clear finish on its face.

WHAT IF...
You want to make baseboards appear thicker?

Sometimes you'll want to increase the thickness of a molding—particularly a baseboard—to give it a more substantial look. Although you could simply buy thicker lumber, doing so could be costly. Instead, consider adding strips to the back of the baseboard to give it the bulked-up look without breaking your budget.

   You can apply spacers to the back of the baseboard itself or nail furring strips directly to the wall.

In this example, the thin strip applied to the back of this ¾-inch baseboard makes its thickness equal to the 5/4 stock that will be applied above it. As an additional benefit, the strips at top and bottom add the value of a back cut, explained above.

Sometimes it's easier to nail strips to the wall instead of the baseboard. Snap a chalk line on the wall to indicate the position of the upper strip. Locate the studs, then mark their position with pieces of tape on the wall. At the base, you'll nail into the wall's bottom plate.

WORKING AROUND OBSTRUCTIONS

Items once considered modern conveniences are now basic necessities. These utilities punctuate your walls with heat registers; electrical outlets and switches; and telephone, cable, and data ports.

In some cases, you can modify your design to avoid obstacles such as electrical outlets. But when that's not possible, adding a block and extending the electrical box is a reasonable approach. Carefully executed, the block is an effective solution.

Another approach is to relocate outlets so that they integrate into the design. For example, installing a wide baseboard provides a new site for wall outlets that will be virtually out of sight if you choose sockets and plates that coordinate with the molding. The location will look as if you planned it—precisely because you did plan it.

Heating registers and cold-air returns are much more difficult and costly to relocate, but there are ways you can work around them so they become an attractive part of the installation—not a distraction from it.

1 Have your electrician place the wire for a baseboard outlet near the floor. Be sure to have the electrician leave plenty of extra wire length so you can fine-tune the outlet's location later. It's best to have the circuit disconnected, but have the wires individually capped in case the line is accidentally energized. Measure the position of the wire so you can transfer its location to the baseboard.

2 Make certain that the location for the box doesn't fall directly over a stud. Otherwise, you won't have enough depth for the electrical box. Using the template that's often supplied with the old work box (or by tracing the box itself), mark its position on the face of the baseboard. To visually center the box, position it ½ to ¾ inch above center.

WHAT IF...
You need to work around a baseboard register?

Baseboard registers can seem problematic at first, but the solutions are straightforward. If the height and thickness of the baseboard are such that it will butt against the register, you have a simple solution with square cuts. The main caution in this case is to avoid making the fit too snug. Otherwise, you'll create a problem for yourself if you need to remove the grille later.

The next solution involves supersizing the baseboard so that the grille doesn't appear pinched in. In this case, you'll probably want to junk the old register and buy a new grille. Your local home center should have a good selection, and mail-order suppliers offer even greater choices.

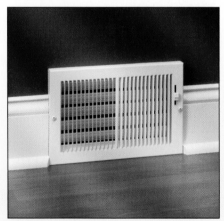

This kind of wall register makes baseboard installation quite simple. Revitalize your grille with a fresh coat of paint or consider replacing it if shows wear.

When you replace the baseboard, consider cutting a notch in it and replacing the old protruding register with a flush surface-mounted grille. Consider whether you want the grille to blend or become a decorative accent.

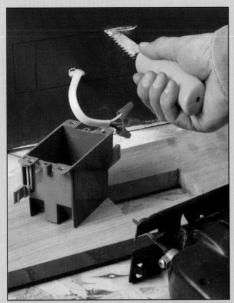

3 Drill a starter hole for your jigsaw blade, and cut the hole through the baseboard. Test the fit of the box to make certain it installs easily. Hold the baseboard against the wall, then mark the perimeter of the hole. Add 1 inch at each end so that the ears of the box will open. Cut outside the marked lines to ensure an easy fit.

4 Put the box into the front of the baseboard, and insert the wire. Turning the screws at each end, rotate the ears that secure the box to the board. Tighten the screws and nail the baseboard in place.

5 Choose socket and plate color to coordinate with your baseboard. In this case, the brown socket and plate blend nicely with the dark finish of this white oak baseboard.

Add a block to an outlet or grille

Sometimes your best solution is to set an electrical box into a block. That way, molding elements can terminate against a flat surface. This idea works well when you're running wall frames and simply can't work around the location of the wall outlets.

You can apply this thinking to wall-mounted heat registers or cold-air return grilles. These grates may be in the way when you're installing running molding high on a wall, such as a picture-hanger molding or wall frame. For this larger version, though, consider making a frame composed of mitered strips, then simply screw the metal on top of the wood assembly.

Mounting an outlet on a block makes your moldings fit flat against the surface so the installation looks like a solution, not a problem.

STANLEY PRO TIP

Install a box extension

When you add thickness to a wall, you should add an extension to electrical boxes. Purchase an extension that matches the shape of the box and provides the amount of extension required to bring the front surface flush with the wall.

BASE SHOE MOLDING

In most homes, base shoe molding teams up with baseboards in rooms with hard flooring surfaces such as tile, stone, sheet vinyl, hardwood, and laminate. For years, quarter-round molding (an obvious name based on its end view) was considered *the* base shoe. The only real question was whether you chose ½- or ¾-inch quarter round. But there is actually a wide range of base shoe profiles, or you can make your own moldings—even in a modestly equipped shop.

The small scale and simple lines of most base shoes make it easy to cope the inside corners. After cutting the copes in a roomful of baseboard, it will seem like a quick and easy job. The flexibility of base shoe enables you to bend it to conform with the wavy floors that are almost universal in older homes and still quite common in new construction.

The most important thing to know about shoe molding is that you always nail it into the wall, never the floor.

1 To make a shoe molding dive into casing, first cut the strip to length, then butt it against the casing. Angle your pencil to get a line as close to the casing as possible and draw a vertical mark. Before committing to your finished molding, you may want to practice this step and the next on a few scrap pieces of molding to get the exact fit you want.

2 Set your mitersaw to make a 45-degree cut, then remove the tiny nick of wood that ends at the pencil line. If you're working with a stained molding that has a clear finish, a stain marker will take away the raw-wood look in a hurry. (See *page 231*.)

STANLEY PRO TIP

Cardboard protects flooring

Protect your finished flooring with a square of cardboard in the area where you're hammering by hand. By keeping the side of the hammerhead in contact with the cardboard, you'll drive nails parallel to the floor with almost no risk of scratching.

Base shoe choices

This sampling merely hints at the wide range of commercially available base shoe profiles. Quarter round ranges from a dainty ¼-inch size up to a truly massive 1 1/16-inch dimension. A true base shoe is taller than it is wide, enabling it to conceal a large vertical gap without appearing chunky.

With a tablesaw and router, you can easily make custom baseboard and base shoe profiles. The set above fits the Arts and Crafts style. It features simple chamfers along quartersawn white oak lumber. The baseboard is ¾×7 inches with a ⅛-inch chamfer along its top edge. The base shoe measures ½×1 inch with a ¼-inch chamfer. A ½-inch quarter round tops the baseboard.

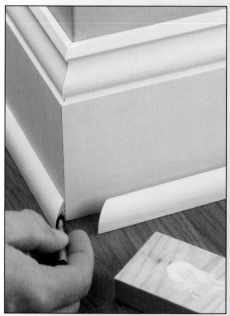

Outside corners of base shoe molding are mitered—like the baseboard itself. Adding a touch of glue is inexpensive insurance that the joint will stay closed. To avoid splitting this small-scale lumber, resist the urge to drive nails too close to the end.

Cope inside corners for tight-fitting joints that look great even if the corner is out of square. (And the corner is almost always out of square.) Coping most base shoes is a simple matter of following a smooth line. For coping techniques and tips, see *pages 208–209*.

Pushing down on thin base shoe molding makes it conform to a wavy floor for a no-gap fit. A pneumatic brad nailer makes driving fasteners a one-handed task and eliminates the tedious job of burying each head with a nail set. A wood block keeps your hand safely back from the nail gun.

WHAT IF...
You want to scribe the baseboard to the floor?

1 Temporarily secure the baseboard against the wall by partially driving nails. Find an offset that will make a continuous line along the bottom edge of the board without removing an excessive amount of stock. In this case, a mechanical pencil laid flat on top of a ⅛-inch-thick spacer is just right. Simply pull the pencil and spacer along the board to mark it. Other scribing tips and techniques are on *page 213*.

2 If there's a significant amount of stock to remove, tilt the base of your jigsaw about 15 degrees, and cut to the waste side of the pencil line—but don't let your cut touch the line. Although the tilt isn't absolutely necessary, it significantly reduces the amount of stock you'll need to remove in the next step. In addition, it eliminates potential points of contact with the floor, which could spoil the fit.

3 Complete the stock removal with a belt sander, carefully working right up to the line. By tilting the sander less than you did the saw, you'll remove a minimal amount of stock, speeding the process. A small block plane is a quieter and less dusty way to work up to the line. Test-fit the baseboard and make any minor corrections required.

CROWNING TOUCHES

Crown moldings are popular, yet installation of these large moldings intimidates many homeowners. That's understandable because even the simplest mitering method requires you to position the molding upside down and backward in the miter box.

A compound mitersaw has several advantages over manual cutting: It removes much of the physical effort, it usually results in a cleaner cut, and it allows you to place the molding flat on the cutting table. Knowing exactly how to place the molding is the trick.

Secrets revealed

In this chapter, you'll see the step-by-step processes involved in cutting and installing crown molding, whether you have an economical manual cutting guide or the latest sliding compound mitersaw. You'll see how to make templates that speed setups and virtually eliminate mistakes as well as how to use a special protractor to measure out-of-square corners (corners are almost always out of square).

Choose your crown

By combining stock moldings, you can create a unique installation for your home. If your taste runs to massive moldings, take a look at the choices offered by lightweight plastic crown moldings. The intricate patterns cast into the moldings give your home the charm of old-world craftsmanship without heavy expense or heavy lifting.

Uplights and crown moldings

Imagine soft uplights from a crown trough adding drama to an entry foyer or gently glowing down the length of a hall. In an entertainment room, they'll virtually eliminate reflections from the television screen while still maintaining a comfortable lighting level. Along one wall or all the way around a room, uplights add a great look.

Coffered ceilings

Coffered ceiling construction techniques go back to ancient times. Some of the rooms found in Egyptian pyramids have coffered ceilings. But you can add a coffered ceiling to your home without recruiting a workforce of thousands of people. In fact, one helper and perhaps a drywall lift will be all the help you'll need.

Crown moldings and other decorative treatments will have your ceilings and walls looking up.

CHAPTER PREVIEW

Installing crown molding
page 142

Compound mitersaw
page 145

Crown molding and other variations
page 148

Crown molding with uplights
page 150

Uplighting—provided by economical rope lights—adds dramatic soft lighting above this room's crown molding.

Plastic crown molding
page 152

Coffered ceiling
page 154

INSTALLING CROWN MOLDING

Crown molding is installed at the juncture of the wall and the ceiling. Although it looks like a hefty piece of wood, most crown molding is relatively thin material. The secret of its appearance is the way it is installed. Rather than being a solid block nailed into the corner, crown moldings are installed on the diagonal between the wall and ceiling—there is nothing in the corner. Moldings installed this way are said to be sprung into place.

The tricky part about installing crown molding is cutting the joints. Because the molding is installed at an angle, it cannot be cut lying flat in an ordinary miter box; as you make the cuts, you must hold the molding at an angle. To cut crown molding flat, you need a compound mitersaw. See *page 145* for that technique.

PRESTART CHECKLIST

☐ **TIME**
About 4 hours for a regular room with four straight walls

☐ **TOOLS**
Tape measure, framing square, miter box or mitersaw, hammer, nail set, coping saw, utility knife

☐ **SKILLS**
Measuring and laying out, driving nails, crosscutting moldings, mitering moldings, making coped joints

☐ **PREP**
Walls and ceiling should be finished and painted, molding can be prefinished

☐ **MATERIALS**
Crown molding, 8d finishing nails, wood for blocking

1 Start by determining how far out from the wall the edge of the molding will fall. Place a piece of the crown inside a framing square to find this measurement. Mark this distance on the ceiling near the corners and at several points along the length of the wall.

2 Start with the wall opposite the door. Cut the molding to length with square cuts on both ends. Hold it in place and nail it first to the wall studs with 8d nails and then to the ceiling joists.

Installing plaster-faced crown molding

In the heyday of the plasterer's craft, elaborate crown moldings in fine homes often were cast in place from plaster rather than made of wood. Today, thanks to a new molding material, you can create the same effect with less skill than it takes to install wood molding. This new material has a very lightweight core of expanded polystyrene—the same material used to make a plastic foam cup. The polystyrene comes coated with gypsum plaster, so you really are getting a plaster surface.

The good news for do-it-yourselfers is that the molding is attached to the wall with any lightweight sandable joint compound. No nails are needed and joints with gaps up to ⅛ inch are easy to fill with the same joint compound used to install the molding. Also, inside miter joints are used instead of coped joints. Cut the molding with a miter box or mitersaw and finish it with the same paint you use on the other trim in the room.

1 Cut the molding as you do wood molding, except make miter cuts instead of copes for inside corners. Use a putty knife to apply a ⅜-inch-wide swath of sandable joint compound to the top and bottom edges of the crown.

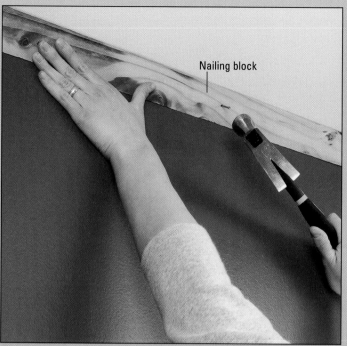

Nailing block

3 If the wall runs parallel to the ceiling joists, there may be no framing members in position to nail the molding to the ceiling. In this situation, cut some triangular nailing blocks to attach to the wall studs. Size the blocks to allow a ¼-inch gap between the block and the back of the crown.

4 The second piece of crown is cut square on one end and coped on the other. To cut the cope, start with an inside miter cut. Hold the crown in your miter box upside down (as if the base of the box were the ceiling and the fence were the wall) and backwards (if the cope is on the right end of the piece, the cut will be on the left as the piece rests in the miter box).

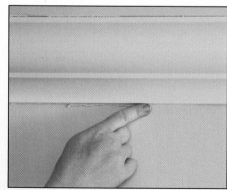

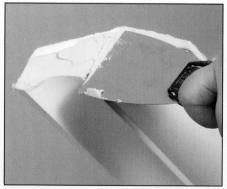

2 Press the molding into place, causing the joint compound to ooze out along the length. Where the molding meets the ceiling and wall, smooth the excess with your finger.

3 To join two pieces in a straight run, use a butt joint. Wherever one piece of molding joins another, coat the adjoining face of the second piece with joint compound before you press it into place. Wipe off the excess squeezeout with a damp sponge.

4 After the adhesive dries, smooth joints with a fine-grit sanding sponge, which will conform to the shape of the molding. Dab in joint compound to fill any gaps. Sand again as needed.

INSTALLING CROWN MOLDING (continued)

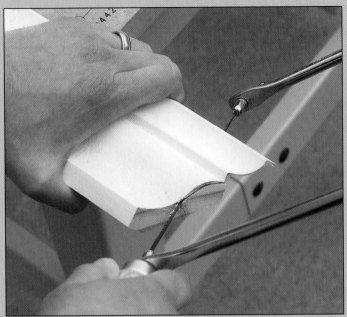

5 Create the cope by sawing along the intersection of the miter cut and the face of the profile. Angle the saw slightly so the joint is undercut. Test the fit against a piece of scrap molding and fine-tune the piece with a utility knife. Nail the piece in place as before. Proceed around the room, making square cuts on one end and coped cuts on the other end of each piece. Make coped cuts on both ends of the last piece.

6 For outside miters, the pieces also are held in the saw upside down and backwards, but the cut is angled in the opposite direction. To get a tighter fit in both outside and inside corners, flex and twist the pieces slightly before driving in the nails closest to the joint.

WHAT IF...
You need to end crown molding without running into a wall?

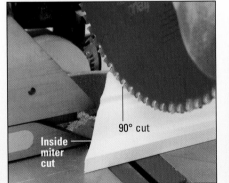

90° cut

Inside miter cut

You may need to end a run of crown molding that doesn't turn a corner or run into a wall. If so, stop the molding with a triangular return piece. To cut this piece, place a scrap of crown upside down in the chop saw or miter box and make an outside miter cut. Then set the saw to 90 degrees, cut off the triangle,

aligning the blade to the point where the miter ends at the back of the molding. Attach the return piece with yellow carpenter's glue. Use masking tape to hold the piece in place until the glue sets. For further details on cutting returns, see *page 214*.

STANLEY PRO TIP

Burnish corners to cure gaps

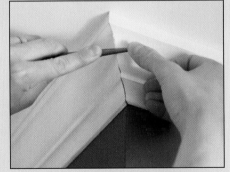

In spite of careful work, not every joint will fit perfectly. If you find a slight gap in an outside miter, force a little glue into it, then burnish the edges using the side of a nail set. Burnishing the corners folds over the thin wood fibers, bridging the gap.

COMPOUND MITERSAW

In recent years, two woodworking trends have helped fuel each other—the popularity of crown molding installations and the proliferation of compound mitersaws.

One of the major problems in using a compound mitersaw is visualizing how to position the crown molding on the saw before you make the cut. To overcome this problem, you'll make four templates—one for each of the basic saw positions used for running crown around a flat ceiling.

You'll need two more items before starting the project. The first is the chart of miter and bevel settings on *page 147*. You'll also need an accurate protractor—preferably with legs at least 18 inches long. (See "Resource Guide" on *page 236*.) You'll utilize the protractor for each outside corner in the room and for inside corners that are not exactly 90 degrees. Because you'll cope an inside corner against a square-cut piece that butts into a corner, you don't have to be so finicky about the inside angles. Back-cut the cope and you'll easily fit corners.

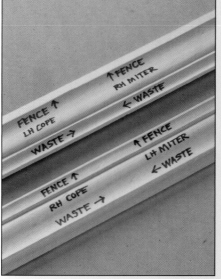

1 Cut two lengths of crown molding about 24 inches long. Lay them on your workbench so their bottom edges are near each other, then duplicate the writing shown in the photo above.

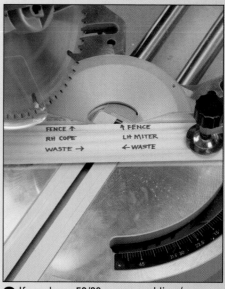

2 If you have 52/38 crown molding (see "Understanding the spring angle" *below*), set the miter at 31.6 degrees left and bevel the blade 33.9 degrees left. Some compound mitersaws have a miter stop at this setting. If you're working with 45/45 molding, the miter angle is 35.3 and the bevel is 30 degrees. Slice apart the LH cope/RH miter templates.

Understanding the spring angle

52/38 crown molding — 52° 38° 52°

45/45 crown molding — 45° 45° 45°

The spring angle of crown molding refers to the angles that the flat back of the molding makes with the ceiling and the wall. There are two common types: the 52/38 molding and the 45/45 variety. As you'll notice in the drawings, the first angle also describes a complementary angle, the slope of the installed molding relative to the floor. When buying molding, make sure all the pieces have identical spring angles.

Choosing the correct template

The left hands and right hands you marked on the template do not refer to directions on the stick of molding. Instead, they refer to the corner of the wall where the molding is installed. The drawings identify right and left as judged when you're facing the corner—whether it's an inside or outside corner. After you make the templates, hold them up to walls to understand how the directions relate to each other.

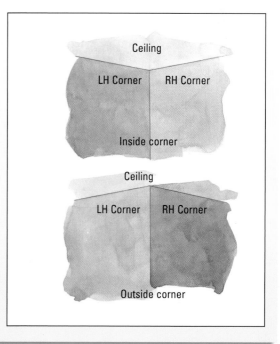

Ceiling
LH Corner   RH Corner
Inside corner

Ceiling
LH Corner   RH Corner
Outside corner

Compound Mitersaw (continued)

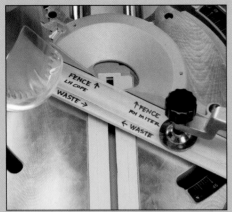

3 Without changing the bevel setting, swing the miter angle to the right side of the zero mark and all the way to the opposite setting you made in the first cut. In this case, that is 31.6 degrees right. Cut apart the LH cope/RH miter templates.

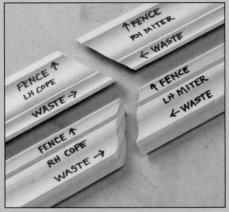

4 The completed templates will last a long time. Consider painting part of the wood a bright color to make them easy to find— even if one gets accidentally mixed in with some molding scraps.

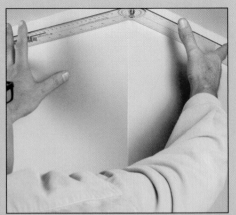

5 Measure an outside corner with your protractor, holding it where the bottom of the molding will hit the wall. A protractor with long legs will give you a more accurate reading because it will measure beyond the immediate vicinity of the corner. Because that area was formed by the drywall finisher who applied the compound at the corner, its surface may not truly represent the angle between the walls.

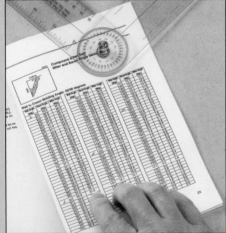

6 Lock the protractor's angle (in this case, by turning a small brass knob). Check that the setting didn't change when you turned the knob, then read the angle on the protractor. Refer to the angle chart on the opposite page for the spring angle of the molding you have—either 52/38 or 45/45. Set your bevel setting to the angle listed in this chart or the chart packed with your compound mitersaw.

7 Place the appropriate template sample for the right- or left-hand miter onto your saw table, then set the miter to match the direction of the cut on the template. The exact miter angle you set will be the one you found on the chart in the last step. Observing how the molding is oriented on the table (bottom or top toward the fence), slide the template away from the fence and place your molding in the same relative position. Move the template out of the cutting path, then make the cut.

8 Swing the miter setting to the same number but on the other side of zero to make the matching miter cut. You can now install the two pieces of crown molding for a crisp outside miter.

CROWN MOLDING CUTTING ANGLES

Angle Between Walls	52/38° CROWN MOLDING		45/45° CROWN MOLDING		Angle Between Walls	52/38° CROWN MOLDING		45/45° CROWN MOLDING	
	Miter Setting	Bevel Setting	Miter Setting	Bevel Setting		Miter Setting	Bevel Setting	Miter Setting	Bevel Setting
67°	42.93°	41.08°	46.89°	36.13°	124°	18.13°	21.71°	20.61°	19.39°
68°	42.39°	40.79°	46.35°	35.89°	125°	17.77°	21.34°	20.21°	19.06°
69°	41.85°	40.50°	45.81°	35.64°	126°	17.42°	20.96°	19.81°	18.72°
70°	41.32°	40.20°	45.28°	35.40°	127°	17.06°	20.59°	19.42°	18.39°
71°	40.79°	39.90°	44.75°	35.15°	128°	16.71°	20.21°	19.03°	18.06°
72°	40.28°	39.61°	44.22°	34.89°	129°	16.37°	19.83°	18.64°	17.72°
73°	39.76°	39.30°	43.70°	34.64°	130°	16.02°	19.45°	18.25°	17.39°
74°	39.25°	39.00°	43.18°	34.38°	131°	15.67°	19.07°	17.86°	17.05°
75°	38.74°	38.69°	42.66°	34.12°	132°	15.33°	18.69°	17.48°	16.71°
76°	38.24°	38.39°	42.15°	33.86°	133°	14.99°	18.31°	17.09°	16.38°
77°	37.74°	38.08°	41.64°	33.60°	134°	14.65°	17.93°	16.71°	16.04°
78°	37.24°	37.76°	41.13°	33.33°	135°	14.30°	17.55°	16.32°	15.70°
79°	36.75°	37.45°	40.62°	33.07°	136°	13.97°	17.17°	15.94°	15.36°
80°	36.27°	37.13°	40.12°	32.80°	137°	13.63°	16.79°	15.56°	15.02°
81°	35.79°	36.81°	39.62°	32.53°	138°	13.30°	16.40°	15.19°	14.68°
82°	35.31°	36.49°	39.13°	32.25°	139°	12.96°	16.02°	14.81°	14.34°
83°	34.83°	36.17°	38.63°	31.98°	140°	12.63°	15.64°	14.43°	14.00°
84°	34.36°	35.85°	38.14°	31.70°	141°	12.30°	15.25°	14.06°	13.65°
85°	33.90°	35.52°	37.66°	31.42°	142°	11.97°	14.87°	13.68°	13.31°
86°	33.43°	35.19°	37.17°	31.14°	143°	11.64°	14.48°	13.31°	12.97°
87°	32.97°	34.86°	36.69°	30.86°	144°	11.31°	14.09°	12.94°	12.62°
88°	32.52°	34.53°	36.21°	30.57°	145°	10.99°	13.71°	12.57°	12.28°
89°	32.07°	34.20°	35.74°	30.29°	146°	10.66°	13.32°	12.20°	11.93°
90°	31.62°	33.86°	35.26°	30.00°	147°	10.34°	12.93°	11.83°	11.59°
91°	31.17°	33.53°	34.79°	29.71°	148°	10.01°	12.54°	11.46°	11.24°
92°	30.73°	33.19°	34.33°	29.42°	149°	9.69°	12.16°	11.09°	10.89°
93°	30.30°	32.85°	33.86°	29.13°	150°	9.37°	11.77°	10.73°	10.55°
94°	29.86°	32.51°	33.40°	28.83°	151°	9.05°	11.38°	10.36°	10.20°
95°	29.43°	32.17°	32.94°	28.54°	152°	8.73°	10.99°	10.00°	9.85°
96°	29.00°	31.82°	32.48°	28.24°	153°	8.41°	10.60°	9.63°	9.50°
97°	28.58°	31.48°	32.02°	27.94°	154°	8.09°	10.21°	9.27°	9.15°
98°	28.16°	31.13°	31.58°	27.64°	155°	7.77°	9.82°	8.91°	8.80°
99°	27.74°	30.78°	31.13°	37.34°	156°	7.46°	9.43°	8.55°	8.45°
100°	27.32°	30.43°	30.68°	27.03°	157°	7.14°	9.04°	8.19°	8.10°
101°	26.91°	30.08°	30.24°	26.73°	158°	6.82°	8.65°	7.83°	7.75°
102°	26.50°	29.73°	29.80°	26.42°	159°	6.51°	8.26°	7.47°	7.40°
103°	26.09°	29.38°	29.36°	26.12°	160°	6.20°	7.86°	7.11°	7.05°
104°	25.69°	29.02°	28.92°	25.81°	161°	5.88°	7.47°	6.75°	6.70°
105°	25.29°	28.67°	28.48°	25.50°	162°	5.57°	7.08°	6.39°	6.35°
106°	24.89°	28.31°	28.05°	25.19°	163°	5.26°	6.69°	6.03°	6.00°
107°	24.49°	27.95°	27.62°	24.87°	164°	4.95°	6.30°	5.68°	5.65°
108°	24.10°	27.59°	27.19°	24.56°	165°	4.63°	5.90°	5.32°	5.30°
109°	23.71°	27.23°	26.77°	24.24°	166°	4.32°	5.51°	4.96°	4.94°
110°	23.32°	26.87°	26.34°	23.93°	167°	4.01°	5.12°	4.61°	4.59°
111°	22.93°	26.51°	25.92°	23.61°	168°	3.70°	4.72°	4.25°	4.24°
112°	22.55°	26.15°	25.50°	23.29°	169°	3.39°	4.33°	3.90°	3.89°
113°	22.17°	25.78°	25.08°	22.97°	170°	3.08°	3.94°	3.54°	3.53°
114°	21.79°	25.42°	24.66°	22.65°	171°	2.77°	3.54°	3.19°	3.18°
115°	21.42°	25.05°	24.25°	22.33°	172°	2.47°	3.15°	2.83°	2.83°
116°	21.04°	24.68°	23.84°	22.01°	173°	2.15°	2.75°	2.48°	2.47°
117°	20.67°	24.31°	23.43°	21.68°	174°	1.85°	2.36°	2.12°	2.12°
118°	20.30°	23.94°	23.02°	21.36°	175°	1.54°	1.97°	1.77°	1.77°
119°	19.93°	23.57°	22.61°	21.03°	176°	1.23°	1.58°	1.41°	1.41°
120°	19.57°	23.20°	22.21°	20.70°	177°	.92°	1.18°	1.06°	1.06°
121°	19.20°	22.83°	21.80°	20.38°	178°	.62°	.79°	.71°	.71°
122°	18.84°	22.46°	21.40°	20.05°	179°	.31°	.39°	.35°	.35°
123°	18.48°	22.09°	21.00°	19.72°					

CROWN MOLDING AND OTHER VARIATIONS

Successful architecture is like the story of Goldilocks and the three bears—you don't want your molding installation too big or too small. You want it to be just right.

For example, a multi-element installation could be the perfect scale in a room with a ceiling that's 10 feet high. But nail those identical moldings in a room with an 8-foot ceiling and you'll feel that you need to duck to avoid bumping your head. On the other hand, combining base and cove molding can be the right proportion in a room with an 8-foot ceiling, but it would be lost on top of a 10-foot wall.

As a general rule, the need for restraint diminishes as ceiling height increases. When a wall reaches a height of 10 feet or more, you can pretty well throw caution to the wind and pursue any molding combination your ambition and budget allow.

The best way to judge the scale of a molding installation is to assemble a sample that's 2 or 3 feet long, then tack it at ceiling level. After looking at it for a few days, you'll be able to tell whether it's too big, too small, or just right.

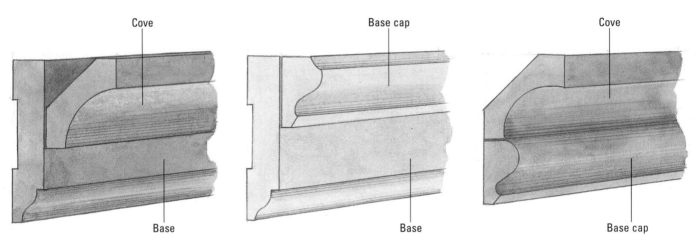

Cove

Base

Option 1

Base cap

Base

Option 2

Cove

Base cap

Option 3

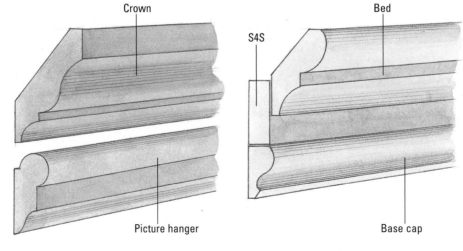

Crown

Picture hanger

Option 4

S4S

Bed

Base cap

Option 5

Combining standard moldings

There are thousands of ways to combine the hundreds of standard molding profiles to achieve exactly the look you want. These examples merely hint at the variety that's available. To see other possible mix-and-match candidates, turn to "Molding Gallery," beginning on *page 196*.

In multi-element installations, you'll often see baseboard molding applied to the wall, as in Options 1, 2, and 8, but sometimes it goes on both wall and ceiling, as shown in Option 7. Option 6 shows a similar effect, but this time you apply casing to the ceiling. By using the same base and casing profiles you installed elsewhere in the room, you'll unify the design.

Don't let the molding names get in the way of assembling a pleasing crown molding. In fact, you can achieve the effect of crown molding without using actual crown molding. Study the combinations of cove, base cap, and bed moldings shown on these pages. Several of the options show S4S stock, which is lumberman's lingo for smooth four sides. Your lumberyard will probably have stain-grade S4S in a variety of sizes, or you can rip your own from dimensional lumber.

Options 9 and 10 show rectangles with Xs, which indicate lumber that serves as blocking. The blocking is 1×, and 2× lumber provides nailing surfaces and support for the moldings.

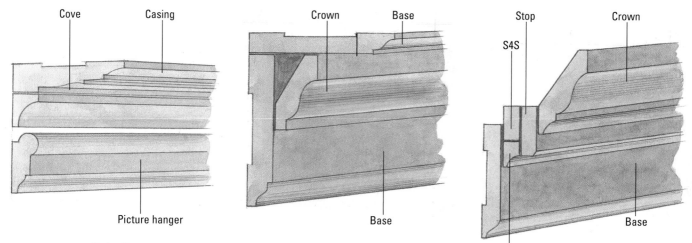

Option 6

Option 7

Option 8

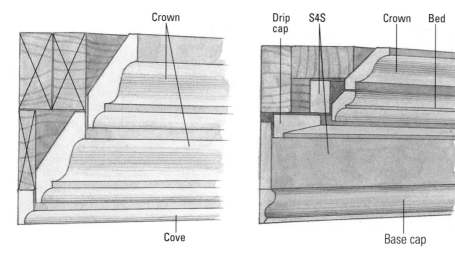

Option 9

Option 10

CROWN MOLDING WITH UPLIGHTS

This project combines the architectural interest of crown molding with the soft glow of indirect lighting, whether it's along one wall or all the way around the room.

The project is no more difficult than a standard installation of crown molding—in fact, it's easier because you don't have to worry about fitting the molding tightly to the ceiling. Ripping the nailer strip is an additional step, but it's an easy task if you have a tablesaw. No saw? Visit a local cabinet shop and you may be able to get the strips cut for a reasonable cost. The 1½-inch thickness of standard 2× lumber produces the right nailing strip height for the 4-inch crown chosen for this project. If you downsize to a 3-inch crown, cut the strips from 5/4 stock, which measures about 1 inch thick.

Paint the inside of the lighting trough to maximize light output from inexpensive rope lighting. You'll find the painting is easy because you roll or brush it before installing the components.

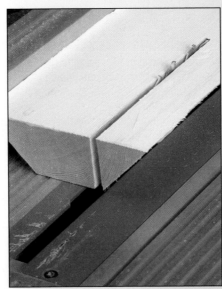

1 Paint primer and a coat of white topcoat onto one side of the 2×6 lumber that you'll use for the nailing strips. Apply an identical finish to the back of the crown molding. Tilt your tablesaw blade to match the spring angle of your crown molding. For 52/38 crown, tilt the blade to 52 degrees, and make the cuts with the painted side of the board against the table. Return the blade to vertical, and slice off the angled nailing strips.

2 Cut a 24-inch length of the nailing strip and crown molding, then tack-nail them together to make a mock-up of the light trough. Hold the end of a length of rope light in the assembly, and position it against the wall at varying heights until you're pleased with the lighting effect. Don't place it too close the ceiling or you won't have room for the outlet box. Make a mark at the bottom of the nailing strip—4½ inches from the ceiling in this case.

Getting power to the trough

You may be able to install a switched outlet near the trough from an existing wall switch. See *Stanley Complete Wiring* for details and installation instructions or hire a professional electrician to do the job.

Wire the circuit with a separate switch for the trough outlet so you can control it independently of the existing overhead light. That gives you flexibility in setting the lighting level and mood. You can either expand an existing single box to a double or purchase a double switch that fits into a single box.

Rope lights that run off a low-voltage transformer bring an additional consideration: the transformer may be too bulky to fit into the trough. If there isn't room in the trough for the transformer, find a place for it in an adjoining room or basement.

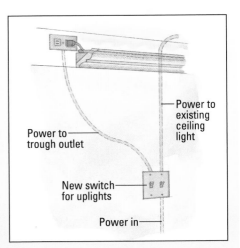

Power to existing ceiling light

Power to trough outlet

New switch for uplights

Power in

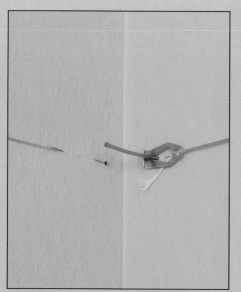

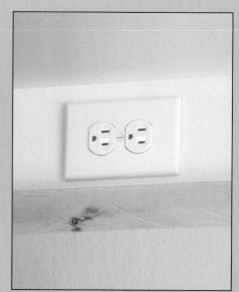

3 At each corner of the room, make a mark at the measurement you determined, and snap chalk lines connecting the marks. Resist the urge to check whether this line is level; as long it is parallel to the ceiling, it will look fine. If you run a level line below a nonlevel ceiling, the out-of-parallel situation would draw attention to the defect.

4 With a stud finder and short strips of masking tape, mark the position of all wall studs. Nail or screw the nailer strips around the perimeter of the room. The white-painted edge of the strip faces upward—an easy check for proper placement. End each strip about 4 inches away from each inside corner to allow butt-fitted ends of crown molding to extend all the way to the wall.

5 Install a switched electrical outlet box at a convenient location. Refer to "Getting power to the trough" on the opposite page for ideas on getting power to the outlet. Position the box close to the edge of the nailing strip, but leave enough space to install the cover plate.

6 Proceed with the installation of the crown molding, butting its backside against the strip and nailing it in place. Coped corners require a special technique so that the rope lighting can make the turn. Hold the coped piece against the piece butted against the wall, and run a pencil along the back side of the coped molding to mark a cutline.

7 Remove the waste from the butt-fitted piece with a fine-tooth saw and chisel. Your cut doesn't need to be pretty because it won't be seen—it's merely necessary to create clearance for rope lights. Everything else in the installation follows the usual procedures.

8 Lay the rope lights neatly into the trough, and turn on the power to admire the effect.

PLASTIC CROWN MOLDING

If you want the latest thing in crown molding, here's one word of advice: plastics.

You'll find a wide range of styles, from relatively plain to incredibly intricate. They resemble the best work crafted in plaster and found in stately vintage homes, but the low density of the plastic material slashes weight and cost.

Another appealing aspect of cast plastic moldings is the fact that the skill level required for successful installation is quite modest. With nothing more complicated than square cuts when you utilize corner and connector blocks, it's a project that's very accessible to many people. You'll need just a few basic tools; you can even get by without a mitersaw. The material has about the same density as pine, so even a hand-powered cut through the widest molding will barely cause you to break a sweat.

As you shop around, you'll discover several styles and sizes of molding and corner blocks. Be certain that the blocks you select coordinate with both the proportion and character of the molding.

1 Through each tab of the blocks, drill a ⁵⁄₃₂-inch shank clearance hole so that the threads of a #8×2-inch roundhead screw don't hang up on the plastic. Note that there are three styles of block: an inside corner block, an outside corner one, and a connector block. If you need to use a connector block, position it in the middle of a run or evenly space a series of connectors along a wall.

2 Screw the blocks to the wall, making certain that you install them squarely to the ceiling. Don't overdrive the screws or you'll risk breaking the plastic. To end a run, simply cut a tab off a block with a handsaw. Referring to the depth dimension supplied with the molding (or by measuring it), make a reference mark near each block and about every 4 feet along the run of the molding. The depth dimension is the height of the installed molding on the wall.

Corner blocks for wood crown

Your home center may stock wood corner blocks that you can use in conjunction with wood crown molding. Be sure to check that the entire end of the molding you choose will land on the block with no overhang.

As the photo shows, you can also mix media by utilizing plastic blocks with wood molding. As long as the completed installation is painted, no one will be able to detect the difference in the materials.

WHAT IF...
You don't use the corner blocks?

You don't absolutely need the corner blocks for plastic moldings, but you don't install the material exactly like it's wood molding. Here are a few key differences:

■ If you need to join two pieces of molding along a wall, do not cut a scarf joint. Simply make a butt joint and apply adhesive at the seam. If necessary, touch up the joint with vinyl spackle and sand it smooth.

■ You'll utilize butt joints at the ends of the molding. But eliminating the midrun block means that you need to create a temporary anchor point so you can spring the slightly overlong molding into place. This anchor point is nothing more complicated than a wood block temporarily screwed to the wall. For an extremely long molding run, you'll leapfrog the position of the wood block along the wall to install each piece.

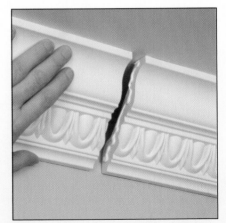

■ If you sand through the factory-applied primer, touch it up with a compatible primer before painting.

■ Cut miters instead of copes for inside corners, and apply adhesive to the joint.

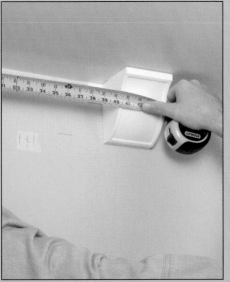

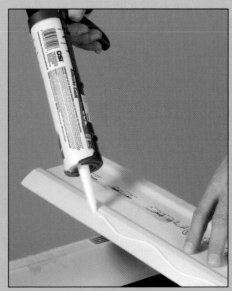

3 With your stud finder and strips of masking tape, mark the location of each stud on the wall. Measure between a pair of blocks and add ¼ inch to ensure a snug fit; mark this dimension on a length of molding.

4 Cut the molding to length. A mitersaw will do the job quickly, but a handsaw is just as effective. If you choose the manual route, make sure you cut straight across the molding and squarely through it.

5 To ensure a snug fit, apply the adhesive recommended by the manufacturer to the bedding edges of the molding. (The bedding edges are the molding surfaces that contact the wall and ceiling.) Don't overdo the adhesive or you'll create a mess when you install the molding.

6 Because you cut the molding a bit long, you'll snap it into place between the blocks. Having a helper makes this part considerably easier because you need to ensure that the bottom edge of the molding meets the depth dimension marks you made earlier.

7 Secure the molding with a 2-inch trim-head screw driven into each stud. The slim square-drive trim screws usually don't require a pilot hole. You could drive finishing nails, but be aware that a misplaced hammer blow could smash details of the molding. Screws are far less risky.

8 Remove excess adhesive with a putty knife and mineral spirits. Fill the screw holes with a paintable caulk that's compatible with the molding. Also caulk any gaps along the wall and ceiling. Follow the manufacturer's paint recommendations.

COFFERED CEILING

The coffered ceiling is adaptable to a variety of treatments by changing the number of steps and by adding moldings. You'll build each step from 2× lumber, which measures 1½ inches thick, plus a layer of ½-inch drywall. As a result, each step adds 2 inches of thickness.

A room with a standard 8-foot ceiling can easily tolerate a 2-inch loss of headroom in the name of style. A second layer in that room isn't out of the question. But if you want to add a third step, your original ceiling height should be at least 8 feet, 6 inches or higher to avoid a claustrophobic feeling.

The engineering is straightforward, as you can see in the section view drawings *below*. The two-step ceiling has a 2×4 strip above the second strip. This additional lumber width provides a nailing surface if you want to add moldings. Cove, crown, or bed moldings are three possibilities. The addition of moldings has two positive benefits: The millwork adds style and interest, and you don't need to be as precise with your drywall work when the inside corner is covered.

1 Measure out the desired distance from the walls, and snap chalk lines to define the perimeter of the 2×2 framework. To make a step 16 inches wide, for example, snap the chalk lines 15½ inches from the walls to account for the thickness of the ½-inch drywall on the edge of the frame.

2 Using your stud finder, mark the position of the ceiling joists. Make your lines right on the ceiling between the chalk lines and the walls, because the new drywall will cover that area. Attach the 2×2 strips to the ceiling with construction adhesive and screws driven into the joists. For the strips that run parallel to the joists, adopt one of the solutions explained in "What If" on the *opposite page*.

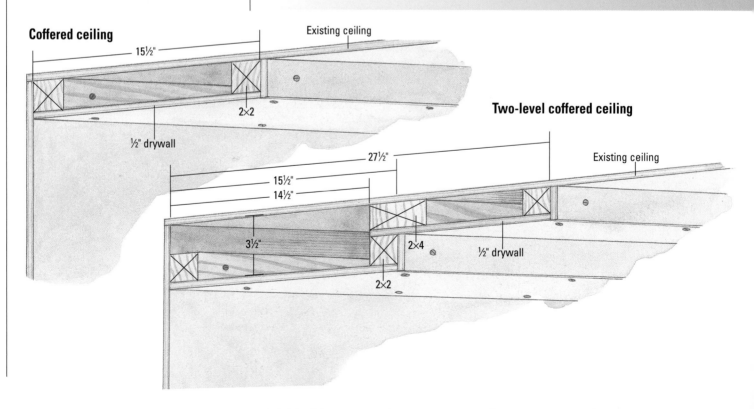

Coffered ceiling

Existing ceiling

15½"

2×2

½" drywall

Two-level coffered ceiling

Existing ceiling

27½"

15½"

14½"

3½"

2×4

½" drywall

2×2

3 Screw or nail a 2×2 strip around the perimeter of the room where the walls and ceiling meet. Again, use construction adhesive and drive fasteners into the studs. Don't use a level to establish a perfectly flat plane for these strips—that will merely emphasize any out-of-level condition your ceiling currently has.

4 Cover the framework with drywall, attaching it with construction adhesive and screws. Add a strip of drywall along the edge of the 2×2.

5 Nail metal corner bead along the edges of the drywall, mitering the corners with tin snips for a neat fit. For best results, drive 1⅝-inch ringshank nails through the metal instead of through the holes punched in the metal. Add drywall tape to the inner corners and apply joint compound to the inside and outside corners. See *page 109* for tips and techniques.

WHAT IF...
There's no joist where you need to attach a strip?

At first, you might be tempted to simply attach the strip to the ceiling with construction adhesive and toggle bolts. But that's not a good idea because it makes the drywall on the ceiling support the load of the strip plus the weight of the drywall you'll attach to it. Doing that would exceed the drywall's limits because it was not engineered to handle such an application.

The right approach is to add blocking between the joists so that the screws through the strips hit a solid anchoring point. This blocking can be 2× stock bridged between the joists or a continuous length of lumber added to the side of a joist. If you're redoing the entire ceiling in the room, add blocking while the joists are exposed. If you have access to an attic above the ceiling, you can add

blocking without disturbing the existing surface. As a last resort, you'll need to cut away the existing ceiling between joists to add the blocking. That's not as big a deal as it sounds, because you'll be adding drywall and spreading joint compound anyway. A little more area to cover is not a significant problem.

STANLEY PRO TIP

Mitering corner bead

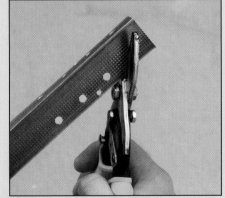

Before you install strips of metal corner bead along an inside corner, make a miter nip at the end of each piece with a pair of tin snips. Otherwise, you'd have the bulk of two thicknesses of metal overlapping at the corner.

GREAT IDEAS THROUGHOUT THE HOUSE

If you want inspiration for some dramatic changes that will energize your home, this is the chapter for you. You'll discover how easy it is to install soaring columns, reface your kitchen cabinets, and transform wood cabinet doors with glass panes.

Columns of choices

After you see how easy it is to install columns, you'll be looking for more places in your house to install them. Although this chapter features half-round columns, you'll also find quarter columns that fit inside corners or three-quarter models that wrap around outside corners. You'll also see fully rounded columns that can even be used structurally indoors or out.

Reface instead of replace

Many kitchen renovation projects stop dead in their tracks when the homeowner looks at the bids for replacement cabinets. As long as your kitchen cabinets are structurally sound, you can reface instead of replace at a fraction of the cost. This is also a good time to replace droopy shelves and drawers that are falling apart or stick so badly you can barely open them.

Let in the light

Maybe you've admired the look of glass-paned kitchen doors but didn't like the price tags on cabinets that have them. If your kitchen cabinets have doors with wood panels, you can upgrade to glass yourself for only the cost of a piece of glass and a few pieces of hardware.

In just a few hours, you can add inspiring touches to your home to enjoy for decades.

CHAPTER PREVIEW

Installing decorative columns
page 158

Kitchen cabinet makeover
page 162

Changing a wood panel to glass
page 166

*In an afternoon, you can upgrade
a kitchen cabinet with a new
glass panel.*

INSTALLING DECORATIVE COLUMNS

If you want to add a distinctive and timeless touch of class to your home, consider adding columns. After making the initial commitment, there are many more decisions to come. First, you need to select appropriate locations—where the columns actually appear to be performing a supporting role, even if they are purely decorative. Second, choose the material of the column. You'll find stain- and paint-grade hollow-wood columns, as well as synthetic materials such as the fiberglass version shown here. Third, select a style that's appropriate for your home. Although it's tempting to select the most ornate version, a bit of restraint goes a long way.

When you order your columns, you'll probably have to purchase a stock size slightly longer than the finished size. Also check on the availability of factory-split columns, such as a quarter column, half (shown in this installation), or three-quarter. The manufacturer may be able to supply other designs to suit your needs also.

PRESTART CHECKLIST

☐ **TIME**
About 1 hour per column, plus drying time for the finish

☐ **TOOLS**
Tape measure, rasp, level, saw, drill and bits, caulking gun, combination square

☐ **SKILLS**
Sawing, drilling, using a level

☐ **PREP**
Carefully measure installation site, order column and its capital (top) and plinth (base)

☐ **MATERIALS**
Columns, screws, lumber for backerboard, caulk, tapered shims

1 Measure the height of the installation site so you can place the order for the columns. Also ensure that the site is large enough to accommodate the width and depth of the capital and the plinth.

2 Subtract ¼ inch from the measured height, then mark the cut line near the base of the column. See *below* for more information on cutting columns. Triple-check the measurement, then cut the column to length with a handsaw. The edges of a fiberglass column, like the example shown, can be very sharp, so dull them with a few passes of a rasp.

Straight talk about columns

When you shop for columns, you may discover that the shaft does not have a consistent diameter along its entire length. For example, the factory made the columns in this installation with a straight section along the bottom one-third of its length and a taper along the upper portion. This is why columns are sold in a variety of lengths and why you must trim them from the bottom only, never removing more than one-third of the total length.

You may also discover columns that have sides that bulge slightly. The ancient Greeks discovered that perfectly straight columns didn't look right—the sides seemed to curve inward. That's why Greek architects introduced the concept of entasis, which is a very slight convex curve along the column's shaft. This swelling overcomes the illusion of concavity and makes the eye see the column as straight.

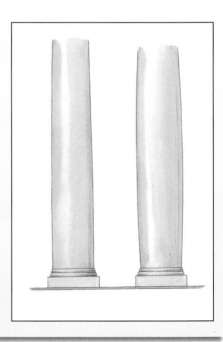

3 Mark the side-to-side centerline on the surface where you'll set the base of the column. Make certain that the platform is sturdy enough to support the column's weight. Just as important, this base surface must have a substantial appearance because those viewing it will assume that this column plays a role in supporting your house.

4 Transfer the horizontal centerline into a vertical centerline for the column. Extend this line all the way to the top of the installation. Extend the centerline onto the ceiling, then mark about 2 inches toward the center of the room.

5 Measure the inside diameter at the top of the column, then rip a piece of ¾-inch-thick lumber into a backerboard that will fit inside the column for the top one-third of its height. If the column tapers, ignore it and simply get a decent fit at the top. Mark the centerline at the top end of the board, check its edge for plumb, and fasten it to the wall with nails or screws.

WHAT IF...
You're installing full-round columns?

If columns support a structural load, you'll need to cut them to exact length, and in remodeling, that usually means that you have to jack up the structure, insert the columns, then lower the structure onto the top of the columns. A square cut at both the top and bottom of the column is very important in order to have an even distribution of the load through the shaft's section.

Your local building codes may prescribe that exterior structural columns also be able to resist uplift—the roof-raising force that can occur during hurricanes or tornadoes. If you plan to cut into a structural column or attach another load to it, you'll need to consult the column's manufacturer and possibly seek the services of a structural engineer as well.

With either decorative or structural full-round columns, you need to remember to

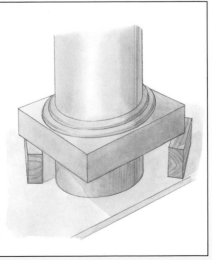

slip the plinth and capital collars onto the shaft before sliding it into position.

Sand holds column for sanding

Fiberglass columns can have a rough surface, and that may be a good base if you're applying a textured paint treatment, such as one that simulates rough granite. But if you want a polished stone look, you'll need to sand the columns.

The easiest time to do that is prior to installation. Immobilize the column so it doesn't roll away as you're working on it. Bags or tubes of sand provide an easy and inexpensive anchor.

INSTALLING DECORATIVE COLUMNS _(continued)_

6 Drill countersunk screw shank clearance holes through the edges of the column for screws that you'll drive into the backerboard. The capital will cover the topmost screws. Space additional screws no farther than 12 inches apart until you reach the bottom of the backerboard.

7 Mark a centerline at the top and bottom of the column's face. Drill angled countersunk screw shank clearance holes at the centerline near the column's top and bottom ends.

8 If you're working with a tall column, recruit a helper for the next steps. Hoist the column into position, then drive tapered shims under the end on each side until the top of the column touches the ceiling. Make certain that the column's centerline matches the horizontal one on the support surface.

Faux finishes

Faux finishes—paint finishes that mimic materials such as marble—were once the exclusive domain of talented artisans. But the popularity of these surface treatments has inspired paint manufacturers to craft carefully blended colors and specialized tools to make these decorative looks more accessible to do-it-yourselfers.

Although convenience packaging doesn't completely remove the need for painting skill from the project, you can inexpensively try your hand at creating a marble or granite finish. Craft stores and paint dealers usually sell materials along with decorative-painting books with step-by-step instructions.

Granite is one of the easier stones to fake. It generally has a very regular appearance throughout the entire piece. Instead of relying on your memory or imagination when it comes to the stone's appearance, purchase a piece of granite tile for reference. A tile dealer will likely have several samples from which you can choose. As you study the sample, notice that the stone has a dominant tone but also a wide range of tones in other colors.

Marble requires more artistic skill to convincingly mimic. Again, purchase a tile or two for reference, and aim for boldness instead of fussy detail.

If you ultimately discover that you're not a faux finisher, you can hide the evidence under a coat of primer and paint. After all, the purest marble is snowy white.

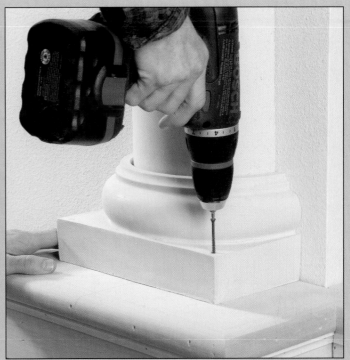

9 Drive a screw to secure the bottom of the column. Stop the screw as soon as it touches the column so you don't strip the hole or misalign the column. Drive a screw at the top centerline of the column and along both edges into the backerboard.

10 Drill countersunk screw shank holes through the plinth (base), then drive screws to secure it to the mounting surface. Again, stop driving as soon as the screw makes solid contact with the material.

11 Drill countersunk screw shank holes through the capital (top), then drive screws to secure it to the ceiling.

12 Apply caulk along all the seams. Then you're ready to apply the finish.

KITCHEN CABINET MAKEOVER

The first impulse when considering kitchen remodeling is to replace all the old cabinets. That idea often lasts only until you get the cost estimates.

While recovering from sticker shock, you can consider other options, such as refacing. Unless you want to shuffle the location of the appliances or change the kitchen layout, there's no compelling reason to replace cabinets that are structurally sound. An application of plywood and veneer will give the ends and face frames a fresh look. New doors, drawers, and hardware will completely update the cabinets. Refacing can be far less disruptive, messy, and time-consuming than a complete overhaul.

Home centers and woodworking specialty stores are sources for refacing supplies, tools, doors, drawers, slides, hinges, and other parts and hardware. Many dealers offer installation tips and information about measuring for replacement doors. (See the Resource Guide on *page 236*.)

1 Empty the contents of the kitchen cabinets into boxes, and move the boxes into another room. Remove all doors, drawers, hardware, and moldings. Make sure the cabinets are tightly attached to the walls and to each other, adding screws if necessary. Degrease the cabinets by wiping them with denatured alcohol. Fill dents and holes with wood filler. Lightly sand all surfaces with 100-grit sandpaper. Vacuum the dust to start with a clean work area.

2 If the edge of the face frame projects past the cabinet's end panel, bring the surfaces flush with a hand plane or with a flush-trim bit in a router. Cut a piece of ⅛- or ¼-inch-thick plywood to size for the end panel. Position the panel so that it barely extends past the face frame— an overhang that's just enough to snag your fingernail is plenty. Attach the plywood with panel adhesive and brads.

Paint freshens a cabinet's interior

As long as you have a cabinet empty, it's a good time to prime it and then apply a coat or two of white enamel—either latex or oil-based. A regular 9-inch roller can be a bit unwieldy inside a cabinet, so downsize to a 7-incher. The job will go surprisingly fast, and your cabinets will look cleaner and brighter. They may even look better than they did when brand new.

STANLEY®   PRO TIP: **Center the veneer pattern**

When you're applying strips of veneer or sheets of plywood, the results always look better when the joint line of the veneer pattern is centered.

When plywood and veneer sheets are made, the manufacturer butts together relatively narrow strips of veneer, creating a joint line that usually is a mirror image of the wood's grain pattern on both sides of the line—this is called bookmatching. Centering this line on wide elements, even if it means creating some waste, is worthwhile because it's a sure sign of high-quality work.

Avoid joint lines, if possible, when you're veneering rails or stiles that are 2 inches wide or narrower. That's because it will make that small-scale part appear as if it were pieced together.

3 Trim the end panel flush with the face frame by using a plane, a router with a flush-trim bit, or sandpaper in a hard rubber sanding block. Be careful to keep the corner square. This will ensure that the veneer on the face frame will have a firm foundation at this outer edge.

4 Apply a coat of water-based contact cement to the face and edges of each stile (the vertical elements of the face frame). When the contact cement dries in about 30 minutes, it will act as a bonding agent to improve the grip of the pressure-sensitive adhesive on the back surface of the veneer.

5 Make a pencil mark on the upper and lower rails 1 inch to the side of each stile. Measure the size of the stile and then cut a piece of veneer that's 2 inches wider (for intermediate stiles) and 1 inch longer. For stiles at the end of the ends of the cabinets, cut the strip about 1¼ inch wider. Start to strip away the backing and align the edge of the veneer with the marks on the rail. Work downward, peeling the backing and patting the veneer into place.

Shelf replacement is fast and easy

If your kitchen is ready for a makeover, you'll probably have a few worn or bowed shelves. Replacing them with melamine-covered shelves is faster and easier than repainting the old ones. You can purchase the plastic-covered shelf material in a variety of widths and lengths at a home center. You might also consider adding some intermediate supports for heavily loaded shelves so you won't have a repeat problem with bowing or sagging.

Replacement drawers

In some cases, you may be able to simply remove the existing drawer front and screw on a replacement. Or you may be able to salvage a drawer by performing some minor corrective surgery. But total replacement has a powerful allure, especially when you're already replacing other parts.

If you have a woodworking shop, consider making your own drawer boxes. Or subcontract this job to a company that specializes in drawer boxes. Depending on the amount of money you're willing to spend, you can purchase knocked down or fully assembled hardwood boxes with dovetailed corners, plywood or laminate-clad sides, and rabbeted or doweled corners. You can even purchase metal sides that have built-in drawer slides—you complete the box by cutting front and back panels and sliding in a plywood bottom.

It's easy to assemble drawers that are shipped as components. Brush water-resistant glue into the joints, then clamp. Make sure that the drawer is flat and square while the glue dries.

KITCHEN CABINET MAKEOVER (continued)

6 To ensure a good bond between the veneer and stile, rub the veneer with a smoothing tool. Woodworking catalogs have tools especially designed for this purpose, or you can substitute a piece of hardboard with its edges fully rounded over to blunt them.

7 To wrap the veneer around the stile, slice along the edge of the rail. Put a new blade into your utility knife, then cut with a sawing motion, exerting pressure only on the forward stroke. Repeat this slice at the top of each stile.

8 Bend the veneer around the edge of the stile with your fingers. Press it with your smoothing tool to ensure a secure bond. Don't worry if you have some minor cracking of the veneer as it goes around the stile. You can sand that smooth later.

New slides glide smoothly

The selection of drawer slides dictates the side clearances and influences the maximum height of the box, so it's a good idea to choose the style of slides before ordering the drawers.

The economical drawer slide shown in the photo is often called epoxy-coated because of its durable and low-friction finish. It requires ½ inch of clearance on each side, so order a drawer box that's 1 inch narrower than its opening. The ½-inch clearance is also standard on many side-mounted drawer slides. These ball-bearing units are more expensive, but you can choose full-extension and even over-extension models that allow easy access to the back of the drawer.

Bottom-mounted slides require precise dimensions between the bottom of the drawer and the lower edges of the sides. After installation, these slides are virtually invisible, and that can be an important consideration if you want to show off the dovetailed sides.

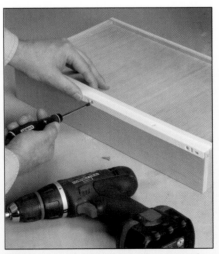

Simply screw the drawer members to each side of the drawer box. Screw the cabinet members to the side of the carcase or utilize a socket for mounting to the cabinet's back.

Attaching the drawer front

Joining the drawer box with its new false front is a relatively easy process. Install the drawer box into its opening; make certain that the hardware works smoothly. Put several strips of cloth double-faced tape onto the drawer front.

Draw marks on strips of tape applied to the cabinet's face frame to position the new false front. As you hold the false front in position, reach inside the cabinet, and press the drawer box against the false front. Gently remove the assembly, then drive screws through pilot holes to permanently join the pieces.

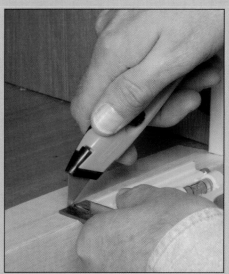

9 With a steel straightedge as a guide, slice away the excess veneer in a straight line across the rail. To trim the veneer flush with the bottom edge of the rail, stroke your utility knife blade along the back edge of the veneer two or three times, then gently wiggle the piece back and forth until it breaks. Use this same technique to trim the veneer flush with the edges of the wrapped stile.

10 On the inside of the cabinet's bottom, run a strip of masking tape so its edge touches the back of the stiles. Brush contact cement onto the rails and up to the tape. Cut a veneer strip 1 inch wider than the rail. Square-cut the one end by using a framing square and utility knife. Butt the cut end against the veneer on a stile, then mark the other end with a knife nick.

11 Cut the rail veneer to length, then apply it using the same procedures as for the stiles. By holding your utility knife blade against a framing square, you can easily slice through the veneer folded into the cabinet. Peel away the masking tape to reveal a smooth edge. Use 120-grit paper in a sanding block to tackle any splinters and sharp edges. Apply stain, if desired, then the clear finish.

Choose and install your hinges

There are two broad categories of hinges you can choose for the new cabinet doors: overlay hinges and Euro hinges. Overlay hinges screw to the back of the door and to the surface of the face frame. Installation requires no fancy tooling or jigs. Euro hinges also are named 35mm hinges because that's the diameter of the hole you need to drill to mount the hinge cup. The mounting screws require pilot holes that are precisely positioned. Instead of resorting to tedious marking for each hinge, you can purchase a drilling jig; shop around, some jigs are relatively inexpensive and others cost up to several hundred dollars. Be sure to pair your hinges with mounting plates designed for face frame application.

Gauge the installation spot for an overlay hinge at the width of one hinge leaf from the end of the door.

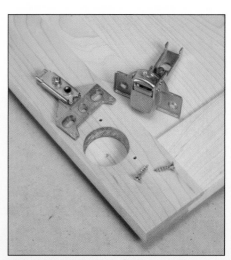

Here's a Euro hinge for a ⅜-inch overlay door with a baseplate that allows face frame mounting. The hinge has three-axis adjustability to ensure a great fit.

CHANGING A WOOD PANEL TO GLASS

Cabinet doors with glass panels are a hot look in custom kitchens. Clear glass in door panels allows you to show off china and glassware tucked safely in a cabinet. Cabinets fronted with fluted, pebbled, or frosted glass don't show off cabinet contents as clearly but do give the kitchen a lighter, airier look than doors with solid wood panels.

If your existing cabinet doors are sound and serviceable and are constructed with stiles and rails surrounding a wooden panel, follow the steps on these pages to replace the wood panel with glass for a new look.

The method is direct and fast, utilizing a jigsaw to remove most of the panel. A hammer, chisel, and locking-grip pliers then come into play to split out the remaining waste. Work carefully to remove the panel without damaging the door's framework.

PRESTART CHECKLIST

☐ **TIME**
About 1 hour per door, plus drying time for the finish

☐ **TOOLS**
Jigsaw with blades, drill with bits, chisel, locking-grip pliers, sanding block with paper, utility knife, hammer, router with ¼-inch straight bit (optional)

☐ **SKILLS**
Sawing, drilling, chiseling, routing with a guide

☐ **PREP**
Remove door and its hardware

☐ **MATERIALS**
Touch-up paint or stain and clear finish, glass, retainer clips with screws

1 After removing the door and its hardware, place the door face down on your worktable. Drill an entry hole for your jigsaw blade, then slice out the central portion of the door panel, leaving a perimeter of approximately 1 inch around the door's framework.

2 Stand the panel vertically, supporting it in a vise if possible. Drive a chisel along the grain of the panel to split the wood. Be careful that the chisel tip doesn't scar the door's rail. Make a second split about 1 inch from the first one. (Plywood doesn't split as easily as solid wood.)

WHAT IF...
You don't have a router?

Conduct some exploratory chisel work near the end of the panel on each frame member to find the depth of the groove. Draw a line to connect these points, then cut the line with a metal straightedge and utility knife. Tap a chisel downward along each line to remove the waste.

3 Solidly clamp the jaws of your locking-grip pliers onto the wood between the chisel marks. Hold onto the pliers, and give them a strong smack with a hammer to complete the splits and yank out the piece of wood. To avoid damage, make certain the hammer's path is parallel to the door. Also make sure the pliers or your hand won't hit the opposite rail when the chip is freed.

4 After you've removed the first piece of the panel's perimeter, getting out the remainder is relatively easy. If you wiggle the pieces, move them side to side only to prevent accidentally splitting the door frame. Always pull toward the panel's center. Placing a carpet remnant or scrap of carpet padding between your worktable and the door will help prevent scratches.

5 With the panel removed, you can accurately measure the depth of the groove in the door frame. Chuck a ¼-inch straight bit into your router, and use an edge guide with your router to remove the rear lip. This will convert the groove into a rabbet. If you don't have a router, switch to the method described *opposite below*.

6 A sharp chisel easily squares the corners of the rabbet. Inspect the entire perimeter of the rabbet and employ your chisel or a sanding block to smooth away any irregularities or puddles of finish that seeped into the groove.

7 Apply finish to the rabbet so that it matches the rest of the door. Take the doors with you to the glass shop to ensure an accurate fit. Consider double-strength glass, which measures ⅛ inch thick and is only slightly more expensive than single-strength. Many glass shops also can cut plastic glazing materials to fit the opening.

8 Select a glass retainer that will hold the pane firmly. The selection in the photo includes models that reach in to meet the glass, ones designed to secure glass that's flush with the wood, and a screw-adjust version that handles virtually every thickness—even bulky leaded-glass panels. Glass clips are available from woodworking dealers and hardware stores.

CHOOSING TOOLS

As you walk through the tool aisles of any well-stocked home center or hardware store, the choices will seem overwhelming. The following pointers will help you purchase the best tools for your purposes without spending more money than necessary.

Never buy a tool before you need it. A tool purchased because you think you might need it someday is destined to years of collecting dust.

When you need a tool, purchase the best quality you can afford, especially when it comes to edge tools, such as chisels and planes. Any chisel or plane will last a lifetime, but lower-cost, lower-quality tools cost you in time, convenience, and precision—cheap chisels don't stay sharp, and cheap planes don't cut flat and don't adjust smoothly. The metal on all hand tools should be flawlessly machined, and handles should be tight-fitting, hefty, and comfortable.

Power tools

When it comes to power tools, the shopping strategy is a little different. Consider whether you need to buy the tool at all. If, for example, you don't expect to do much trimwork after you remodel the den, consider renting a power miter box instead of buying one.

If you do decide to purchase a power tool, you probably don't need the top-of-the-line contractor's model. These tools are worth the money to pros who use them day after day. For your purposes, a lighter-duty saber saw will do a fine job, for example, of notching wainscot boards around electrical boxes.

Although you don't need the most heavy-duty power tools, you do need tools that are well made. Check that parts are well finished. Look for knobs that are hefty enough to tighten and loosen easily—stamped-steel wing nuts are a sign of a cheap tool. Inevitably you will dangle a power tool by its cord as you lower it from a ladder to the ground, so make sure the cord is sturdy and reinforced where it enters the housing.

The horsepower rating of a tool means little; amperage rating is a truer measure of power. Finally, before you buy a tool, pick it up and make sure it feels comfortable in your hands.

Start out with the best-quality hand tools you can afford—they pay off in the long run.

CHAPTER PREVIEW

Measuring and layout tools
page 170

Demolition and construction tools
page 172

Power cutting tools
page 174

Drilling and shaping tools
page 176

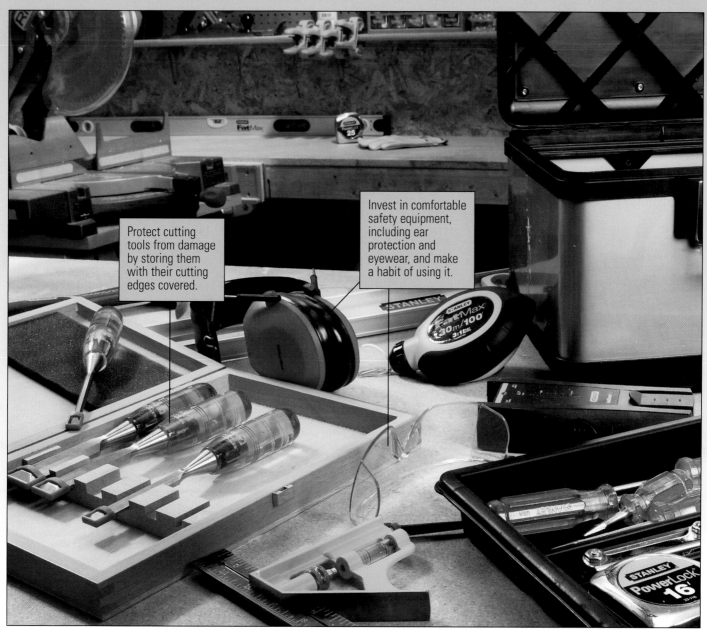

Protect cutting tools from damage by storing them with their cutting edges covered.

Invest in comfortable safety equipment, including ear protection and eyewear, and make a habit of using it.

Carpentry and remodeling involve a variety of tools and supplies. To protect your investment, store tools in toolboxes when not in use. Keep like tools together in individual carriers so they are easier to find when needed.

Choosing a mitersaw
page 178

Which blades do I buy?
page 180

Pneumatic tools
page 182

Accessories
page 184

MEASURING AND LAYOUT TOOLS

As you assemble a collection of tools for remodeling work, remember that you don't have to purchase everything at once. Start by purchasing only those tools you need for the job at hand, then add to your collection as the scope of your work expands. As a do-it-yourselfer, you probably do not need top-of-the-line tools. But buying high-quality tools from the start ensures many years of service from your purchase.

Tools for measuring
Carpenters live by three rules: plumb (pieces are vertically straight), square (pieces are 90 degrees perpendicular), and level (pieces are horizontally straight). The need for these rules starts from the ground up. A foundation that isn't level and square inevitably leads to trouble throughout a house as construction progresses. Learn to adhere to these standards, and your work

will look professional and create fewer problems as you go.

Working on an older home, however, teaches you that plumb, square, and level are often ideals rather than realities. In an older structure, you may have to compromise between what is right and what looks right. The two are often quite different.

The tools shown here come in handy as you plan, lay out, and build. A **tape measure**

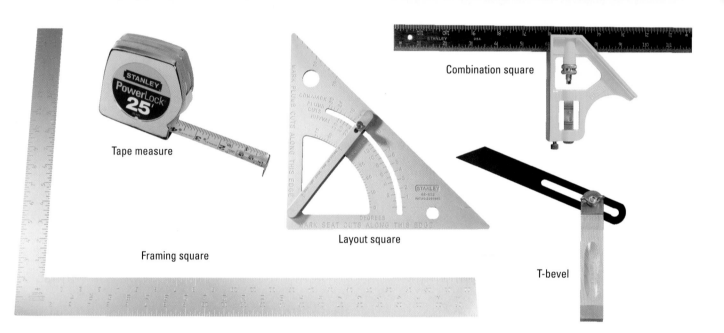

Combination square

Tape measure

Framing square

Layout square

T-bevel

Checking a square for square

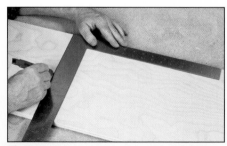

1 A framing square that is truly square is a valuable tool; one that is almost square is next to worthless. To check the accuracy of a framing square, hold the square along the edge of a straight board and draw a line.

2 Flip over the square and draw a second line right over the first. If the lines coincide, the square is square.

3 You can adjust a framing square by striking it with a center punch and hammer. Punch the square near the outside corner to close the angle. Punch it near the inside corner (as shown above) to open it up.

provides a compact ruler for all measuring tasks. A 25-foot model is the most common, although a 16-footer proves adequate for most jobs. A **combination square** allows you to draw square lines across boards for crosscutting. It is also handy for marking layout lines a specific distance in from the edge of a board. A **layout square** does many of the same tasks and can serve as a guide when crosscutting with a circular saw or jigsaw. A **framing square** (also called a carpenter's square) can be used for larger layouts. A **T-bevel** transfers angles from one place to another.

To check for level, you'll need a good **level** or two. They come in many lengths; a 3- or 4-foot model is a good first purchase. A **plumb bob** is simply a heavy, pointed weight.

When dangled from a string, a plumb bob and the string provide a vertical reference. A **chalk line** is used to mark long, straight lines. Many chalk lines have cases that can serve as plumb bobs. A **stud finder** is used to find framing studs in walls. Electronic and magnetic finders detect the nails in a wall but can be fooled by wires and pipes. New models sense the density of the studs.

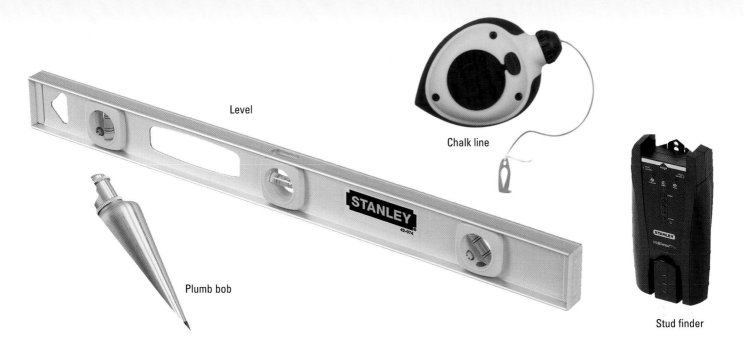

Level

Chalk line

Plumb bob

Stud finder

Using a tape measure

The hook on the end of a tape measure is loose for a reason. When taking an inside measurement, it slips up tight to the end of the tape, its thickness becoming part of the measurement. When hooked over the end of a board, it slides out to compensate for the missing thickness.

Snapping a line: Mark the ends of the line. Hook the chalk line at one mark, stretch it taut, and hold it at the other mark. Lift the line straight up and then let it go to make your mark.

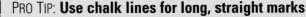

Chalk for chalk lines comes in a variety of colors. For marking complex layouts, use two or more lines, each with its own color.

DEMOLITION AND CONSTRUCTION TOOLS

You probably already have some basic carpentry tools around the house. To handle the demands of a remodeling project, make sure the tools you have are good quality and in good condition. If not, purchase new ones.

One of the most basic tools is the hammer. A **16-ounce framing hammer** is an essential. It is heavy enough to drive the large nails used for framing, yet small enough for use when installing moldings. Add a **22-ounce framing hammer** for heavy work. **Straight** and **Phillips screwdrivers** are necessary for installing hardware and occasionally for opening a paint can. A **utility knife** does everything from sharpening your pencil to cutting drywall. Keep plenty of blades on hand and replace them often so you always have a sharp cutting edge ready.

You'll find **nail sets** handy for driving finishing nails below the surface of moldings and extending your reach into hard-to-hammer places. An **awl** is a sharp-pointed tool you'll use for marking hole locations and starting screws. For cutting and pulling small nails, nothing beats a set of **end nips.**

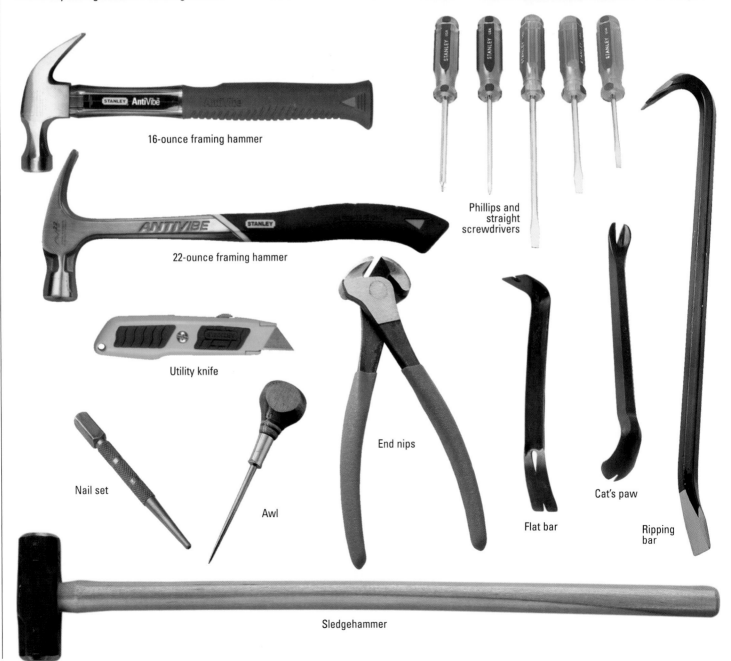

16-ounce framing hammer

Phillips and straight screwdrivers

22-ounce framing hammer

Utility knife

End nips

Cat's paw

Flat bar

Ripping bar

Nail set

Awl

Sledgehammer

Along the same line, three tools will handle your prying tasks: a **cat's paw** for pulling big nails, a **flat bar** for general prying, and a **ripping bar** for heavy-duty demolition. A **sledgehammer** is also useful for demolition and for nudging wayward walls into position.

For cutting wood, you'll need some chisels, saws, and other edge tools. A **toolbox saw** packs a lot of cutting capability into a compact size. A **coping saw** is indispensable for cutting moldings at inside corners. For making accurate crosscuts and miters in molding, you'll need either a **miter box** or a power mitersaw. For paring and fine-tuning the fit of door hinges and other hardware, you'll want a set of **chisels** (blade widths of ¼ inch, ½ inch, ¾ inch, and 1 inch). A **block plane** makes short work of fitting a door. A **putty knife** is a multipurpose tool. Its obvious use is for applying putty to fill nail holes, but it is also useful for prying off moldings without damage. A pair of heavy-duty **metal snips** comes in handy for a variety of cutting tasks, including the installation of metal studs.

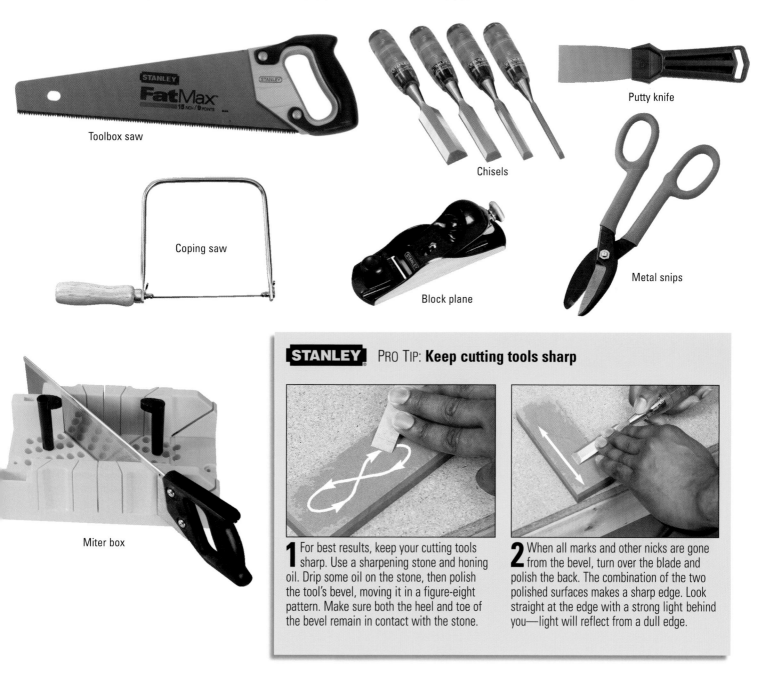

Toolbox saw

Chisels

Putty knife

Coping saw

Block plane

Metal snips

Miter box

STANLEY PRO TIP: **Keep cutting tools sharp**

1 For best results, keep your cutting tools sharp. Use a sharpening stone and honing oil. Drip some oil on the stone, then polish the tool's bevel, moving it in a figure-eight pattern. Make sure both the heel and toe of the bevel remain in contact with the stone.

2 When all marks and other nicks are gone from the bevel, turn over the blade and polish the back. The combination of the two polished surfaces makes a sharp edge. Look straight at the edge with a strong light behind you—light will reflect from a dull edge.

POWER CUTTING TOOLS

There are three types of power saws that will accomplish almost everything you'll need to do. The most useful is a <u>circular saw.</u> It will crosscut lumber and plywood to the right size, making straight cuts with ease. The most common saw uses a blade with a diameter of 7¼ inches. Most come with a steel-tipped combination blade, adequate for all the projects in this book. Steel blades dull quickly, though, so purchase a more durable carbide-tipped combination blade as a replacement. If you buy only one power saw, this is the one to get.

A **jigsaw** (sometimes called a saber saw) also crosscuts and rips lumber, though not as fast as a circular saw. Its chief characteristic is its ability to cut curves. Some models feature variable speed control, which is handy for cutting materials other than wood, such as plastic or metal. Some jigsaws feature orbital cutting; the blade moves forward and back in addition to up and down, making the saw cut much faster than one without orbital action.

A **reciprocating saw** is handy for demolition work. It utilizes a variety of blades with teeth designed to cut different materials, including wood, nails, screws, and even steel pipes. Its blade can reach into tight places to make a cut, such as between framing members.

A **biscuit joiner,** also called a plate joiner, is not a saw but does have a cutting blade. It cuts mortise slots for cracker-thin biscuits—loose tenons that join two pieces of wood. But unlike traditional mortise-and-tenon joinery, you can make strong biscuit joints quickly and easily with minimal skill. When you apply glue to the compressed and dry beech biscuit, it expands to tightly fill the slots. Some joiners allow you to vary the slot's depth or change the blade to accommodate a number of standard biscuit sizes.

Circular saw

Jigsaw

Reciprocating saw

Biscuit joiner

CIRCULAR SAW
Buying one that's right for you

There are dozens of models of circular saws on the market. Here are some tips for selecting the one that's right for you.

First, look for a good-quality saw in the popular sidewinder or helical-drive style, so named because the motor shaft is aligned beside the blade and drives the blade through gears. The blade is usually to the right of the handle, but some models come with the blade on the left. Find the model that's most comfortable for you. A good one will easily handle any project in this book.

You probably don't need a worm-drive saw. These heavy, relatively expensive tools are designed to withstand all-day framing jobs. The worm-gear drive places the motor behind the shaft that drives the blade. This makes it easy to see where the blade is cutting but awkward for novices to use.

Second, don't concern yourself with a saw's horsepower rating, which is usually measured when the saw is not under load. A saw's amperage rating is a better indication of its power. Find a saw rated at least 12 or 13 amps.

The saw should have a solid extruded or cast base, rather than a light stamped-steel base. Check that the tilt and height adjustments work smoothly and tighten easily and firmly. Large knobs or wing nuts tighten easily; levers work even better.

Finally, make sure the saw is comfortable to use. If you can try different saws at the store, make some test cuts. Make sure you like the grip and the position of the switch and safety-guard lever.

Using a circular saw

Crosscutting: To make a crosscut with a circular saw, draw a line across the piece, then cut on the waste side of the line. Support the piece so the waste falls freely away from the blade. The wider part of the saw's base (or shoe) rides on the part of the board that is supported.

Guided crosscutting: If you need a precise cut, use a layout square as a guide. Line up the blade with the cut at the edge of the board. Then hold the square across the board with one edge against the side of the saw base. Push the saw along the square to make the cut.

Cutting plywood: Mark your layout lines with a chalk line. Support both sides of the cut with a series of 2×4s on a pair of sawhorses. Clamp a straightedge or board on the piece as a guide for the bottom plate of the circular saw. Set the saw to cut slightly deeper than the plywood thickness.

SAFETY FIRST
Preventing accidents and injuries

The importance of safety for home improvement and remodeling projects cannot be overemphasized. Mistakes can have serious consequences. Before starting any project, review all the steps involved. If you are uncomfortable with any procedure, find a carpenter or other knowledgeable person to help you.

Safety equipment should be among the first tools you purchase. Start with a pair of **safety glasses** or **goggles.** If you wear prescription glasses, get goggles that fit over them or invest in a pair of prescription safety glasses. Try them on before purchasing. Find a pair that is comfortable so you

won't mind wearing them whenever you're working. Make a habit of wearing safety glasses whenever working, period. That way you won't be tempted to make "just one quick cut" without them.

Next is hearing protection. There are many types of **earplugs** and **earmuffs** available. Earmuffs provide more complete protection. Again, try them on if possible to test for comfort.

Dust masks are necessary during demolition and drywall finishing. Check the label before you buy and match the mask to the type of work you are doing. In general, masks with a single strap are rated for nuisance dust.

These keep sawdust out of your lungs. For sanding drywall or ripping out plaster, you'll want a mask rated for fine dust. These thicker masks usually have two straps for better protection.

Protect your hands with **work gloves** when handling work such as unloading materials, demolition, and cleaning up debris. Do not wear them when you are working with power tools. You are more likely to lose your grip or fumble a tool or piece with gloves on. In addition, gloves may get caught in a spinning blade or drill bit.

Finally it is always a good idea to have a **first aid kit** on hand.

Safety goggles

Earmuffs

Safety glasses

Earplugs

Work gloves

Dust masks

First aid kit

DRILLING AND SHAPING TOOLS

Along with power saws, you also will need a power drill or two and an assortment of bits and cutters for making holes. The tool to start with is a **corded variable-speed reversible (VSR) drill,** with a ⅜-inch-diameter chuck. This tool handles 90 percent of your drilling needs. Along with the drill, purchase a set of **twist drill bits,** used for boring things such as pilot holes for screws. For larger holes, a set of **spade bits** does the trick. For really large holes, such as those for a lockset in a door, use a **hole saw,** which fits into a drill.

The next drill to acquire is a **cordless drill/driver,** which comes in a variety of voltages ranging from around 7 to 24. The higher the voltage, the more powerful the tool (and the more money it costs). For most remodeling, a 14-volt model is ideal. Spend a little more money to purchase an extra rechargeable battery, so the drill won't run out of power in the middle of a project. A cordless drill/driver is handy for odd jobs and is probably most useful as a power screwdriver, especially when hanging drywall. To equip a drill as a screwdriver,

buy a **magnetic bit holder** and a variety of **screwdriver bits.**

One of the nicest features most cordless drill/drivers have is a clutch, which causes the drill to slip out of gear when it reaches a certain amount of torque. This helps prevent overdriving screws and stripping out the holes or the screwheads.

A **router** and a variety of **router bits** are useful for shaping decorative moldings and cutting mortises for door hinges.

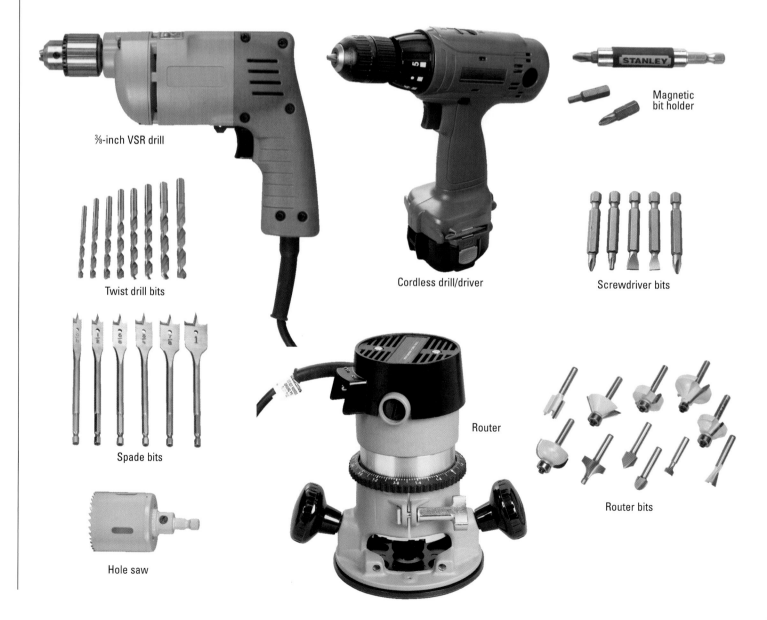

⅜-inch VSR drill

Twist drill bits

Spade bits

Hole saw

Cordless drill/driver

Router

Magnetic bit holder

Screwdriver bits

Router bits

FINISHING TOOLS

Installing and finishing drywall and repairing plaster requires a specialized set of tools. For laying out and guiding the cuts on a sheet of drywall, nothing beats a **drywall square.** After laying out the cut lines, cut with a **utility knife.** For interior cutouts, such as those around electrical boxes, use a **jab saw** to plunge through the drywall and saw out the scrap piece. For slight trimming, such as when you want to plane an edge flush at a corner, use a **Surform plane.**

Once the drywall is installed, the finishing process begins with spreading joint compound over the fasteners and taping and spreading compound across the joints between the drywall sheets. The tools used for spreading the compound are called **taping** or **drywall knives.** These come in a variety of widths. For most purposes a 6-inch, a 10-inch, and a 12-inch will handle the task. Along with the knives, get a **mud pan** to hold a supply of joint compound (often called mud).

The final stage of finishing drywall consists of smoothing the dried compound. The traditional method involves sanding with **abrasive paper,** which is fine for small jobs. For larger expanses of drywall, invest in **sanding screens** and a **holder** to mount them on. Some holder models have a dust pickup that attaches to the hose of a **shop vacuum.** Be sure to replace the filter in your vacuum with one designed to handle drywall dust. For an almost dust-free environment, smooth the walls with a wet **drywall sponge,** which has a tough abrasive plastic layer laminated on one side.

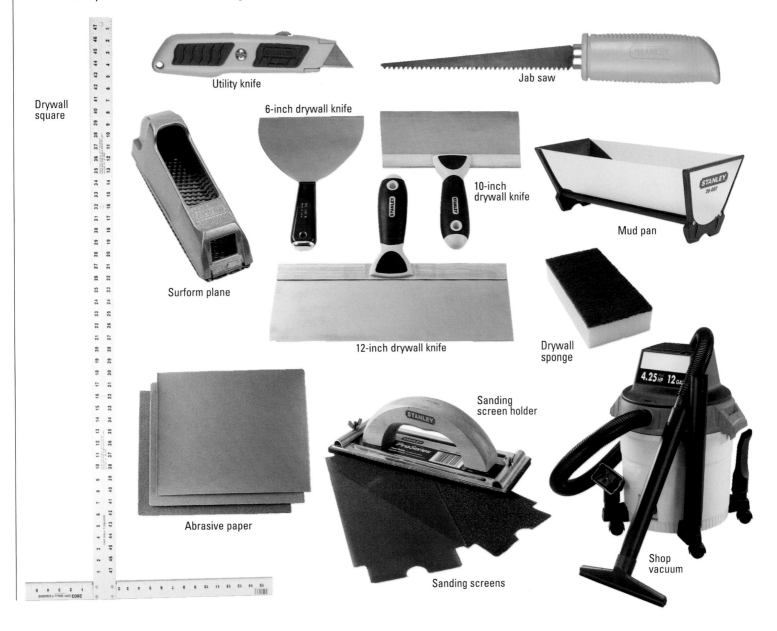

Utility knife

Jab saw

Drywall square

6-inch drywall knife

10-inch drywall knife

Mud pan

Surform plane

12-inch drywall knife

Drywall sponge

Abrasive paper

Sanding screen holder

Sanding screens

Shop vacuum

CHOOSING A MITERSAW

There are four types of mitering tools that you can purchase. Two of them are manual, and two substitute electrical power for arm and shoulder strength.

The manual miter guides are highly affordable, but they require consistent technique to achieve good results. At the bottom of the price line is the simple **miter box** made from plastic or wood. The model shown *below left* features holes in the base that accept cam pins. Turning the pins supplies clamping pressure to immobilize the wood you're cutting. Although you could miter with a standard handsaw, you'll get better results with a **backsaw** like the one

shown in the photo. This saw gets its name from the rigid metal spine on top of the blade. Unfortunately, the plastic miter-guide slots can widen after you've made a number of cuts, and that can defeat the accuracy you need. The guide's usefulness is also limited by the fact that it's set up only for crosscuts and a few fixed angles right and left of square.

The next step upward in price and accuracy also has holes in its base for clamping cams. But that's where the similarity ends. This model features a fine-tooth blade in a frame that's tensioned to give it rigidity. In addition, the columns

support the body of the saw so you're not relying on the sides of the blade for control. As a result, this guide doesn't have the self-destructing tendency of the less-expensive model. Its usefulness also is improved by the fact that you can easily set virtually any angle you need.

One serious shortcoming of both manual guides is their inability to accurately slice a tiny amount from the end of the board—a task that's easy with a power mitersaw.

Power mitersaws
Power mitersaws used to be called chop saws, a name that accurately describes

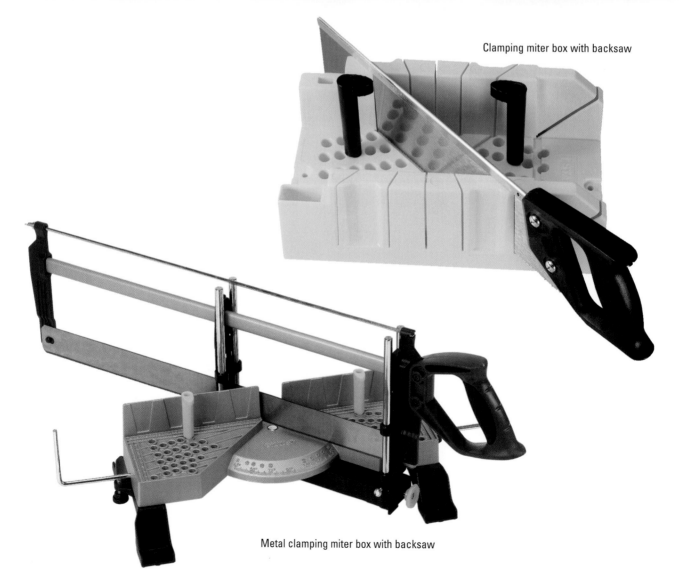

Clamping miter box with backsaw

Metal clamping miter box with backsaw

the saw's straight downward cutting action. A simple adjusting knob allows you to accurately lock in any angle. Some saws have a wood cutting platform that can be replaced periodically; others have a slot that moves as you change the cutting angle. Because the blade moves through a fixed arc, it has a limited crosscut range and an even more restricted capability for angled cuts.

Most manufacturers no longer make straight chop saws. Instead, two more-versatile power mitersaws have taken the lead in popularity. The first major type is the **compound mitersaw** shown *below left*. The blade moves in a fixed arc, and the head of

the saw can also tilt to produce a cut that's both mitered and beveled. With this type of saw, you can make the compound cut for crown molding corners with the molding laid flat on the saw table—a real convenience.

The **sliding compound mitersaw** *below right* is a step up in price and function. This saw has the miter- and bevel-cutting functions of the compound model, but the saw head also slides on a carriage. The sliding action significantly increases its cutting capacity without increasing the size of the blade. Saws with a 10-inch blade are the most common, but you'll also see models with 12-inch blades.

Which one to select?

A well-built mitersaw will last a long time, so carefully consider its capabilities against the amount of money you're willing to invest. It's understandably tempting to want a professional 12-inch sliding compound mitersaw with its impressive cutting range. But you may never actually need to cut lumber that large for your home projects.

Most 10-inch compound mitersaws will easily handle everything from tiny moldings to miter cuts in 2×4 stock. The compound and sliding-compound simplify crown molding installation; the sliding function increases the cutting range.

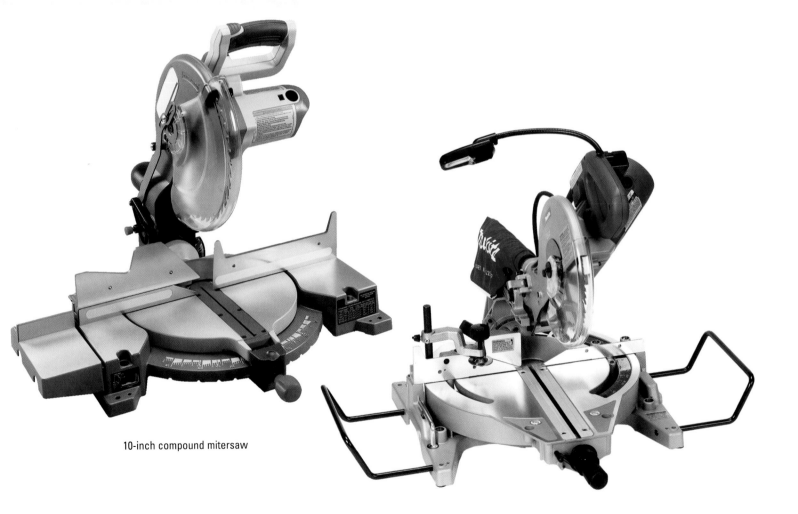

10-inch compound mitersaw

10-inch sliding compound mitersaw

WHICH BLADES DO I BUY?

Circular saw blades

Equipped with the right blade, a portable **circular saw** can cut tough jobs down to size in a hurry. The following recommendations are for a 7¼-inch saw—the most popular size. For rough cutting and framing jobs, choose a carbide-tipped blade with 18 to 24 teeth. For demolition jobs in which you may encounter embedded fasteners, select a blade that is rated for nail cutting. For finish cuts in both solid wood and plywood, reach for a 36-tooth blade. Inexpensive steel blades are useful for rough carpentry work.

For your tablesaw, the 10-inch blade is the most common. Today you can find nearly a dozen different categories of blades to cut everything from ferrous and nonferrous metals to wood and plastics. Some of the more useful blades for cutting wood are shown below.

Reciprocating saw blades

This tough saw can be a remodeler's best friend, rapidly chewing through demanding demolition tasks. A 6-inch blade with 6 teeth per inch (TPI) is a good choice for most jobs because it combines ample capacity with fast cutting and ample rigidity. For demolition jobs, it pays to buy good-quality blades that will slice through nails without complaint. For jobs where you're

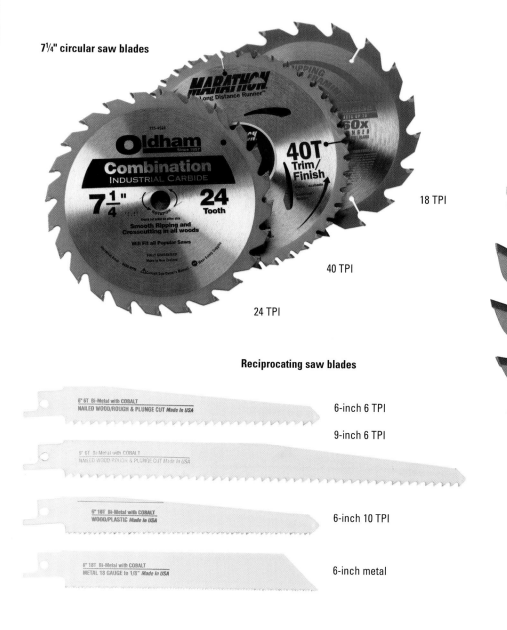

7¼" circular saw blades

18 TPI

40 TPI

24 TPI

Reciprocating saw blades

6-inch 6 TPI

9-inch 6 TPI

6-inch 10 TPI

6-inch metal

attacking thicker material, move to a longer blade such as the 9-incher shown in the photo *opposite left*. Like the shorter version, this blade also has 6 TPI.

A blade with 10 TPI will yield a smoother surface, but you'll rarely use a **reciprocating saw** for finished cuts. For metal cutting, select a blade that's engineered to handle the job. Choose a blade with 18 to 24 TPI depending on the thickness of the metal—the thinner the stock, the more teeth.

Jigsaw blades

Recommendations for jigsaw blades closely follow the advice for the reciprocating saw: 6 TPI for rough cuts and 10 TPI for smoother cuts. For cutting a tight radius, choose a blade that has a narrower body—this is typically called a scrolling blade.

If your **jigsaw** has a provision for switching from reciprocating to orbital action, you'll gain greater control over your cut. A reciprocating (straight up and down) motion yields a smoother surface but

requires more time. Orbital action gives a faster but rougher cut.

Coping saw blades

The most-used **coping saw** blade has 15 TPI and gives a fast cut. Because the cut surface is usually not seen, its smoothness is not a concern in blade selection.

But if you need to cope intricate small moldings, choose a finer blade (18 to 20 TPI), not for the smoothness but because its narrower body will turn a tighter corner.

JIGSAW BLADES

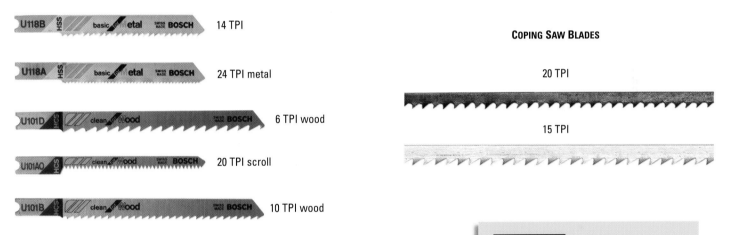

U118B — 14 TPI

U118A — 24 TPI metal

U101D — 6 TPI wood

U101AO — 20 TPI scroll

U101B — 10 TPI wood

COPING SAW BLADES

20 TPI

15 TPI

Extend the life of your blades

How will you know when it's time to sharpen your blade? Here's a simple test: If you can't nick your nail when you drag it across one tip, its time to visit a reliable sharpening shop.

Other telltale signs include:

- Burn marks on both sides of material
- Slower feed rate required
- Undesirable burnished (polished) end grain
- Pitch buildup on teeth
- Visible chips in teeth

Don't despair if pitch builds up on your blade. Clean a dirty blade by soaking it overnight in kerosene, then scrub it with an old toothbrush.

Recommended tablesaw blades

It's challenging to recommend ideal blades for every shop, but many woodworkers would list these as their favorite 10-inch carbide-tipped tablesaw blades:

- 40T ATB (alternate top bevel) General Purpose—crosscuts and rips lumber and sheet materials
- 24T FT (flat top) Rip—ideal for ripping hardwoods and thick softwood stock
- 80T ATB Finish—a blade for finish cuts through your best hardwoods

STANLEY PRO TIP

Switch to a new blade

Trying to coax additional cuts out of a dull blade is false economy. It wastes your time, wears out your arms, stresses your saw's motor bearings, and overheats your patience. In addition, a burned surface is nearly worthless from a gluing standpoint. Switch to a new blade as soon as you sense that a cut requires additional effort.

PNEUMATIC TOOLS

Pneumatic (air-powered) tools save enormous amounts of time and physical energy, making them the mainstay of virtually every professional trim carpenter. But they have three other important advantages that recommend them to amateur home-improvement enthusiasts:

■ You eliminate the need for repeated hammer blows that can throw an assembly out of alignment.

■ You drive and countersink with one trigger squeeze, banishing unsightly hammer tracks caused by blows that miss the nail.

■ There's no more fumbling with individual nails—align the trim with one hand and trigger the nailer with the other.

Two pneumatic tools will handle virtually every interior trim job in your house. Adding a third optional driver will let you install even tiny moldings flawlessly.

The first is a **finish nailer** that drives fasteners from approximately 1¼ to 2½ inches in length. This range covers many molding jobs as well as installation of doorjambs. Some less expensive nailers utilize 16-gauge fasteners, but the more robust 15-gauge nails in the better drivers have superior bend resistance. Another

decision is whether you should choose the straight magazine (at 90 degrees to the head) or an angled design. Many finish carpenters believe that the angled design is easier to maneuver in cramped corners.

A **brad nailer** typically drives 18-gauge fasteners from approximately ⅝ to 1¼ inches. As you can see in the photo below, the brad nailer is considerably smaller than the finish nailer.

The third driver is a **headless pinner**, and it drives fasteners from approximately ½ to ¾ inch. The absence of the head on the fastener reduces its holding power, but that is usually not a problem because it's

Finish nailer

Headless pinner

Brad nailer

A finish nailer (top) and a brad driver (bottom) will handle virtually all of your trim carpentry projects. Add a headless pinner (center), and you'll be able to fasten tiny moldings without splitting them.

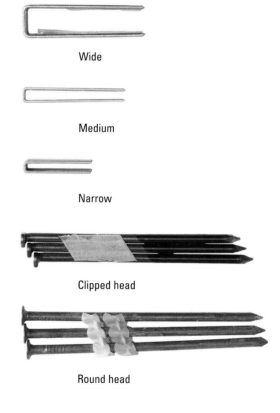

Wide

Medium

Narrow

Clipped head

Round head

Check whether your local building code requires fasteners with a round head or permits the use of clipped heads. The size designation of crown staples (narrow, medium, and wide) refers to the distance between the fastener's legs.

designed to hold small moldings, not structural components. On the plus side, the small gauge of the fastener rarely splits the wood and leaves a minute hole for you to fill.

Framing nailers and crown staplers

Rough-in carpenters rely on framing nailers to shoot headed fasteners up to 3½ inches long to assemble the structural components of a house. If you're starting with a stack of lumber to build your own home, purchasing a framing nailer makes sense. But for building an occasional partition wall, it's a tough purchase to justify. Even renting this tool for a small job is a questionable proposition—you can probably nail the studs and plates by hand in less time than it takes to make a round-trip to the rental store.

A crown stapler produces excellent holding power because of the twin legs and the crown that bridges them. But this structural advantage comes with a serious drawback for trim projects—the crown produces a huge hole that will need filling. For that reason, a crown stapler works best in applications in which the fasteners will be hidden, such as attaching plywood backs to cabinets. A few pneumatic drivers combine a crown stapler and brad driver into a single unit.

How big an air compressor do I need?

With an **air compressor,** big can mean any of four things: the volume of the storage tank, the size of the motor, the weight of the unit, or the price tag.

A 2-horsepower motor and a 4-gallon tank should comfortably supply plenty of air power for trim carpentry. If you have other pneumatic tools on your want list, consider those needs before you open your wallet. Choosing a larger motor will probably mean longer life, but larger compressors draw more power, leading to nuisance tripping of the 15-amp circuits that predominate in most houses. A larger tank means that the motor will start less frequently. (A large tank is more important for air-hungry applications such as spray painting.)

Before you buy a compressor, consider its portability. Just because it has a handle doesn't guarantee you can actually carry it for any distance without strain. Wheeled models ease movement on level surfaces, but steps can be quite a barrier if you don't have a strong helper.

Choose a compressor that combines adequate air delivery with portability and affordability.

Set up your driver for single-shot operation

When you unpack a pneumatic nailer, you'll probably find that it's set up for both trigger-fire and bottom-fire operation. In the trigger-fire mode, you depress the nosepiece against the wood and then squeeze the trigger to shoot the fastener. But if you continue to hold down the trigger, you engage the bottom-fire mode, driving a fastener every time you depress the nosepiece against the wood. The bottom-fire mode is handy for repetitive jobs like securing roofing shingles, where speed is more important than accuracy of placement. But for interior trimwork, you'll probably use the trigger-fire method more often.

Many manufacturers offer a free conversion kit that allows you to change your gun to fire only in the trigger mode. This easy changeover also makes your gun safer by guarding against unintended firings.

For safer operation, consider swapping the stock trigger for one that requires you to squeeze to drive each nail. Many manufacturers supply a restrictive-fire trigger at no cost—some companies even provide a toll-free number to request one.

Check your fastener supply

Even with an empty fastener magazine, a pneumatic driver will punch a hole into wood, so you need a more reliable test to make sure the gun is loaded. Most tools have a visible fastener supply, so make a habit of glancing at it every time you pick up the gun. That way, you'll avoid the embarrassing problem of moldings without nails.

ACCESSORIES

Several items make working with hand and power tools easier, starting with one or two **extension cords.** Purchase heavy-duty ones—the wires should be 12 gauge. Lighter weight cords could overheat, posing a fire or shock hazard, and they will rob the tools of the power they need.

Sawhorses hold lumber at a comfortable working height. You can create an impromptu worktable by laying a sheet of plywood across two horses. Wooden horses are heavier than metal models, but they do have some advantages. You can nail a couple of 2×4s across them for added stability, and should you happen to cut into one, you won't damage your saw blade. Metal and plastic/composite sawhorses are sturdy, lighter, and often fold for easy storage. If you use a metal sawhorse, bolt a 2×4 laid flat on top of the crosspiece (countersinking the bolt heads) to help prevent damage to saw blades.

If you're doing any work overhead, a **stepladder** provides a safe, comfortable work platform. A 6-foot ladder will be adequate for most tasks.

A bright **work light** makes a big difference if you are working in dimly lit spaces (where most remodeling projects take place). Halogen lights are bright and often come with adjustable stands. They become hot when left on for a long time, however, and some models should not be used indoors.

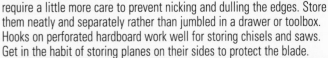

Sawhorses

Extension cord

Work light

6-foot stepladder

3-foot stepladder

STANLEY PRO TIP: **Save your sawhorses**

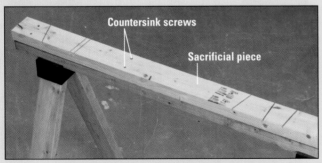

Countersink screws

Sacrificial piece

As they age, the top edges of most sawhorses become scarred from use. To make your horses last longer, add sacrificial pieces of wood to the top edges. These can be screwed in place and replaced as needed. Be sure to countersink the screws deeply to keep saw blades from striking the screwheads.

Storing and protecting your tools

Caring for your power tools is easy—just keep them away from dust and moisture. One handy way to keep them organized is to store them in plastic milk crates. The crates have handles for easy carrying, and they serve as impromptu step stools.

Hand tools with cutting edges—handsaws, chisels, and planes—require a little more care to prevent nicking and dulling the edges. Store them neatly and separately rather than jumbled in a drawer or toolbox. Hooks on perforated hardboard work well for storing chisels and saws. Get in the habit of storing planes on their sides to protect the blade.

A great way to protect the cutting edges of your chisels and handsaws is to purchase a length of ½-inch-diameter clear plastic tubing. Slit the tubing open with a utility knife and cut it to lengths to fit your tools.

RENTING

Several tools are useful to remodelers but are too expensive to own for the few times they will be used. Check with a local rental shop, hardware store, or home center to see what is available for rent by the hour, day, or week. A **drywall hoist** takes a lot of the stress and strain out of hanging drywall. If you have enough space to make use of one, renting a hoist is money well spent. For drop ceilings, nothing beats a **laser level** for setting the initial layout line around the perimeter of the room. Specialty saws are extremely useful for remodeling projects. For example, a **jamb saw** slices away the bottoms of door frames. The undercut enables you to slide tile, hardwood, and laminate flooring under the jambs for a seamless look.

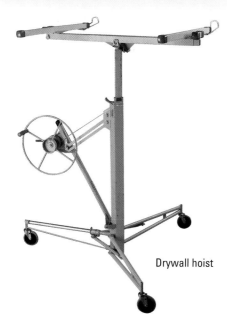

Drywall hoist

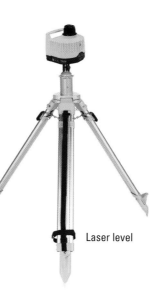

Laser level

Jamb saw

 PRO TIP

Build a stable work platform

Most overhead work can be accomplished using a ladder, but there are times when a larger elevated work platform is needed. The pros often use a scaffold. You can accomplish the same thing by resting a 2×12 across the rungs of two stepladders. Clamp the board to the ladders to prevent it from slipping. For safety, don't use this method to span more than 12 feet.

Choosing a tool pouch

A tool pouch may seem like a luxury, something only pros really need. And it's true, you probably don't need a double-bag tool rig with built-in padded suspenders.

Yet even if you are a weekend warrior, a good tool pouch is the best timesaving and frustration-preventing item you can buy. Without one, your work will be constantly interrupted as you fetch tools you forgot to have on hand.

To be truly quick on the draw, purchase a compartmentalized side pouch with its own belt. The exact configuration of these pouches varies, but most have a large pocket with a smaller pocket attached to the outside. The large pocket has plenty of room for your layout square and tape measure plus your chalk line when you need it. The smaller pouch is for nails or screws. Flanking the smaller pocket are usually two pockets: one sized to hold your utility knife, the other for a chisel or putty knife.

Attached to the flanking pockets will usually be four narrow pockets suitable for pencils and nail sets.

Most nail pouches have loops that hold a hammer, but few carpenters use it for that. It's much more efficient to have a separate hammer loop on your hammer-hand side with the pouch on the other side. If you will be driving screws, you can replace the hammer loop with a drill/driver holster.

PANEL AND CONSTRUCTION ADHESIVES

Most people think this category contains only a single product. But go to a well-stocked store and you'll discover that there is an entire family of **adhesives**. There are special formulations for drywall, foamboard, subfloors, tub surrounds, and many other specialty applications. Each type has its own advantages. For example, the one designed for paneling and moldings has a quick-grab feature. You'll even find a clear adhesive in a self-dispensing can as well as the familiar tan formula in a resealable squeeze tube.

Read the label carefully and you'll discover that you've probably been skipping a step when using these products in the past. After applying the zigzag bead, press the pieces together, then pull them apart as shown *right*. Wait 3 to 5 minutes, then push the parts together and drive the fasteners.

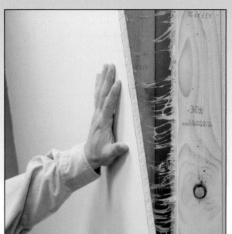

Pull the pieces apart after you've made initial contact (the strings at right are desirable) and wait a few minutes. When you push the pieces together again, the construction adhesive will grab strongly.

At home centers and hardware stores, you'll find general-purpose construction adhesives, as well as special formulations for specific tasks.

WOODWORKING ADHESIVES

You'll find an extensive array of **woodworking adhesives** to help you build secure joints. Ordinary yellow wood glue (carpenter's glue) does a good job, but the water-resistant formula may have more than double the shelf life. Both formulas allow you about 5 minutes for assembly (this is called open time) before the adhesive grabs. Although some people disregard ordinary white glue, it has sufficient strength for most applications, plus it has an open time of about 10 minutes, so you can build more complex assemblies without panic.

A special adhesive for moldings features a thicker consistency to resist drips. If you're working with dark moldings, consider a tinted formula that minimizes the appearance of glue lines. Polyurethane adhesive—one of the newer categories—offers high strength, but its foaming action can make a mess if you're not careful. For joining dissimilar materials, choose polyurethane or epoxy. The quick-setting epoxy formula is handy when you're in a hurry, but the long-setting variety offers superior joint strength.

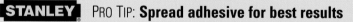

STANLEY PRO TIP: **Spread adhesive for best results**

Most adhesives require only a thin coat; any excess will merely make a mess. Smooth glue into a thin coat with a small brush or a wood spreader. For maximum strength, apply adhesive to both surfaces whenever possible. The disposable acid brush shown here is sold in plumbing departments with soldering supplies.

CLAMPS AND FASTENERS

Clamps

C-clamps are a popular choice, but they have a limited range. In addition, you need to place a scrap board between the clamp and wood to avoid denting surfaces that will be finished. Wood-jaw clamps are a traditional choice that eliminates the need for scrap blocks.

Expand your reach with fast-acting clamps. A few minutes of practice will have you easily operating these clamps with one hand—a real advantage. For even bigger assemblies, choose clamps that screw onto lengths of ¾-inch black steel pipe with threaded ends. Threaded couplings allow you to join pipes to virtually unlimited lengths for those really big jobs.

Screws

There are a great number of different thread styles for screws, but the two you'll probably find at your local hardware store are the **rolled-thread** type and the **cut-thread** type. The photos *below* clearly show the differences between them. The cut-thread style represents the traditional appearance of wood screws and requires a body hole that's larger than the pilot hole. With the rolled-thread style, the body hole is the same diameter as the pilot hole. The charts *below* give the dimensions for the most-used screws.

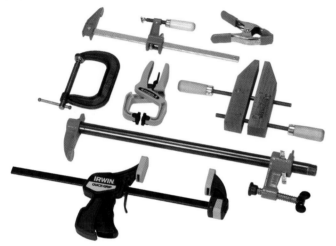

Collect an assortment of clamps so you can have the best ones available for the job.

Traditional cut-thread screws, top, require a body hole larger than the pilot hole. Rolled-thread screws, bottom, have a body hole equal to the pilot-hole diameter.

ROLLED-THREAD SCREWS

Gauge	4	6	8	10	12	14
Head diameter (inch)	7/32	17/64	11/32	23/64	7/16	½
Pilot-hole diameter (inch) hardwood	5/64	7/64	1/8	9/64	5/32	11/64
Pilot-hole diameter (inch) softwood	1/16	3/32	7/64	1/8	9/64	5/32
Phillips screwdriver size	#1	#2	#2	#2	#3	#3
Square screwdriver size	#0	#1	#2	#2	#3	#3

CUT-THREAD SCREWS

Gauge	2	4	6	8	10	12	14
Head diameter (inch)	11/64	15/64	9/32	11/32	25/64	7/16	½
Body hole diameter (inch)	3/32	7/64	9/64	5/32	3/16	7/32	¼
Pilot-hole diameter (inch) hardwood	1/16	5/64	3/32	7/64	1/8	9/64	5/32
Pilot-hole diameter (inch) softwood	1/16	1/16	5/64	3/32	7/64	1/8	9/64
Phillips screwdriver size	#1	#1	#2	#2	#2	#3	#3
Square screwdriver size	#0	#0	#1	#2	#2	#3	#3

Nails

You'll find five types of nails that are useful for most of your home carpentry projects. All of them utilize the penny designation to describe the length of the fastener, but they vary in head style and gauge. Generally speaking, the longer the nail, the larger its shank diameter. Nail diameter is usually expressed in a gauge number that runs backward to the usual method of expressing size. In this case, diameter increases as the gauge number decreases.

Choose galvanized nails (slightly more expensive) for exterior applications and bright nails for interior work.

Common nails are a thick-shank headed fastener useful for heavy-duty joints in rough carpentry, such as wall framing.

Box nails look similar to common nails and are used in many of the same applications, but their slimmer shank makes them easier to drive and thus less likely to cause wood splits. They're also less expensive than common nails because you get more per pound.

Finishing nails have a brad head that's easy to countersink for a concealed appearance in trim applications. For tips on how to properly drive and countersink finishing nails, see *page 210*.

Casing nails look similar to finishing nails but have several important differences because they are generally used for exterior trimwork such as door and window frames. Casing nails are galvanized and have a larger shank than a finishing nail of identical length. In addition, casing nails have a tapered head that's sometimes driven flush to the wood's surface to save the additional labor of countersinking and filling.

Hardwood trim nails have a brad head like finishing nails but a slimmer shank to help prevent splitting—even without drilling pilot holes—in materials as tough as oak. The high carbon content of the steel enables the manufacturer to make these nails slimmer without sacrificing strength. Despite the "hardwood" designation, these fasteners also work well for softwood trim (pine and fir) installations.

Hardwood trim

Casing

Finishing

Box

Common

NAIL SIZES

Nails are sized by the *penny*, using the English abbreviation *d*, as in 8d nails, which refers to length. The origin of the term is fuzzy, but one common explanation is that centuries ago in England, nails were sold by the hundred. The designation told how many pennies each size cost per hundred.

Penny size	Length in inches
2d	1
3d	1¼
4d	1½
5d	1⅝
6d	2
7d	2⅛
8d	2½
10d	3
12d	3¼
16d	3½

STANLEY PRO TIP

Shop for clean nails

Manufacturers of bargain-priced nails may shortchange the cleaning process, leaving behind oil that transfers from your hands to the wood. Though that may not be an issue with rough-in carpentry projects, oil-stained trimwork will create serious finishing problems for your project.

Inspect nails before buying and reject brands that market dirty or oily fasteners.

CHOOSING MATERIALS

Many homeowners today can find two or three home centers plus a locally owned lumberyard within easy driving distance. These companies compete aggressively for your business, and you benefit from their battles to deliver the best prices and customer service. In addition, you'll find a wider range of choices than ever before.

Price is an obvious and easy-to-understand part of every buying decision. When you're shopping for a specific name-brand power tool, for example, it's easy to determine which retailer offers the best value.

But lumber products—even when they bear identical grading stamps—can vary significantly among retailers. When you know the quality points of these products, you'll be armed with the knowledge you need to make better buying decisions.

Know the store's policies

Some retailers may consider that lumber sales are final when you leave the parking lot; others will accept returns of unused materials at the end of a project.

Delivery is another major consideration. If your only vehicle is a compact car, attempting to haul drywall can break the material, damage your car, or both. Some retailers offer delivery, which may even be free, depending on the size of your purchase and the retailer. But don't expect immediate delivery. It may take several days to work your order into the schedule.

You also may find that some stores offer the option of renting a small flatbed truck to haul your materials. Call ahead of time to check whether you need to make a reservation and to learn other details of the rental agreement.

Seeking professional help

Many retailers pride themselves on the personal qualifications of their employees, many of whom are former tradespeople who are willing to share their knowledge and experience with you. Don't hesitate to ask for advice on material selection, specialized tools, or installation procedures.

If you're about to embark on a complex project, review your plans with personnel at the retailer's service desk. These folks should double-check your materials estimates and offer insights.

Spending extra time to select top-quality materials prevents frustration in the long run.

CHAPTER PREVIEW

Lumber
page 192

Sheet stock
page 194

Molding gallery
page 196

With your plans decided, it's time to select the materials that will make your project a reality. In this chapter you'll learn how to choose the right materials when you visit the lumberyard or home center.

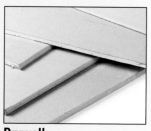

Drywall
page 200

Jamb kits save time
page 201

LUMBER

Lumber makes up the structure of most houses and will probably play a big part in your remodeling project. For framing (building the skeleton of walls), most of the wood you use will be 2× (two-by) material. When it was sawed to size, the wood was about 2 inches thick. But it lost some of its thickness to shrinkage and planing. So the pieces you buy are actually about 1½ inches thick. Boards for trimwork, nominally 1 inch (1× material), actually measure ¾ inch thick.

The same size shrinkage holds true with regard to the width of lumber—the actual dimension is narrower than the stated sizes, which is called the nominal size. The length of lumber is usually accurate. In fact, you may find boards that measure fractionally longer than stated.

For the most part, you will be using 2×4s (1½×3½ inches) and 2×6s (actually 5½ inches wide). Occasionally you may need something wider, such as a 2×8 (7¼ inches wide), 2×10 (9¼ inches wide), or even 2×12 (11¼ inches wide). Widths of 1× boards are the same.

Many home centers have two or more grades of lumber. The grades indicate the relative quality of the wood. The better the grade (#1 vs. #2), the fewer defects the pieces have and the higher the price. Usually you will not need the greater strength that characterizes better grades of lumber, but better grades also are more consistently straight, a desirable quality.

Along with grade, the species of the wood makes a difference in the price. In the Northeast, for instance, lesser grades of 2×4 studs are lumped into a category called SPF, which stands for spruce, pine, and fir. The better studs are Douglas fir or occasionally hemlock. These two species command a higher price because they tend to yield stronger, better-quality wood.

Steel studs match the size of wooden studs and are used for similar situations. They are light and fireproof and are cut with tin snips and attached with screws.

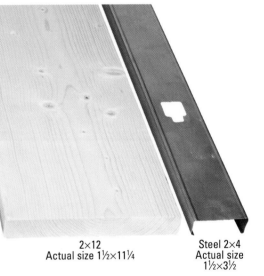

2×4
Actual size
1½×3½

2×6
Actual size 1½×5½

2×8
Actual size 1½×7¼

2×10
Actual size 1½×9¼

2×12
Actual size 1½×11¼

Steel 2×4
Actual size
1½×3½

Which grade to buy?

For most remodeling projects, buying a higher grade of lumber is a waste of money. If you have the opportunity to select each piece of wood, which is usually the case at home centers or lumberyards, you can avoid the worst pieces of the lesser grades and return home with pieces of wood suited to your purposes. High-grade lumber may be worth the extra cost if the wood will remain visible in the finished result.

The grade stamp on a piece of lumber tells you where the wood came from and what grade it received at the mill. The smaller the grade number, the higher the quality of the wood. Instead of a number, 2×4s are often stamped "STUD" to indicate they are suitable for this purpose. "Hem-Fir" means the wood is either hemlock or fir, two equally strong species. "W" means the wood was graded under Western Wood Product Association rules, and "134" is the number assigned to the mill where the wood was processed.

Selecting lumber

Look for defects: Start by looking over each piece for obvious defects. Tight knots are no problem for framing lumber. Reject pieces with knotholes or knots that are loose enough to move with your fingers. Also reject pieces with checks (splits and cracks) and wane (missing corners or edges).

Check for straightness: If a piece seems free of defects, hold it at one end and sight along the edges to see if the piece is straight. A slight warp is OK, but reject boards that are severely bowed or twisted.

Remove hazards: As you handle stock, watch for staples and other metal hardware that may be embedded in the wood, waiting to ambush your saw blade. Although not a reason to reject a good piece of lumber, staples are a hazard. Remove them immediately after purchase.

STANLEY PRO TIP

Buying the right length

Most framing lumber comes in lengths starting at 8 feet and then increasing in 2-foot increments. Keep this in mind as you make your shopping list; you may be able to cut a single long piece into the shorter pieces you need. For example, if you need several 5-foot 2×4s, cut 10-footers into two 5-foot sections rather than cutting down 8-footers and leaving 3-foot-long scraps.

Many suppliers stock what they call precut studs. These are 2×4s that are 92⅝ inches long (just under 8 feet), the right size for 8-foot walls (the top and bottom plates add 4½ inches to the overall wall height, and flooring and ceiling drywall subtract an inch or so).

Marking your purchases

As you select lumber, note the use of each piece, according to your materials list (page 28), for example, a wall stud or a bottom plate. As you place each piece on the cart, use a lumber crayon to write on the wood itself exactly what it is for. This prevents the frustration of spending several hours at the lumberyard selecting stock for your project, getting it home, and then needing to sort it all over again.

SHEET STOCK

Along with framing lumber, trim, and drywall, you may find use for different types of sheet stock. This category includes plywood, particleboard, oriented strand board (OSB), medium-density fiberboard (MDF), and medium-density overlay (MDO). These products come in 4×8-foot sheets, in thicknesses from ⅛ to 1¼ inches (although the thickest and the thinnest sizes may be harder to find). Along with full sheets, many home centers offer quarter and half sheets.

Plywood, an engineered wood product, is made of a sandwich of thin layers of wood called plies, or veneers. Each successive ply is laid with the grain running at 90 degrees to the previous layer. The resulting sheet is dimensionally stable and very strong.

Construction plywood, made of softwood veneers, is graded according to the quality of the veneers that make up the two outside faces. These grades, from best to worst, are A, B, C, and D. One of the most common grades of plywood used in construction is **CDX,** meaning the sheet has one face graded C and the other D. The X stands for exterior, referring to the glue that bonds the veneers. Builders use this grade for sheathing and roof decking. **AB plywood,** a better grade of plywood, is a good choice for shelving and utility cabinets.

AB plywood

Oak veneer plywood

CDX plywood

Birch veneer plywood

Reading the plywood stamp

When shopping for construction plywood, look for a grading stamp that says "APA The Engineered Wood Association." This stamp's meaning varies according to the intended use of the panel. For example, if the plywood is graded for sheathing outside walls, it will include the stud spacing on which it should be attached. For interior remodeling, the appearance of the face veneers is most important. Here are the characteristics of each face grade:

A—A smooth, paintable veneer free of knots and possessing only neatly made repairs that are parallel to the grain. It can be finished with a clear coat (rather than paint).

B—A solid-surface veneer that allows only small round knots, patches, and round repairs. Acceptable for the inside surfaces of a painted shelving unit.

C—Allows small knots, knotholes, and patches. Probably not used for an exposed face inside the house unless you are going for a rustic look. The lowest grade allowed for permanent exterior exposure.

D—This veneer can include large knots and knotholes. Acceptable only for a hidden face, such as the surface of a sheathing panel that faces inside the wall.

Hardwood plywood is faced with hardwood veneers and is used primarily for furniture and cabinetry. Home centers usually carry **oak** and **birch veneer plywood.** If you want another species, such as cherry, you can order it through a home center or contact a plywood distributor (look under "plywood" in the phone directory).

Other sheet goods are not as recognizable as wood, although they are wood products.

Particleboard is made of coarser wood particles. It is commonly used as floor underlayment and occasionally for inexpensive cabinets (often with a vinyl wood-print veneer). It also is frequently used as the bottom layer for countertops. **OSB,** another engineered sheet made of bigger pieces of wood, is stronger than either MDF or particleboard, although not as strong as plywood, and is commonly used for sheathing and roof decking.

MDF is made of fine wood fibers that have been pressed and glued together. The resulting sheets are very smooth and flat. MDF paints well and is a good choice for interior shelving and painted cabinetry. **MDO** has a paper face designed to take paint beautifully. It is commonly used to make outdoor signs.

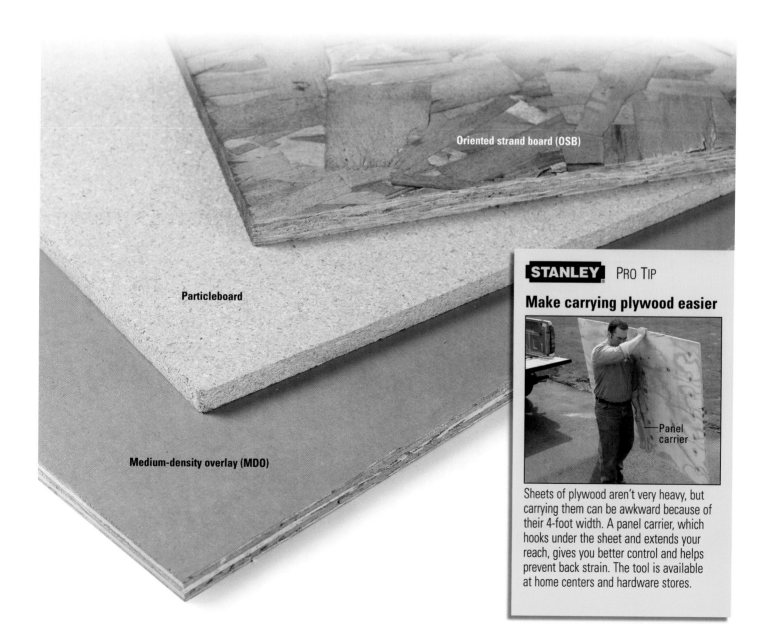

Oriented strand board (OSB)

Particleboard

Medium-density overlay (MDO)

STANLEY PRO TIP

Make carrying plywood easier

Panel carrier

Sheets of plywood aren't very heavy, but carrying them can be awkward because of their 4-foot width. A panel carrier, which hooks under the sheet and extends your reach, gives you better control and helps prevent back strain. The tool is available at home centers and hardware stores.

MOLDING GALLERY

When you visit a lumberyard or home center, you'll find hundreds of molding profiles to chose from. Don't be fooled by the molding names. For example, base cap was first milled to rest on top of baseboards, but it makes an excellent chair rail when teamed with a flat board. And you'll find many multi-element crown treatments that incorporate chair rail.

Red oak hardwood examples are shown on these pages; you'll also find two softwood varieties—stain grade (jointless) and paint grade, which has finger joints you'll conceal with paint. Where applicable, an HWM code is shown; this identifies a standard hardwood profile milled by members of the Wood Moulding & Millwork Producers Association. (WM denotes a softwood molding.) Some profiles don't have a standard designation. See *page 236* for details about contacting the association.

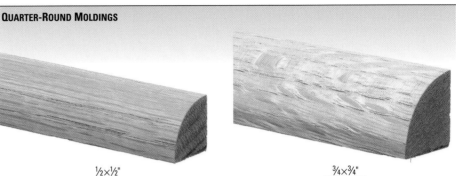

QUARTER-ROUND MOLDINGS

$\frac{1}{2} \times \frac{1}{2}$"
HWM 105

$\frac{3}{4} \times \frac{3}{4}$"
HWM 100

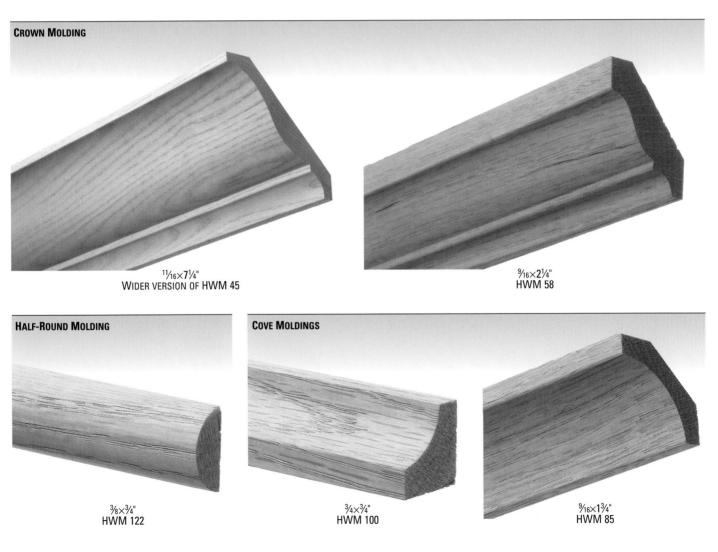

CROWN MOLDING

$\frac{11}{16} \times 7\frac{1}{4}$"
WIDER VERSION OF HWM 45

$\frac{9}{16} \times 2\frac{1}{4}$"
HWM 58

HALF-ROUND MOLDING

$\frac{3}{8} \times \frac{3}{4}$"
HWM 122

COVE MOLDINGS

$\frac{3}{4} \times \frac{3}{4}$"
HWM 100

$\frac{9}{16} \times 1\frac{3}{4}$"
HWM 85

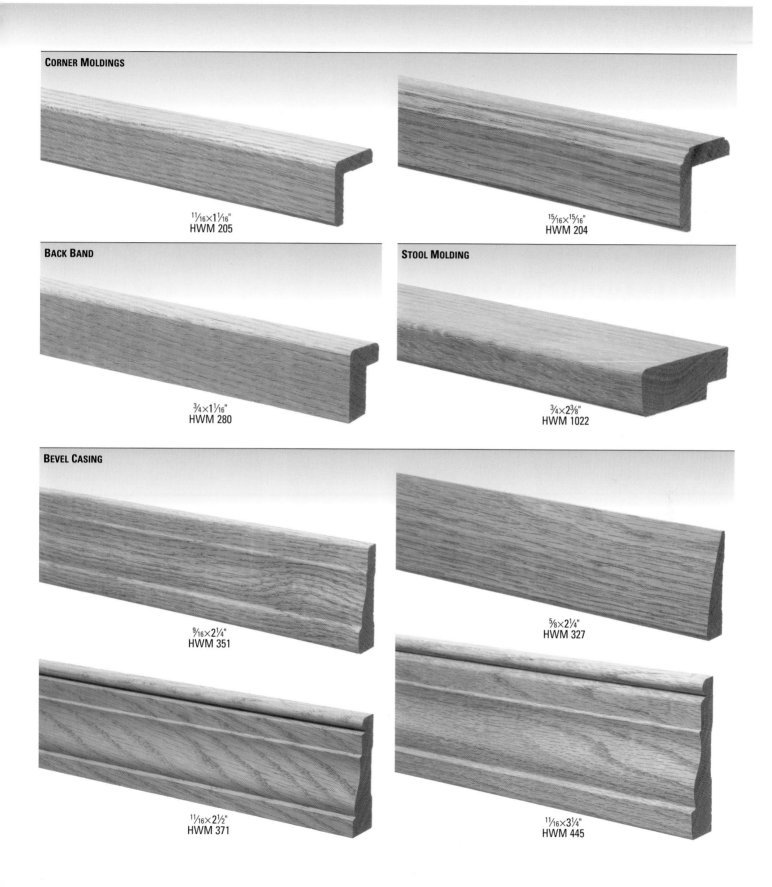

CORNER MOLDINGS

$^{11}/_{16} \times 1^{1}/_{16}$"
HWM 205

$^{15}/_{16} \times ^{15}/_{16}$"
HWM 204

BACK BAND

$^{3}/_{4} \times 1^{1}/_{16}$"
HWM 280

STOOL MOLDING

$^{3}/_{4} \times 2^{3}/_{8}$"
HWM 1022

BEVEL CASING

$^{9}/_{16} \times 2^{1}/_{4}$"
HWM 351

$^{5}/_{8} \times 2^{1}/_{4}$"
HWM 327

$^{11}/_{16} \times 2^{1}/_{2}$"
HWM 371

$^{11}/_{16} \times 3^{1}/_{4}$"
HWM 445

MOLDING GALLERY *(continued)*

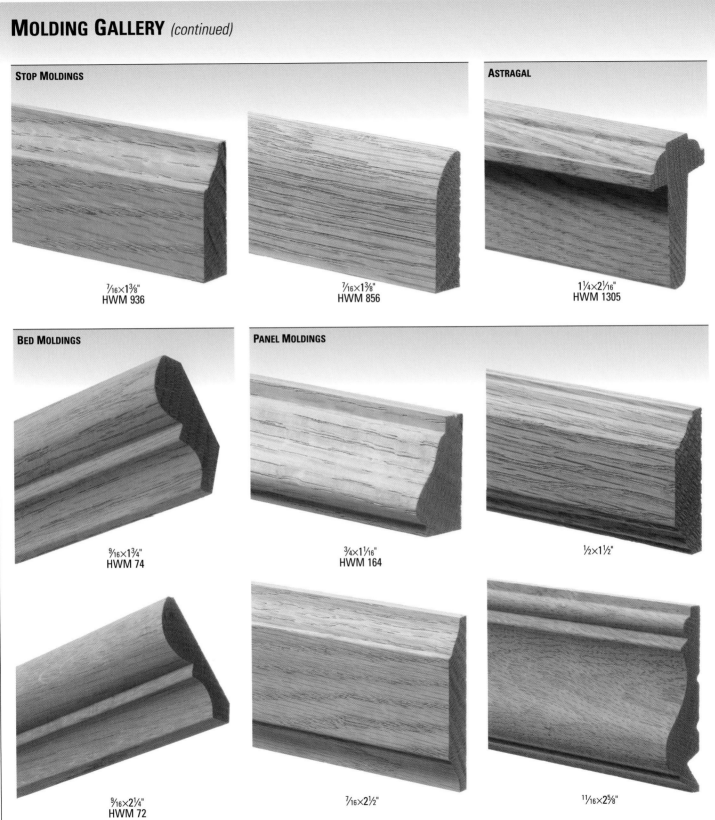

STOP MOLDINGS

$^7/_{16} \times 1^3/_8$"
HWM 936

$^7/_{16} \times 1^3/_8$"
HWM 856

ASTRAGAL

$1^1/_4 \times 2^1/_{16}$"
HWM 1305

BED MOLDINGS

PANEL MOLDINGS

$^9/_{16} \times 1^3/_4$"
HWM 74

$^3/_4 \times 1^1/_{16}$"
HWM 164

$^1/_2 \times 1^1/_2$"

$^9/_{16} \times 2^1/_4$"
HWM 72

$^7/_{16} \times 2^1/_2$"

$^{11}/_{16} \times 2^5/_8$"

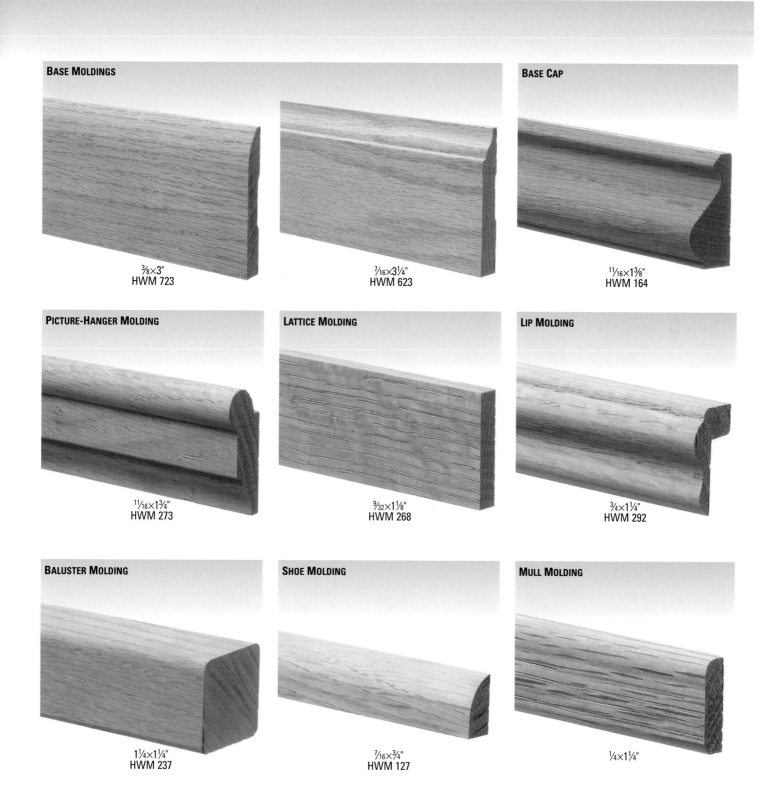

BASE MOLDINGS

$\frac{3}{8} \times 3"$
HWM 723

$\frac{7}{16} \times 3\frac{1}{4}"$
HWM 623

BASE CAP

$\frac{11}{16} \times 1\frac{3}{8}"$
HWM 164

PICTURE-HANGER MOLDING

$\frac{11}{16} \times 1\frac{3}{4}"$
HWM 273

LATTICE MOLDING

$\frac{9}{32} \times 1\frac{1}{8}"$
HWM 268

LIP MOLDING

$\frac{3}{4} \times 1\frac{1}{4}"$
HWM 292

BALUSTER MOLDING

$1\frac{1}{4} \times 1\frac{1}{4}"$
HWM 237

SHOE MOLDING

$\frac{7}{16} \times \frac{3}{4}"$
HWM 127

MULL MOLDING

$\frac{1}{4} \times 1\frac{1}{4}"$

DRYWALL

The wall surface found in most modern homes is a material called drywall, made of a thick layer of gypsum sandwiched between two layers of paper. The paper and gypsum work together, forming a strong building material. Drywall commonly comes in sheets that are 4 feet wide and 8 feet to 16 feet long and in four thicknesses—¼ inch, ⅜ inch, ½ inch, and ⅝ inch. The long edges of the sheets are tapered to help create a flat seam where two pieces join. The ends are left at full thickness.

The longer the pieces you use, the fewer end-to-end seams you'll have to tape and fill. This convenience comes at a price: The added length means added weight. Recruit a helper or two before you hang (attach) the drywall, and make sure it fits into the work area before you order a load of 16-foot pieces. For ceilings, see *page 105* for a handy drywall lift to consider renting.

Most walls and ceilings are covered with ½-inch drywall. In cheaper construction, you'll occasionally find ⅜-inch. The thinner size also works well when covering old plaster walls to renew them. For top quality, ⅝-inch drywall is the way to go. It is stiffer than the thinner sheets, which makes for a flatter wall. It also has more sound-deadening qualities. Your local building code may require ⅝-inch drywall as fire protection in certain situations, such as a wall between an attached garage and the house. On ceilings, ⅝-inch drywall tends to sag less than thinner sheets, especially when attached to 24-inch on-center trusses.

To cover curved surfaces, use two layers of ¼-inch drywall (⅜-inch will work if the curve isn't too severe).

Moisture-resistant (MR) drywall (sometimes called greenboard because its paper facings have a greenish tint) is designed for damp locations such as bathrooms or laundry rooms. MR drywall is somewhat more flexible than regular drywall and tends to sag, especially when damp. It should not be used for ceilings unless the joists are spaced 12 inches on center.

Moisture-resistant (MR) drywall: For use in humid or damp locations

¼-inch drywall: Good for curved surfaces

⅜-inch drywall: Good for covering old walls and some curves

½-inch drywall: General purpose for walls and ceilings

⅝-inch drywall: Good for firewalls and top-quality work

Transporting drywall

Drywall is heavy and not very strong, particularly when it is unsupported. If you try to transport a stack propped up on a tailgate or otherwise wedged into a car or van, the bottom sheets may break. To avoid such trouble, place a couple of 2×4s underneath to add support. Another concern: The weight of a big stack may damage your vehicle. Make two or more trips if necessary, or have it delivered.

JAMB KITS SAVE TIME

For most applications, you'll find that purchasing a jamb kit is a real timesaver. You'll free yourself from the tedious work of selecting the stock, cutting it to width and length, and machining the rabbet or dado at the top inner edge of each leg to receive the head jamb. None of the individual steps is particularly difficult, but when you take a hard look at the price of clear softwood lumber, you may discover that making your own jambs literally doesn't pay.

The components of a standard 2×4 interior wall covered with ½-inch drywall add up to a thickness of 4½ inches. The jamb kit is minutely oversized at 4⁹⁄₁₆ inches wide. If the walls are both covered with ⅝-inch drywall, the computed thickness matches the jamb stock width of 4¾ inches.

If you're going to paint the woodwork, you can save a considerable amount of money by choosing paint-grade jambs. The finger-jointed stock may look a little weird while you're installing it, but the patchwork appearance disappears under the primer and paint. Stain-grade jambs may be defect-free solid lumber or veneers of top-quality wood adhered to a plywood backing. A few purists may cringe at the concept of veneered jambs, but they actually have several advantages over solid stock. Plywood construction has high dimensional stability, meaning that it resists changes in width and shape (such as cupping) that can plague solid lumber. Price is another distinct advantage. The oak veneered stain-grade jamb kit in the photo *below* costs a fraction of the solid hardwood you'd need to purchase, and you would still have to do all of the machining steps yourself.

Rabbet or dado?

Some jamb kits feature a rabbet at the top of the jamb legs; others will have a dado, which is a groove that's cut across the grain. In a jamb made from solid wood, a dado does a better job of restraining potential cupping of the head jamb. If you purchase the rabbeted style, you may want to add some blocking or shims between the top end of the jamb leg and the header to counteract cupping forces.

Paint-grade jamb

Stain-grade jamb

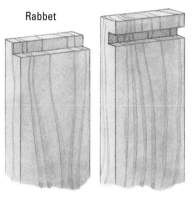

Rabbet

Dado

PRO TIP: **Use setting-type joint compound for strength**

You'll find joint compound packaged two ways: premixed in a bucket or the setting variety in a bag. The setting type is stronger, but the premixed version is easier to apply and sand. After the premixed type cures, smooth it with a sponge, which is faster and creates less mess than abrasive paper.

The other formula is setting-type joint compound, which comes as a powder that must be mixed with water. The bag will be labeled 90, 45, or 20. The numbers indicate how many minutes it takes for the compound to set up. The safest approach is to use the 90-minute mix. If you want it to set faster, mix it with warm water.

Once set, setting-type compound cannot be softened with water. It is harder to sand flat than premixed is, but it is much stronger. Professional drywall finishers often use setting-type for the first coat of mud, especially at outside corners, which are vulnerable to damage. It is also useful when patching drywall, as it helps reinforce the repair. Because this compound sets up so fast, you may be able to apply two or more coats in a day.

When you mix setting-type joint compound, mix only what you can use in the time indicated on the label. Otherwise the compound will set before you can apply it. Be sure to use clean water and a clean bucket. Pouring water into the fine powder raises a lot of dust, so put the proper amount of water in the bucket first, then add the powder, stirring as you go until you reach a consistency (similar to oatmeal) that spreads easily but sticks to the drywall without running.

Tapered jamb edges

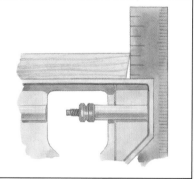

You'll notice that some jamb edges taper a few degrees, flaring inward toward the stud to which it's nailed. This helps ensure that the edge of the casing will fit tightly along the jamb. If you make your own jambs, you can create a similar angle by tilting the tablesaw blade about 5 degrees for the rip cuts.

TECHNIQUES AND TIPS

While it's certainly true that practice makes perfect, it's equally true that knowing a shortcut will get the job done faster.

Of course, when you're into a carpentry or trimwork project, you need to strike a balance between speed and accuracy. That's why this chapter provides you with a solid foundation of knowledge for many of the skills you need. And you'll also discover what to do when things turn out less than perfect.

Abilities for many jobs

Accurately measuring and leveling are skills you'll utilize at every step of the construction process. Mastering the mitersaw is invaluable because this tool has so many applications. Whether you're chopping studs to length or mitering a delicate molding, your familiarity with the mitersaw will keep your project moving.

At first, you may think that cutting a cope joint is more baffling than understanding baseball's infield-fly rule. But when you follow the step-by-step technique, you'll catch on quickly.

Even more techniques

Following proper technique is essential to obtaining good results, whether you're wielding a tool as versatile as a biscuit joiner or as basic as a nail set. This chapter provides insights into producing better results with both.

Many beginners get frustrated trying to remember which way to position plywood for the smoothest cuts at the tablesaw (good face up) and with a handheld circular saw (good face down). But instead of merely committing this knowledge to rote memory, you'll also learn why tearout occurs. With that understanding, you'll get smoother cuts every time—with a coping saw, jigsaw, or any other saw you own.

Tips and secrets

Until someone invents a molding stretcher, you'll need to know how to cut scarf joints and how to make them virtually invisible.

Working alone—by choice or necessity—can be a rewarding experience. For example, you'll learn how to easily make jigs that solidly support moldings when you're the entire crew.

Add these techniques to your home-improvement skills, and you'll save time on every project you tackle.

CHAPTER PREVIEW

Accurate measuring and marking
page 204

Cutting miter joints
page 206

Cutting coped joints
page 208

Biscuit joinery
page 212

Learning tips and shortcuts for miter cuts will make the best use of your time and money.

Making a return
page 214

Minimizing tearout
page 215

Making scarf joints
page 219

Fixing the fit
page 221

ACCURATE MEASURING AND MARKING

Accurately transferring measurements is one of the most fundamental skills in carpentry. It's so basic, in fact, that most people assume they already know how to do it. But that assumption wilts when drywall has to be cut not once but three times, and every joint in the trimwork has a sizable gap.

First off, you need to start with quality measuring tools. And you need to know the two key ingredients to accurate measuring: consistent technique and practice. Also knowing a few tricks of the trade can't hurt.

It's a good idea to keep the concept of accuracy in a reasonable perspective. For example, you don't need a perfect fit between sheets of drywall. A gap up to ¼ inch is tolerable because the discrepancy will disappear under the tape and joint compound. If you're working with trimwork that will be painted, simply reach for the painter's caulk to conceal misalignments that are as wide as a hairline (or two or three). The acceptable tolerance level tightens up with clear-finished woodwork. But while absolute perfection is the goal, you also have to remember that you're building a house—not a jewelry box.

Sizing the tape measure to the job is a sound ergonomic principle that will save effort every time you pick up a tape measure. Although the jumbo-sized tapes have a macho appeal, you don't need a 25-foot tape to handle a 3-inch measuring job. Choose a smaller tape by feel: Select a case that feels comfortable in your hand.

Inside measurements can be tricky, but here's an accurate method. A folding rule with a brass extension is a time-proven classic. You can read the measurement, but it's quicker to simply mark the wood directly from the rule. Your tape measure's case tells the amount to add for the length of its body.

REFRESHER COURSE
Leveling

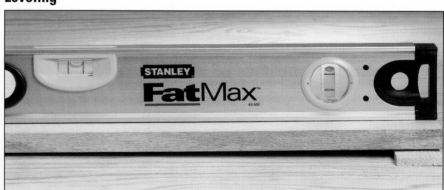

Modern manufacturing methods produce levels with impressive accuracy, but that quality takes a beating every time you drop the tool. Shocks can dislodge a vial's mountings and misalign the frame itself by warping or twisting. Here are a few tips on testing a level and preserving its precision.

Check your level's accuracy by placing it on a flat board on top of your workbench. Put shims under the board to center the bubble in the vial. Rotate the level end for end (don't flip it) and check the vial. Any error will be doubled. Some expensive levels can be recalibrated, but replacing the level is the usual cure.

To transfer a measurement to the wood's surface, first press on the edge of the tape to roll the marks next to the wood. Put your pencil point at the line, and pull it away to the left. Repeat with another short line snapped to the right. The V-shape is highly visible but its tip is small enough to retain accuracy. Stow a pocket-size pencil sharpener in your tool belt and use it often.

A mechanical pencil is a great tool for high-precision marking. Hold it upright at the point of the V-mark, then gently slide the blade of your combination square up to it. Brace the square, then make your mark. To minimize mistakes, develop the habit of marking an X on the waste side of the cut.

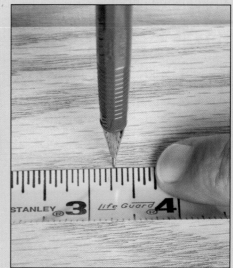

Here's a trick to accurately measure to 1/32-**inch** without squinting at tiny marks. Utilize the 1/16-inch scale on your tape measure and visually split the divisions in half. Assign a plus or minus to identify your location. For example, you could call the location in the photo "3¼ plus" or "3⁵/16 minus," whichever is easier to remember.

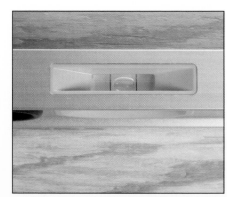

A "top reading" level has a viewing slot in the edge of the tool's frame. This is a real convenience when you're working on projects that are either too high or low to permit a comfortable view of the vial from the side.

Protect your level by storing it in a protective case. Just as important, secure the case so it doesn't get knocked over, rattling the level. These precautions preserve the level's appearance and accuracy, multiplying its longevity.

Need to draw a circle? Here's a simple and accurate method that doesn't require a compass. Drill a hole in scrap material (something the dimension of a wooden ruler is ideal) for your pencil. After marking the radius (half of the diameter), lightly secure the other end with a nail, *above*. Now mark the arc with your pencil.

CUTTING MITER JOINTS

The miter joint, where the ends of the pieces to be joined are cut at an angle (usually 45 degrees), is one of three joints used most often to install trim. The others are the coped joint *(page 208)* and the butt joint, where two square faces meet. Miter joints are used for outside corners, while coped joints handle most of the inside ones. Both allow molding profiles to continue around a corner without interruption.

To cut miters quickly and accurately, use a power mitersaw, commonly called a chop saw, or a handsaw and a miter box. Most professionals use a chop saw for its speed and accuracy. A miter box can be just as accurate; however, it takes longer to make a cut by hand. If your budget is tight and you plan to do a limited amount of trim work, opt for a miter box. You can buy a professional-quality integrated miter box and mitersaw for the price of an entry-level chop saw.

Practice making miter cuts on pieces of scrap, both to improve your skills and to check the accuracy of your tools.

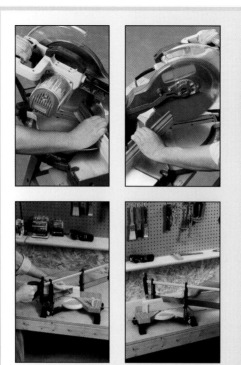

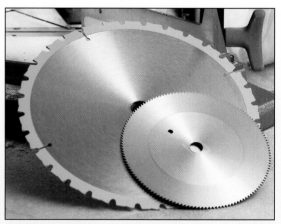

1 Set your saw to cut a 45-degree angle with the blade angled to the left. Make a test cut in a scrap piece of molding. Swing the saw to cut a 45-degree angle with the blade angled to the right. Make a matching cut in a second scrap piece held on the other side of the blade.

2 Check to see if a saw makes accurate 45-degree cuts by holding the test pieces together against a framing square. There should be no gap in the joint. If the saw's stops are not set correctly, consult the owner's manual to learn how to adjust the saw.

STANLEY PRO TIP

Improve the grip of your saw

Whether you use a chop saw or a miter box, the workpiece tends to slide when you make an angled cut. To solve this problem, glue a piece of fine sandpaper to the fence with spray adhesive; it will grip the wood.

REFRESHER COURSE
Buying the right blade

Most chop saws come equipped with a coarse saw blade, which is good for cutting 2×4s and other framing lumber but won't do a good job on trim. For making precise miter cuts, you'll need a fine crosscutting blade. Such blades have more teeth than general-purpose blades do. Look for a blade that has at least 50–80 teeth ground with an alternate top bevel (ATB) pattern. ATB blades excel at crosscutting cleanly; the teeth are ground to shear the wood fibers at the edge of the cut.

If you have a choice, a smaller-diameter blade with more teeth makes much finer cuts than its larger cousin. The smaller diameter means the blade won't wobble as much. The trade-off is that the smaller blade won't cut as wide a piece, but that's not usually an issue when installing trim.

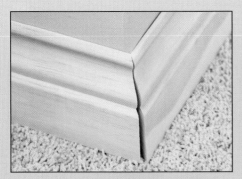

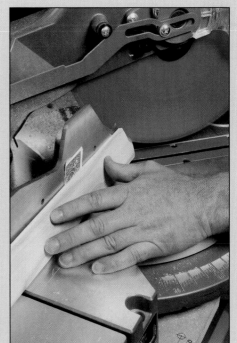

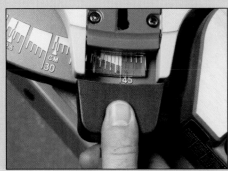

3 Place the test pieces in position. If the miter is open on the outside, adjust the saw to slightly less than 45 degrees. Make test cuts until the angle mates perfectly with one of the original test pieces. Cut one of the pieces you'll install to the adjusted angle, the other to exactly 45 degrees.

4 If the test pieces are open at the back when you place them against the wall, set the saw at slightly more than 45 degrees. Cut scrap until you find the right angle, then cut the angle on one piece you'll install and an exact 45-degree angle on another piece.

5 If you have to make very subtle changes to the miter angle, you may find it easier to insert shims behind the molding rather than trying to shift the blade a slight amount. Plastic-coated playing cards work well for this job; keep a deck in your toolbox.

WHAT IF...
The corner isn't 90 degrees?

With corners that are slightly off 90 degrees, you can achieve a close fit for miter joints by cutting one molding piece to exactly 45 degrees and then making minor adjustments to the saw to "sneak up" on the matching angle for the other piece.

For corners that are intentionally far from square, you'll have to reset the saw to split the angle in half. Fortunately this is easy to do without math calculations. You just need a T-bevel and a compass.

Yet another method involves a protractor that accurately measures the angle. See *page 146* for a demonstration of the protractor in a crown-molding installation.

1 Set a T-bevel against the corner to set the angle. Transfer the angle you want to a board.

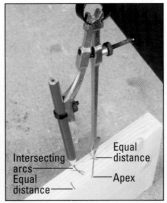

2 Starting at the apex, mark an equal distance along each leg of the angle with a compass. From these new points, draw two intersecting arcs with the same compass setting.

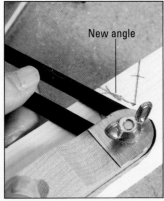

3 Draw a line through the apex of the angle and the point where the arcs intersect. This line bisects the original angle. Transfer the new angle to the saw via the T-bevel.

CUTTING COPED JOINTS

Use coped joints instead of miters for an inside corner. You might have difficulty fitting inside miters, because the wall surfaces tend to give slightly as you nail the pieces in place. Thus a miter joint that looks perfect when held up for a test fit is likely to gap when nailed in place. A coped joint, on the other hand, accommodates such variations.

A coped joint is essentially a butt joint in which one piece of molding runs right into the corner. The end of the adjoining piece is cut to match the profile of the first piece and butts up against it. This is not as difficult as it may sound; coped joints are much easier to cut than they look, and they are fairly forgiving of inaccuracies. The principal tool used is a coping saw.

Even the pros don't cut perfect copes every time. The trick is to take your time and leave the moldings a little long to begin with so you can sneak up on the perfect fit by fine-tuning the cut.

STANLEY PRO TIP

Fine-tune the fit

A small rounded rasp or file works best for fine-tuning coped joints. Filing is slower than using a utility knife but gives you more control when you have just a bit of wood to remove.

1 Start a coped joint by butting one of the pieces of molding into the corner and fastening it in place. When deciding which piece to cope, choose the one that will be least visible as you enter a room.

2 To reveal the line you will cope, miter-cut the end of the piece as though you were going to make an inside miter.

Supporting long pieces

When cutting long pieces of molding with a chop saw or a miter box, make sure that overhanging ends are supported at the same level as the saw or box table. The most important reason to do this is safety—trying to hold an unwieldy, unsupported piece in place is dangerous. In addition, it's much easier to make an accurate cut if the piece is properly supported.

THE LINE YOU WILL COPE
Making the line clear

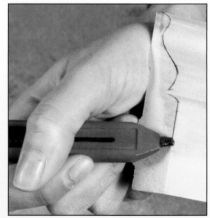

If the molding is prefinished, the profile cut line will show clearly when you make the miter cut. For unfinished molding it can be helpful to run a pencil along the profile to help guide the cut.

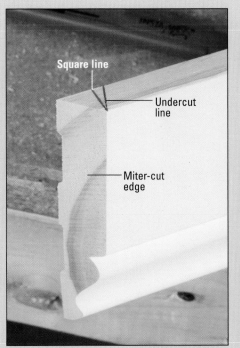

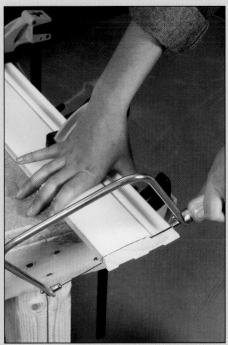

3 In a perfect world, a coped joint would be cut square to the surface (shown by the red line). In reality, a coped joint is undercut (black line) to accommodate any irregularities in the joint.

4 Saw along the cut line with a coping saw, angling the blade slightly to produce the undercut. Brace the molding on a bench or sawhorse. Clamping the molding is an even better idea.

5 Check the fit of the cope against the molding in the corner. If necessary, trim the piece with a utility knife.

Purchasing molding by the numbers

crown - WM 47 - 2 pcs. 14' 2 pcs. 10'
chair Rail WM 276 - 2 pcs. 14'
Baseboard WM 750 - 1 pc. 10'
Baseshoe WM 126 - 1 pc. 8'
casing - WM 371 - 1 pc. 8', 1 pc. 10'

12' 2' 3' 2' 9'6"

Each standard molding has a number (such as WM 51) assigned by the Wood Moulding & Millwork Producers Association (WMMPA). This number indicates a specific profile and its width. Some suppliers will provide you with a catalog of the moldings they stock, but for a comprehensive listing of all molding styles that are manufactured, you'll have to purchase a catalog from WMMPA. There are currently two catalogs: one for softwood and another for hardwood.

When shopping, specify your moldings by the WM number rather than by a name, such as "2¼-inch colonial casing," which might describe several different profiles.

As you calculate how much molding you need, don't simply measure the room and come up with a total number of linear feet. It is better to figure out how long a piece you'll need for each wall and list the moldings that way. This minimizes the number of midwall splices you'll have to make. When listing the lengths needed, add a few extra inches onto each piece to allow for mistakes.

Even when you specify the molding by its WM number, two pieces of the same molding from different suppliers may not match exactly. If possible, select moldings from the same lot number so the profiles match at the joints.

HAMMERING AND COUNTERSINKING

Driving a nail appears easy—until the hammer is in your hand. To turn the odds of success in your favor, take this quick refresher course in hammering and countersinking. You'll learn how to speed up the construction of wall framing, choose the right hammer for drywall, and handle a hammer with skill.

Finish nailing of jambs and moldings requires more finesse. But you'll learn techniques that help you conquer splits and learn how a simple jig can virtually banish hammer tracks from your woodwork. You'll also see how countersinking is a gentle art that is made much more difficult and risky than it needs to be.

 **STANLEY** PRO TIP

Drywall hammers

A specialized drywall hammer features a domed face to drive the nail below the surface but leave a cavity that's easy to fill with joint compound. Don't over-drive the nail, or you'll risk breaking the drywall's paper surface. The checkered pattern on the face transfers to the cavity, helping the joint compound grip the paper.

When you're framing a wall, speed the job by upgrading to a 22-ounce hammer instead of the usual 16-ounce head. Grip the handle near the end and generate power with a sweeping arc of your arm. Brace the other end of the wall against a fixed object; you'll transfer more energy into the fastener instead of scooting the assembly across the floor.

If the wood splits as you're driving a finishing nail, stop! The split will only widen when the larger diameter of the head meets the wood. Work a little bit of glue into the split before pulling the nail. Relocate the fastener, avoiding the split grain line. If you must drive a nail close to an end or edge, drill a pilot hole to minimize the danger of splits.

Don't reach for your nail set until the nailhead is no more than ⅛ inch above the surface of the wood. The set's diameter should not overlap the head and should engage it without slipping. Hold the set firmly against the nail's head, then give it a square blow to drive the head 1/32 inch below the surface.

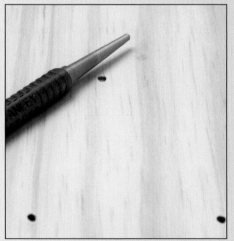

A nail that's countersunk properly makes a hole that's easy to fill. If the set slips off the nail, examine the tool's hardened tip for mushrooming or any other signs of wear. If you find wear, buy a new nail set.

PNEUMATIC NAILERS

If you drive nails by hand, you simply put your hammer in the toolbox at the end of the workday. Air nailers and a compressor require a few more minutes of maintenance, but pneumatic tools are certainly worth the effort because they remove a great deal of the drudgery from door, window, and molding installation.

A hissing sound while the compressor is off means there's a leak somewhere. Check the hoses and connectors until you find the culprit. Disassemble the joint and clean away dried pipe dope with a stiff wire brush. Apply fresh dope or wrap Teflon tape onto the male threads and reassemble the joint. If the hose leaks somewhere along its length, replace it: Fix one spot, and you'll probably soon find another leak.

If you have both a finish nail gun and a brad driver, you'll probably discover that the smaller fasteners demand less air. That could mean resetting the pressure gauge at the compressor every time you switch guns. You can get around this problem by purchasing an in-line pressure regulator valve and adding it to your brad driver's intake. Suppliers typically call this a cheater valve; it's available with or without a gauge. By adjusting the knob, you can set the pressure to the exact amount you need. Once set, you can switch guns back and forth without adjustments.

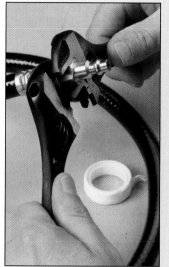

Leaky connections are more than annoying. By wasting air, a leak causes the compressor to cycle on needlessly, eating up electricity, generating noise, and shortening its life. Fortunately the fix is fast and easy. Disassemble the joint, clean the threads, and add new pipe dope or Teflon tape. Tighten securely for a long-lasting fix.

An in-line valve allows you to fine-tune air pressure right at your working position. It's especially handy for reducing airflow to a tool with a lower demand, such as a brad driver, so that you can swap back and forth with one that requires more air—such as your finish nailer—without resetting the compressor's regulator valve.

Many nailers allow you to swivel the exhaust port, directing the blast away from your body and face. Make it a habit to adjust the direction whenever you switch working positions at the job.

PRO TIP

A tip tap tip

Firmly tapping the tip of a nail will decrease the chance that the blunted fastener will split wood. Although it's far from foolproof, it's quicker than constantly drilling pilot holes in moldings. It's worth trying, especially for nails that you'll drive near the end of the molding.

Drill a pilot to avoid splits

For short lengths of molding, drilling a pilot hole gives high assurance against splits. Although drilling takes some time, it's faster than cutting a piece of replacement molding and coping its end. As a rule of thumb, the more work you put into a piece of molding, the more it makes sense to drill pilot holes.

BISCUIT JOINERY

A plate joiner represents a quantum leap in woodworking, permitting amateurs to quickly and easily make joints that rival the strength of those built with traditional mortise-and-tenon joinery. And you'll get those results without serving a year-long apprenticeship. After a few minutes of reading the tool's instruction manual, you're ready to make strong joints.

The biscuit joint is actually a variation of the mortise and tenon, so it shares the element of strength. The biscuit functions as a loose tenon that fits into the arced mortises formed by the tool's circular blade.

By adjusting the depth of cut, you can choose biscuits of various sizes. See the "Pro Tip" *below right,* for additional details on choosing biscuits.

1 To make a butt joint for a box, begin by marking the centerlines of the biscuits' locations onto the boards. These marks are adjacent to the surface where you cut the slots, guiding you to accurately position the tool.

2 Clamp the workpiece to the table. Lock the flip-down fence at the front of the joiner at the 90-degree position. Set the fence's height so that the slot is approximately centered in the stock's thickness. Align the guide notch on the joiner with the centerline, turn on the joiner, then push it forward to cut the slots.

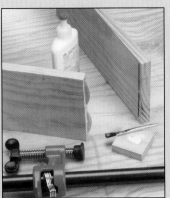

3 Note that you cut the other pair of slots in the board's side. Do a dry assembly (no glue) to check the joint's fit. Squeeze a puddle of glue onto a scrap board and brush glue onto the biscuits and into the slots. Clamp the assembly until the glue sets.

Biscuit joiner shows its versatility

With a little bit of joinery practice, you can make strong edge joints, T-joints, face frame construction, and mitered joints, and even assemble entire cabinets. Jobs that used to be too complicated are now well within your woodworking grasp.

And unlike many woodworking solutions that simplify at the expense of strength, biscuit joinery is extremely durable. Moisture in the glue expands the compressed beech biscuit, filling the slots and ensuring sturdy joinery.

T-joints and biscuit joinery are a perfect match for many assemblies.

STANLEY PRO TIP

Size the biscuit to the job

As a rule of thumb, select the largest biscuit that the width of the stock will allow. This will maximize the biscuit's glue surface to produce the strongest joint. The arc of the cutter creates a slot that's longer than the biscuit itself, so you can't simply measure the biscuit's length when you're making your choice. Instead, refer to the following list of minimum stock widths for the four most common biscuit sizes.

An FF biscuit can handle stock as narrow as 1¾ inches; a #0 biscuit needs a 2½-inch width; the #10 biscuit requires lumber 2¾ inches wide, and the #20 biscuit uses stock 3 inches and wider.

It's also a good idea to make test cuts to confirm the biscuit joiner's setup. Most joiners allow you to fine-tune the depth of cut adjust to ensure that the biscuit seats fully into the slot.

SCRIBING TO FIT

When you're installing drywall or wood moldings, you might run into situations that seem difficult at first glance. One example is hanging drywall next to the irregular stonework of a fireplace. Trying to measure and transfer all of the irregularities to a sheet of drywall would require saintly patience and a lot of time. But if you know how to scribe, you'll produce accurate results within minutes.

Scribing also works well for sheets of wood products, countertops, moldings, and other trim boards. If a wall has a slight bow to it, for example, you probably won't be able to muscle a 1×4 applied flat into the arc. Although pumping a caseload of caulk into the gap is one solution, scribing is more sensible and less expensive.

Another common problem deals with fitting angled pieces of sheet goods. Die-hard engineers will reach for their calculator and trig tables. But the rest of us will get faster results with a tape measure, straightedge, and no math with the procedure shown *below right.*

Solving angled pieces

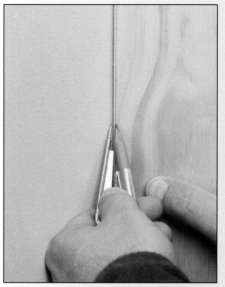

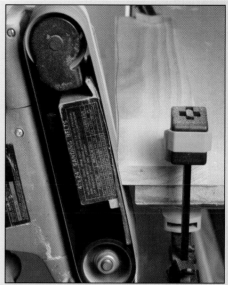

1 Place the wood near the wall and parallel to it. Lock your bow compass at a setting that spans the gap, even at the widest point. Holding the compass at a consistent angle, draw it down the wall, marking the board. In this case, the edge of the compass, not its point, rides along the wall.

2 Securely clamp the scribed board to your worktable, then sand to the scribed line. Tilt the sander slightly backward to undercut the line for a snug fit against the wall. A coarse belt works best. If you have a lot of stock to remove, cut with a jigsaw just to the waste side of the line, removing the bulk of the material before sanding.

STANLEY PRO TIP

Scribing drywall to fit

To cut a piece of drywall to fit against an irregular surface, hold the piece near the surface and trace the outline onto the sheet, using a wood scrap and a pencil as a scribing tool.

Fitting angled pieces

1 Rather than measuring the angle at which a piece must be cut, measure the length of the horizontal run and the vertical rise.

2 Transfer the measurements to the drywall, then draw a cut line between the two marks. Cut and snap the piece along the line.

MAKING A RETURN

Although most people are enthusiastic about the appearance of a wood's face grain, there are very few fans for a wood's end grain. This is the cut—usually on the end of a board—that reveals the wood's annual rings and the tiny structures that moved sap through the living tree. But even after a tree becomes lumber, the ends of these channels suck stain and finish in greater amounts than the face grain. That's why end grain turns unattractively dark.

The ends of moldings or window stools that display end grain have an additional drawback because the design on the face doesn't continue around the end. It looks cut off because it literally is cut off.

A return on the end of a piece of molding solves both of these appearance issues, eliminating end grain and continuing the design around the end. Try it and you'll discover that it's an easy technique that gives your projects an upgraded look.

If you're dealing with painted moldings, you could also try the faux return described *below*. It's a bit more labor intensive, but there may be times you'll want it.

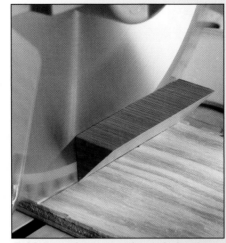

1 Make a miter cut on the end of a piece of molding, then position the wood so that the blade edge will precisely meet the edge of the miter cut. To make the blade's path easy to see, temporarily attach ¼-inch plywood to the saw's base with double-faced tape. Cut a kerf into the plywood to show precisely where the blade cuts.

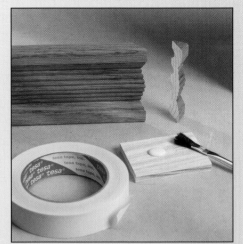

2 Brush a tiny amount of glue onto the return and the mitered molding. Rub the two pieces together until the glue starts to grab. Add a couple of pieces of masking tape to immobilize the parts while the glue dries.

Coping quickly

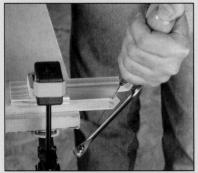

Orient the teeth of your coping saw to cut on the down stroke when holding the saw as shown in the photo. This position gives you maximum power and control. Clamp the wood to slash the total energy required—and reduce the risk of slicing your hand.

A faux return

Here's another way to continue the pattern around the end of the molding. Make a miter cut, then a vertical cope cut along the molding's design. For smoothest results, sand the cut line. Because of the exposed end grain, this technique is more suitable under paint instead of a clear finish.

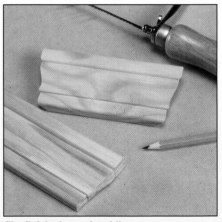

The finished coped molding

MINIMIZING TEAROUT

Each tooth on a sawblade slices though the wood with the action of a miniature chisel. The edges of the wood where the blade enters are usually smooth, because when the cut begins, the blade is like a chisel diving into the lumber. But the exit wound—where the blade leaves the wood—is often messy. That's because the wood fibers split away under the pressure of the advancing blade.

It's easy to understand the entry and exit sides of wood cut with a conventional handsaw because the blade cuts on the push stroke. The teeth enter the wood at the top and exit at the bottom.

But things get a bit confusing when the teeth spin around in the form of a circular saw blade. When mounted in a handheld circular saw, the blade enters the bottom of the wood and exits at the top. But when the blade is in a tablesaw, the teeth enter the top surface of the lumber. Thus, your best board surface should be up when cutting at a tablesaw, the best surface down when cutting with a handheld circular saw.

When you need a clean edge on a piece of plywood, improve your odds by scoring the cut line with a sharp utility knife. The blade severs the face veneer that could chip. Crosscuts are more likely to produce chipping than rip cuts. The X mark on the board indicates the waste side of the cut.

Tape along a cut line will help prevent tearout. The upper surface of a jigsawn board is generally rougher than the bottom, but you can tape top and bottom if you want. If your saw has an adjustment for orbital action, turn it to minimum for smoothest results. See *page 181* for jigsaw blade recommendations.

Stack cuts reduce tearout

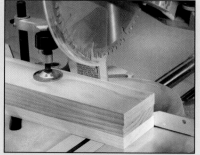

Stack-cutting several flat boards at once keeps tearout to a minimum. The cut line has maximum support along its edges, so the only board with an exit surface on its face is at the bottom of the stack. Placing a sacrificial scrap board at the bottom of the stack ensures that all of the ones on top of it won't have an exit face.

WHAT IF…
I have a sliding compound mitersaw?

When you use the mitersaw like a chop saw, the blade arcs downward and backward. This motion produces a smooth cut on the face and top edge of the stock. You can get tearout on the back surface and lower edge of the wood, but both areas are usually hidden when you install the molding.

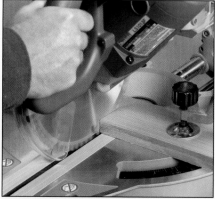

With a push cut, the blade of the sliding mitersaw enters the face of the board that's against the saw's platform. The fuzzy upper face of the board indicates that it is the exit surface. The upward spin also explains the blade's tendency to lift the stock. Note the hold-down at above right.

CIRCULAR SAW CUTS

There are two basic types of cuts to make using a circular saw: a crosscut, which runs across the grain, and a rip cut, which runs with the grain. No matter what type of cut you're making, for best results it should be straight.

The simple homemade cutting guide shown here helps you produce straight, accurate cuts with your circular saw. It is made from a piece of ¼-inch plywood and a straight length of ½-inch-thick stock. You can make the guide any length you like, up to 8 feet long for cutting sheets of plywood.

RIP CUT

Cutting the long way

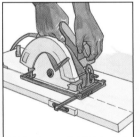

If you need to rip-cut boards, (for example, to make 4-inch-wide baseboards from 1×6s), use a rip guide accessory (available for all circular saws). To make the cut, clamp the board securely across two sawhorses. Set the guide to the required width. Keep the guide firmly against the board.

Making your own cutting guide

1 Start with a piece of ¼-inch plywood that is at least 2½ inches wider than the base of your circular saw. Glue and screw a 2-inch-wide strip of ½-inch-thick stock flush to the long edge of the plywood.

2 Clamp the guide to a pair of sawhorses or on a bench. Place the saw base against the ½-inch stock and run the saw down the plywood, cutting it to width. Make sure the blade won't cut the bench or horses.

3 To use the guide, clamp it to your workpiece with the sawed edge along a marked cutline. Guide the saw along the ½-inch stock to make the cut.

SAFETY FIRST
Setting the correct depth of cut

When cutting with a circular saw, set the depth of cut so the blade extends through the material plus the depth of the teeth. This keeps the amount of exposed blade to a minimum while allowing the blade to cut efficiently. If the teeth reach just barely through the material, the blade may heat excessively and bind in the cut. As you are sawing, remember that the teeth reach past the underside of the board—keep fingers, power cords, and other materials clear.

A PLAN FOR MOLDING INSTALLATION

When you survey a room prior to molding installation, look for a logical starting point. The floor plan of a typical room shows that the baseboard installation consists of eight pieces. Note that the job splits into two sections: pieces 1 through 3, and pieces 4 through 8.

In theory, you could start the installation at the edge of any doorway casing, offering four potential starting points. But the piece marked No. 1 is the preferred starting place for most workers for two good reasons. First, the sequence shown enables a right-handed worker to cut all right-hand copes in the room. (See "Pro Tip," *below)* Second, piece 2 is the longest strip of molding in the installation. If you make a mistake in cutting it, you can still use the strip elsewhere in the room.

As a general rule, right-handers will find it more convenient to cut and install moldings in a counterclockwise direction around a room, and that's what the drawing shows. If you're left-handed and prefer cutting left copes, the installation sequence would be: 3, 2, 1 and then a countdown starting at 8 and ending at 4. A lefty also should modify the cuts to turn the copes left-handed. For example, piece 3 would have two butt ends, the cope and butt would shift ends on piece 2, the end of piece 1 in the corner would be a cope, and its other end would butt against the door casing.

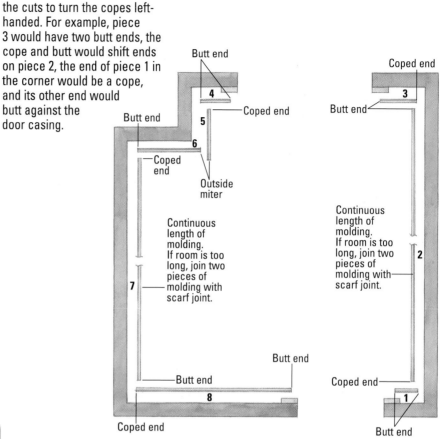

Butt end
Coped end
Butt end
Coped end
Coped end
Outside miter
Continuous length of molding. If room is too long, join two pieces of molding with scarf joint.
Continuous length of molding. If room is too long, join two pieces of molding with scarf joint.
Butt end
Butt end
Coped end
Coped end
Butt end

Right and left copes

The photo shows the coping strategy most right-handers prefer—cutting the delicate top of the molding first. Here's why: If you started from the bottom, the thin top could break off just as you're completing the cut. Left-handers also prefer to start at the top edge but with the miter cut on the end of the molding.

Three prime cuts

You need only three types of end cuts to install moldings around a room: the butt, the cope, and the outside miter. The inside miter cut (not shown) is rarely used because the cope is superior at producing a tight joint, even when corners are slightly more or less than a perfect right angle. The cope also will remain tight even as a house settles and shifts.

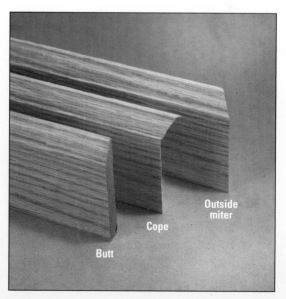

Butt
Cope
Outside miter

SUPPORTING MOLDINGS WHEN WORKING SOLO

It's usually a good idea to find an assistant to help you balance moldings during measuring and installation. But these tasks can become tedious and time-consuming, and the person with the supporting hand can become less supportive as the project drags on. Other times, you simply must work solo.

Whether you're working alone as a matter of choice or necessity, you still need to find a way to deal with the awkward lengths. The solutions on this page all provide a helping hand, and not a single one of them gets impatient or develops an attitude.

But it's also important to keep your own emotions in check during the installation. If you find yourself getting frustrated, take a break. Being agitated can easily lead to mistakes or injury. Return to the job when your mind can focus clearly on it.

Combine a clamp with a stepladder, and you have a support that works great with chair-rail and picture-hanger moldings. Wrap a cloth around the clamp and tape the cloth in place so you won't scar the molding or your wall.

While you're measuring and fitting crown moldings, you need a secure support. Create one by tacking a length of 1×4 that projects past an outside corner. To hold crown molding on a flat length of wall, screw together an L-shape shelf and tack it to the wall. Finishing nails leave such tiny holes that you can easily patch them when the installation is complete.

Get a grip

If wood props slide against the wall, they can scar the paint. And if the jig loses its footing, the molding can come crashing down. Solve both these problems with rubber bumpers. To install, simply peel the bumper from its backing and press firmly on a clean surface.

Here's another easy way to support chair-rail moldings. Simply screw together two lengths of 1×4 for a nearly instant helper. Cut the vertical 1×4 a few inches longer than the distance from the bottom of the molding to the floor. This will position the support at a fairly steep angle for stability.

Add a plywood foot to a molding support for added stability. Position the shelf at the top of the support along the bottom line for the molding.

MAKING SCARF JOINTS

For the best appearance, moldings should run in one continuous strip from one corner of the room to the next. But when the room is longer than your molding, a joint becomes unavoidable. Your task, though, is to make that seam as invisible as possible.

The photo sequence starting at *right* shows you the steps you'll follow to make the joint, but there are several other things you can do to disguise the joint. If you're joining wood that will get a clear finish, join pieces that have the same subdued grain pattern. Joining a wildly grained strip with one that has straight grain will make the difference immediately apparent. If possible, locate the joint where a bed, bookcase, or other large piece of furniture will block it. That way, the only time you'll see the seam is on moving day. Behind the door is another good hiding spot, but be careful of positioning a joint too close to a corner. A seam closer to a corner than 16 inches may look as if you're fixing a mistake—not making a planned extension.

Painted scarf joints are easier to conceal, but they still require careful workmanship and sanding. Paint is merely a finishing coat, not a cure for a poor fit.

If you apply stain and a clear finish before cutting the scarf, you won't have to sand the joint smooth. Although this will save the effort of applying the finish after installation, it means that you'll need to spend extra time to fit the joint as closely as possible. Touch up the joint's ends with a stain pen (see *page 231)* to eliminate the appearance of raw wood.

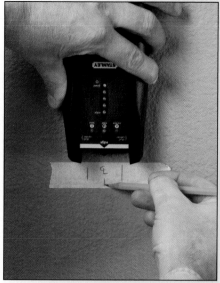

1 Select the location for the scarf joint, positioning it over a stud, if possible. Mark the stud's edges and centerline onto a piece of tape applied to the wall.

2 Fit the end of one molding piece into a corner, then mark the seam cutting line. In this example, the corner at right is fitted first. To help your cutting, mark diagonally across your molding piece.

Scarf sanding success stories

Load abrasive paper into a hard rubber sanding block to level the flat surfaces of scarf-joined moldings. Don't concentrate sanding pressure right at the joint line, but feather out the sanding several inches to each side of the seam line. Remove dust with a tack cloth, then apply primer to the raw wood.

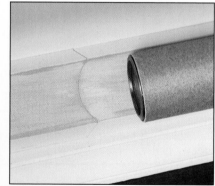

Smooth curved surfaces with sandpaper wrapped around a rod or cylinder that matches the molding. Some good cylinders include round pencils, dowel rods, and PVC plumbing pipe. Pressure-sensitive abrasive (PSA) sticks to the cylinder, making your work easier. Spray adhesive on ordinary sandpaper is a good alternative to PSA.

MAKING SCARF JOINTS *(continued)*

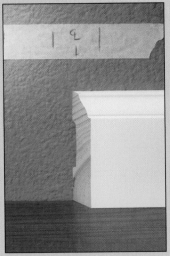

3 Make the first half of the scarf joint with a 45-degree miter cut that opens away from the wall. Nail this piece to the wall at the other stud locations along the wall.

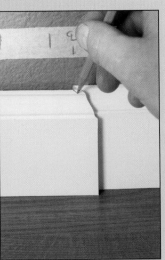

4 Fit the end of the second molding strip into its corner, and mark the location of its scarf joint. Notice that the miter runs in the opposite direction from the cut in the first piece you installed. Make several cuts in order to sneak up to a perfect fit.

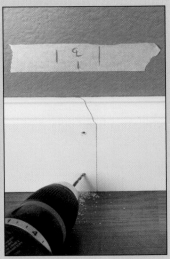

5 Drill pilot holes for the nails that will secure the seam and hold the molding to the wall. Don't neglect this step, because the glue makes the joint slippery, and the pieces can shift out of position as you're driving the fasteners. Slightly angle the pilot holes so the joint doesn't slide apart when you drive the nails.

6 Apply glue to both ends of the joint. Get both nails started through the pilots before you drive either one of them completely. Countersink the nails as little as possible. See *page 210* for countersinking suggestions. Sand the joint smooth and touch up the paint.

Large-scale scarf joints

On some large pieces of trimwork, such as crown molding, you can join lengths prior to installation. Doing this significantly reduces the amount of work you need to perform while standing on a ladder. As a result, you get better joints with less work.

Accurate cutting of the opposing miters for the joint is still an absolute necessity. Follow the recommended setting time so the assembled joint will develop strength in the glue joint before proceeding with installation.

For the wood gusset, *right*, cut the scarf joint, apply glue to the cut ends, and press them together firmly. Align the assembly against a straightedge and apply strips of masking tape to keep the joint shut. Glue and screw a plywood gusset over the seam. As the size of the molding increases, choose thicker plywood, but make certain it doesn't interfere with installation clearances. Steel mending plates, *far right*, are

a good alternative to plywood, lending excellent strength with minimum bulk. Choose coarse-threaded screws for maximum holding power

in softwoods. During installation, don't attempt to drive or shoot nails through the metal plates.

FIXING THE FIT

Sometimes, molding installations speed along at a rapid pace because the walls are straight and the corners are square. But other times, progress is maddeningly slow because of out-of-square corners, bulging drywall, and wavy walls.

Painter's caulk is one solution to the problem of a poor fit between the wall and the wood, but it's not the only recourse you have. In fact, your caulking gun should be your last weapon—not the first.

By checking the walls prior to installation, you can identify and correct problem areas. Shaving down an offending hump of drywall is one solution (see *page 47),* and it's great for fixing big bulges. If the problem area is smaller, however, knock it flat with a block of plywood and a hammer. If you notice a gap between the picture-frame casing of a window and the wall, resist the urge to push the joint flush against the wall. Doing so will open the miter, creating a problem worse than the one you had before.

The scribing technique detailed on *page 213* is a great way to fit a cabinet seamlessly against a wall. But a thin strip of molding is a fast and efficient fix. Sometimes you need a completely different approach, as when you're installing crown molding against a wavy wall. In this case, you build the wall out to meet the molding. It's not as difficult as it sounds.

If your check of the wall uncovers some small waves or bulges, you can sometimes tap them out of existence. Draw a light pencil line to identify the outer edge of the casing, and smack offending areas with a plywood block and hammer. Don't get carried away or you could whack the wall or jamb out of alignment.

If a mitered casing gaps away from the wall, pushing it would open the joint. Instead, gently insert a glued tapered shim at the top to prevent movement. Let the glue set, then trim the shim flush with a fine-tooth saw. With the casing supported, you can now caulk the joint.

To fit a cabinet's rail against a wall, applying a thin molding strip to the surface is much faster and far less dusty than scribing and cutting the rail. If you have a tablesaw, you can quickly slice the piece yourself. For safety, install a zero-clearance throatplate in the saw and utilize a featherboard and push blocks. No tablesaw? No problem. Simply purchase the strip.

WHAT IF...
A wavy wall leaves gaps?

Here's how to build out a wavy wall so that it meets the molding. Make the jig from a piece of scrap molding or ½-inch-thick plywood that's about 12 inches long. Cut a notch to match the molding and screed drywall compound along the jig and into the gap. If the wall is exceptionally wavy, lengthen the jig to taper the compound farther down the wall.

After you've exhausted all of the other tricks to disguise a less-than-perfect fit, reach for the painter's caulk. Buy a good-quality product, making absolutely certain that the label says "paintable."

FINISHING SECRETS

Carpenters know that a careless finishing job can ruin the appearance of the most careful work. On the other hand, a skillful finisher can substantially upgrade the look of less-than-perfect woodworking.

When you're personally responsible for a remodeling project, it pays to put your best efforts into all aspects of the work.

Choose your finish

For some styles of trimwork, paint is the correct choice. You'll also find that paint-grade moldings are significantly less expensive than stain-grade.

Another factor that recommends painted trimwork is the fact that the carpentry skills required are less demanding. You can fill gaps with a number of different products and the repair will be invisible under the final color coat.

On the other hand, the appearance of wood grain has powerful allure. Its richness and subtlety can glow through a carefully applied clear finish. The extra cost of materials and the additional work involved in crafting tight-fitting joints are quickly forgotten once you've completed a high-quality installation.

Don't skimp on prep work

While the beauty of a good finish is literally right on the surface, that final look is the result of careful preparation that goes down several layers.

After careful sanding, remove all dust with a tack cloth prior to staining, dyeing, or applying the first coat of primer. Lightly sand between coats of finish to remove nubs of dust that settled into the wet surface. Tack the surface before each coat, and keep your work area as clean as possible.

Filling the holes

Filling nail and screw holes may seem like an insignificant task, but doing it right—and at the right time—means the difference between blotches or near invisibility. First, you'll learn about the product options you have for both painted and clear-finished woodwork. Then you'll discover mixing and application secrets that will give you confidence and great results.

CHAPTER PREVIEW

After you've worked so hard on a project, make it shine with a great finishing job.

Clear finish or paint?
page 224

Stains and dyes
page 225

The clear truth about wood finishes
page 226

Paint
page 228

Painting walls and painting or finishing trimwork are the final steps in your project. Careful preparation and finishing give the job a professional look.

When to apply finish
page 230

Filling nail holes
page 231

CLEAR FINISH OR PAINT?

Choosing between a clear finish and paint may not sound like a difficult decision, but it can become a fairly complex process that balances personal preferences, historical accuracy, and economics.

Several factors influence the economic part of the equation. For example, if you choose a clear finish for the wood, you'll need to purchase stain-grade millwork, and that can be significantly more expensive than a paint-grade counterpart. One reason is that a piece of paint-grade millwork may be made from a number of finger-jointed short sections of wood, while stain-grade demands an uninterrupted length of defect-free lumber. Installation of clear-finished moldings also requires a greater investment of time to achieve tight-fitting joints. Some carpenters estimate that it takes two or three times longer to install clear-finished millwork because there is no good way to fill gaps. With painted woodwork, you simply pump in a little more painter's caulk.

A desire for historical accuracy also may guide your choice. Genuine Federal and Georgian-era millwork mostly were painted—often to disguise the mixture of wood species used to make the moldings. The distinctive grain pattern of quartersawn white oak was a favorite of the Arts and Crafts movement, but other homes from that era utilized painted trim to accentuate architectural form instead of grain patterns.

Finally, there's the matter of personal choice. If you want a Federal-style doorway in your living room but prefer clear-finished wood to coordinate with the trim in the rest of the house, then that's what you should choose.

Clear finishes require expensive stain-grade softwood or hardwood lumber, as shown on the left. Choose paint, and you can use economical paint-grade millwork, plastic moldings, and medium-density fiberboard.

Painted finishes can conceal, but clear finishes reveal. If you choose the clear route, you'll need to invest extra time to craft tight joints.

Whether you want to restore the original appearance of your home's millwork or transform new construction to a vintage look, it makes sense to pay attention to historical precedents, like this quarter-sawn oak Arts and Crafts example.

WHAT IF...
You can't prefinish the trim or wall?

Keeping stain off a freshly painted wall presents challenges, but if you know a simple trick, you can avoid the problem. Hang strips of waxed paper around the opening, then nail the moldings in place atop the paper. For a window, you'd apply the lower horizontal strip first, the legs next, and the top last. Masking the wall for baseboards could hardly be easier. When the finishing is complete, pull sideways on the waxed paper to remove the strips. If the strip tears, make a clean slice with a fresh blade in a utility knife.

STAINS AND DYES

Choosing the right tone for your millwork is a major decision because changing your mind involves a heavy price in both materials and labor. So it's worth the modest investment to make sample strips of the leading color candidates before making your final choice.

These samples should be more than skinny sticks dipped into a can of stain. Take actual pieces of your millwork (cutoffs work nicely), sanded to the same degree that your installed moldings will be, to the home center.

Use a permanent marker to identify each board with the stain that you're testing. Wipe on the stain, then apply the same number of clear coats that you'll brush on later. To make certain that you're judging the samples under the lighting conditions of the installation site, take the strips into that room. If you've already selected a wall color, go ahead and paint the room or at least make a good-sized swatch to help you visualize how the paint and stain colors influence each other. Don't make a snap decision. Instead, view the samples at different times over several days.

Oil stains are easy to use, but you may need a wood conditioner to prevent blotching, especially on softwoods, such as pine and fir. If you can't achieve the exact look you want with off-the-shelf colors, you can custom-mix a stain. Several cautions: Stir well to ensure consistent results, mix stains only of the same type and from the same manufacturer, and keep careful notes of precise measurements so you can duplicate the tone later.

Dyes are less likely than stains to produce blotching. If you use a dye that mixes with water, prepare the wood by wiping it with a barely damp cloth. Let it dry. Then, using 220-grit sandpaper, remove the whiskers of wood raised by the wetting before you proceed with the dye coat. You also can choose dyes that dissolve in denatured alcohol. Alcohol dries quickly—especially in hot weather—so make certain you allow enough working time to achieve smooth coverage. Whenever you work with solvents like alcohol, provide plenty of ventilation and exercise extreme caution to prevent fires.

Prepare samples with the same care that you'll use on finished moldings so that you can accurately preview the tones.

Using a prestain conditioner can help prevent oil-based stains from blotching your lumber, like the pine sample *above,* bottom piece. Follow label directions closely and ensure identical timing of the conditioner step for consistent results.

Dyes require careful mixing and have greater safety concerns, but they can produce rich clear tones that oil-based stains can't match.

THE CLEAR TRUTH ABOUT WOOD FINISHES

Many people believe that successful wood finishing has more to do with alchemy than chemistry. And taking a quick glance at the wide range of clear wood finishes, you may think it will take a miracle to help you choose the right one.

The ideal finish would combine fast and easy application; quick drying; simple touch-up and repair; complete resistance to moisture, solvents, and abrasion; and low cost. Unfortunately, there's no one finish that combines all these qualities. So choosing a finish involves trade-offs—you select the qualities that are most important to you and decide whether you can live with those you're forced to accept.

Familiarizing yourself with the major categories of finishes will help you narrow your search.

Varnish
Generally speaking, varnish is your best choice as a clear finish for interior woodwork. But selecting varnish involves further choices. Varnish is not a single finish; it's an entire family of products. And like any family, each member is distinctive.

Water-based varnish is environmentally friendly because it eliminates volatile solvents. It's easy to apply with a foam brush, but you have to be careful to minimize bubbles in the finish. (See "Stir gently to minimize bubbles", *below left*.) A water-based varnish doesn't yellow the wood as most solvent-based varnishes do.

A brush is the usual application method for solvent-based varnish. Choose a quality brush for best results. Synthetic bristles are sometimes adequate, but the best varnish brushes are always crafted from natural bristles. Although a high-quality varnish brush can give you a severe case of sticker shock, it's worth it. (Badger bristles are popular with many professional painters.) Cleaned promptly after each use, it will last for years.

Wipe-on varnishes range from thick gels to free-flowing liquids; the one you choose is largely a matter of personal preference. But whichever type you select, be sure to apply it with a lint-free cloth. Worn-out white cotton T-shirts are ideal. Beware of colored fabrics because they may impart a slight tint to your finish. Synthetic fabrics don't flow on the finish as evenly, giving streaky results.

Oil and oil/varnish blends
The so-called pure oil finishes don't contain dryers, so they may remain sticky or emit odors for an extended time. This category includes linseed oil, mineral oil, and tung oil.

But you'll also find a tung oil finish that's actually an oil/varnish blend that contains dryers. Other oil/varnish finishes are sometimes called penetrating oils, but don't confuse this term with the product that loosens rusty bolts. Some common brand names include Watco, Nordic Oil, and Danish Oil.

Applying either pure or blended oils is easy. Simply flood the surface with a liberal amount of product (a brush works fine), let it soak in, then wipe off the excess with soft cloths.

On the plus side, an oil finish offers some protection to the wood without building a surface film and is also easy to repair. On the negative side, oil finishes can require a long finishing schedule—over several days—which is the primary reason they're not often used on architectural woodwork.

To maintain a protective finish, recoat the oil annually.

Stir gently to minimize bubbles

Vigorous stirring whips air bubbles into the finish, which can cause a problem on your woodwork. If the tiny bubbles don't have time to pop and level out before the finish dries, they can impart a gritty feel to the surface.

The flattening agents in a semigloss finish may sink to the bottom of the can during long storage, so gently lift the paddle as you stir to put these tiny particles into suspension. A gloss finish doesn't have these fine grains, so stirring is barely needed.

STANLEY PRO TIP: **Freshness counts**

Even ready-mix finish has a shelf life—even if the can has never been opened. Old shellac thickens and polyurethane that's past its prime may refuse to dry. Chemists formulate water-based finishes so that the products can survive a few (but not an unlimited number of) freeze-thaw cycles during wintertime shipment. Summertime transport can subject finishes to extreme temperatures inside sealed trucks.

Check the container for an expiration date—a common sight on shellac containers. If the varnish cans at your local hardware store are covered with dust, go to a paint store that turns inventory more often.

Lacquer

Many professional finishers choose lacquer because it dries rapidly, which produces two important advantages: airborne dust has little time to settle on a wet surface, and, more importantly, the finisher can apply multiple coats within a single day. The latter enables you to work at your own pace instead of being delayed by drying times.

On the downside, lacquer requires a high-quality spray system that can be a substantial investment for occasional use.

For small-scale work, you can substitute aerosol cans. Wear a respirator to protect yourself from fumes during spray application. Effective ventilation is an absolute necessity because the vapors can be explosive. Unfortunately, lacquer finishes can fail when exposed to moisture or even excessive heat and humidity.

Shellac

Shellac shares lacquer's fast-drying advantage but isn't as durable. Alcohol and other solvents can turn a clear finish white—you may have seen telltale white rings on an antique. But shellac is still valuable as a sealer coat for wood and is compatible with most clear coats. (Check with the finish manufacturer or conduct your own test in an inconspicuous area.) Seal end grain with shellac to limit absorption of stain or other finishes. This even helps under paint.

Polyurethane varnishes

Oil finishes

Clear lacquers

Shellac

PAINT

Ceiling paint

Ceilings usually don't suffer from the contact that trimwork endures or the abrasion that walls sustain, but that doesn't mean that a ceiling is maintenance-free. Over time, cooking vapors, air pollution, and plain old dirt gradually make a ceiling dingy and dull. A fresh coat of paint makes a startling difference and will brighten a room.

If you have a drywall ceiling with spray-on texture (sometimes called popcorn), your builder most likely skipped the paint altogether. Unfortunately, if you try to roll latex paint onto that surface, the roller will remove blotches of texture. To avoid this problem, choose oil-based ceiling paint for roller application (you'll still need a light touch on the roller) or rent an airless sprayer to apply the latex.

Although most ceilings are plain white, you're not restricted to a "vanilla only" menu. Choosing a very pale blue tint gives the room a cooler appearance, while a touch of yellow warms the room. Some manufacturers boast 40-plus shades of white, so you should find something that fits your room.

A flat sheen is the usual choice for ceilings because it hides imperfections well. Choosing more reflective sheens draws more attention to the ceiling.

Wall paint

Many homebuilders specify wall paint with a flat sheen because it helps disguise drywall work that's less than perfect. But if you have an active family, you'll discover that flat paint quickly shows wear. Even mild surface abrasions can register as light streaks and attempts to clean away dirty marks often results in creating a larger smudge.

An eggshell sheen is more forgiving.

Because rollers grab the texture, an airless sprayer is the best solution to repainting this ceiling.

Don't restrict child's-room paint to the playroom or bedroom; it holds up well in bathrooms, hallways, and other high-traffic rooms.

Smooth rolling with paint additives

If brush marks on your painted projects bother you, consider a paint additive that improves flow-out without affecting the durability of the finish. One such product for oil-based finishes is Floetrol. Its companion product, Penetrol, works with water-based finishes.

These products also work well when you're rolling paint onto walls or ceilings. The improved paint consistency reduces spatters and the appearance of roller marks.

The label provides general guidelines for the amount of additive needed, which varies with the type of paint and the application temperature. It takes some experimenting to get the feel of these products.(See the Resource Guide on *page 236*.)

STANLEY PRO TIP

Box the paint

Whenever you buy two or more containers of paint, take a few minutes to mix them together in a larger container, such as a 5-gallon bucket. Doing so ensures a consistent color result throughout your project and is absolutely essential when you're dealing with custom-mixed colors. It's also a good idea with factory-mixed tints, as you may have purchased paint manufactured in different batches. Professional painters call this procedure "boxing the paint."

It produces a surface with substantially upgraded durability without introducing unwanted shine. As you add more reflectivity—such as with a semigloss surface—you'll accentuate waves, dings, and other imperfections in the wall.

Paint stores or home improvement centers have products that are formulated for maximum durability and ease of cleaning. These are sometimes marketed as a "child's-room paint," but they can be used in other demanding locations, such as a kitchen, bath, laundry room, or hallway.

Paint for woodwork

You've probably noticed that doors, windows, and moldings typically have a higher surface sheen than walls and may have wondered why. For one, their higher reflectivity generally means improved durability, which is essential on hardworking elements like doors and windows (because of more physical contact). For another, the difference in reflectivity accentuates the woodwork, creating interest and drawing attention to that part of the room's architecture. To create a noticeable difference in sheen, choose trim paint

that's at least one step glossier than the walls. For example, apply semigloss trim paint if your walls have an eggshell sheen.

An enamel formulation—whether latex or oil-based—often produces a smooth, hard-wearing surface.

Sheens

Four common paint sheens are flat, eggshell, semigloss, and gloss. Manufacturers may choose different names, so avoid surprises by checking actual samples before purchasing your paint.

Flat   Eggshell   Semigloss   Gloss

Latex vs. oil

In the early days of water-based paint chemistry, the quality of the coatings was often inconsistent. So professional painters weren't always sure they'd get a good batch. But nowadays, improved science and quality control enable manufacturers to produce water-based paints that virtually match the durability of oil-based paints.

But many paint professionals—both dealers and appliers—still feel that oil-based primers bond better with raw wood and that oil-based color coats outperform their water-based counterparts for durability, especially in demanding applications like trim and high-traffic rooms. Decide for yourself whether improved longevity is worth the inconvenience of solvent cleanup.

Do you really need a primer?

Many homeowners are in such a rush to complete a project that they skip the primer and go right to the color coats. But they often find that their shortcut backfires because it takes an extra coat of color to get complete coverage. And when they realize that primer is cheaper than finish coats, they discover that they've wasted both time and money.

Primer is specially formulated to bond to raw wood and to seal porous surfaces such as drywall. Primer typically dries rapidly so you get to the finish line sooner. So actually, a good primer saves time, effort, and money. Consider tinting your primer, which improves coverage. A paint store may even tint the primer at no charge.

WHEN TO APPLY FINISH

The answer to when to apply finish consists of two parts. The first deals with sequencing the finishing into the overall construction schedule. The second addresses weather conditions and the workplace environment.

For example, let's say you've remodeled a bedroom, including its ceiling and walls and the replacement of its doors and moldings. Your work now proceeds on two parallel tracks: You'll simultaneously paint the room and also apply the finish to the millwork before nailing it into place.

First, you'll give the ceiling and walls a coat of primer plus two color coats. While they dry you'll work on the moldings, applying stain (if desired) plus two or three coats of varnish. By the time you've completed the moldings, the room will be dry and ready for them.

You need to consider any extremes of temperature and humidity. If you attempt to apply a fast-drying finish (such as lacquer) during humid conditions, moisture can get trapped under the coating. In some cases, the wood will look slightly clouded; in others, the finish turns milky white. During cold weather, a finish may fail because it dried too slowly. In hot weather, it may dry too quickly.

Be sure the finishing site is as clean as possible. Walking on a dirty floor will raise dust that will settle into a wet finish. For ventilation, position a fan so that it moves air out of the room instead of blowing dust into the work area.

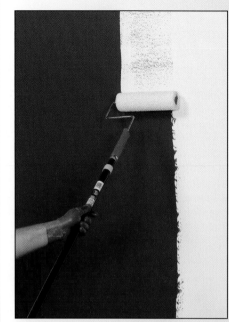

Paint the room's walls and ceilings before applying moldings. Choose a separate work area, if possible, to apply finish to the millwork.

A clean work area is a must for high-quality wood finishing. A fan should pull air and fumes out of the work area. After sweeping, be sure to let any airborne dust in the room settle for 30 minutes or more before painting.

Painter's caulk to the rescue

Painter's caulk provides astonishing results for your project. A small bead squeezed from a caulking gun can eliminate the unsightly line between moldings and wall. This technique also works well for both clear-finished and painted moldings. With the clear finish, however, you need to exercise extreme care so you don't smear it onto the woodwork. Strive to get an even line straight from the gun without having to wipe with your finger. Cutting the plastic tip of the caulk container at an angle improves the bead.

You also can purchase painter's caulk in a can, which is handy for filling any holes or working into tight areas with a putty knife. A close cousin to painter's caulk is a white-tinted putty.

FILLING NAIL HOLES

Painted finish

When you're working with a painted finish, you have a good deal of leeway on the timing of the filler. You can fill holes in raw wood or even after a color coat.

There are two general categories of fillers. One is a dry powder that you mix with water: Durham's Rock Hard Water Putty is one popular brand. The other—available in cans or tubes—is premixed with solvent such as Plastic Wood. Although the solvent-based product has a slight advantage in convenience, it costs considerably more than the powdered type. Evaporation during storage can solidify the unused solvent product, further boosting its expense. If kept dry, the powder form has exceptional longevity.

Applying both filler types is virtually identical. Pack every hole full, then leave a slight mound of extra material to compensate for shrinkage. When the material is dry (the powdered type dries more rapidly), lightly sand the surface to bring the filled hole flush with the surrounding wood. Proceed with the primer and color coats.

Clear finish

Filling holes in a painted finish introduces an additional complication—matching the color of the wood. Do not believe any advertising that claims a wood filler will accept stain and finish like genuine wood.

To see the true filler colors you'll need, first stain the raw wood, if desired, then apply the initial clear coat. Take a sample of the stained and coated wood to the paint store and purchase at least two shades of colored putty—one that approximates the deepest tone of the wood and one that's a close match for its lightest portion. When you get home, scoop out a chunk of each shade and knead them together, but leave the combination slightly streaky. Scoop out a ball of straight dark putty and one of the light putty. With these three, you now have a good palette of colors that will match nearly every tone of the wood.

Painted finish: Slightly overfill holes to allow for the filler's shrinkage. A sanding block will remove the excess while keeping the surface flat.

Clear finish: Buy light and dark putty, then mix the two together to create a medium tone. Rub some putty over a hole, pushing in to firmly seat the putty, then wipe off the excess with your finger (wear rubber gloves). Apply at least one more coat of finish to seal in the putty and give it a sheen that matches the surrounding wood.

Make your mark

Some stain manufacturers also package stain in a felt-tipped pen that makes touch-ups fast and easy. Use it at miters that are slightly misaligned or to eliminate the raw look from exposed cut ends. Choose a lighter tone for end grain because its absorption makes stain appear darker. Draw the marker across the wood, then buff it quickly with a paper towel. Keep the marker handy to minimize the appearance of surface scratches on woodwork.

STANLEY PRO TIP

Kitchen spatula smoothes putty

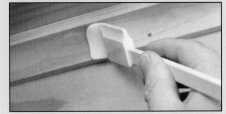

The usual putty-application procedure involves simply rubbing your finger over the hole. But if you've installed several rooms full of trim, you can easily rub your fingertip raw before completing the job. Also, your finger can slightly dip into the hole, creating a slight depression. Use an ordinary kitchen spatula as a solution. It's firm enough to wipe away excess putty and leave a smooth surface. It also conforms to curved surfaces, speeding your work.

GLOSSARY

5/4 stock: Lumber that is surfaced to a lumberyard dimension of approximately 1 to 1¹⁄₁₆ inches thick. This designation, pronounced five-quarter, refers to number of quarter inches of lumber thicknesses prior to drying and milling.

Apex: The uppermost point; also the point of an angle.

Apron: The bottom piece of window casing that finishes the window frame beneath the sill (stool). In better-quality work, the ends of the apron have returned ends to conceal the end grain.

Awning: A type of window that opens with its bottom end pivoting outward. (See also *Casement* and *Hopper.*)

Back cut: The removal of stock along the rear surface of a piece of molding to make it more dimensionally stable and to reduce the amount of contact area between wood and wall that could put the molding out of alignment. Also referred to as a relief cut, the back cut is an angled cut, such as in a coped joint, that removes stock that could interfere with the fit.

Backsaw: A saw designed for precision cutting, as in a manual miter box. The saw gets its name from a stiffening rib of metal along the top (back) edge of the blade.

Baseboard: Trim running along the bottom of a wall to cover gaps between the wall and floor and to protect the wall. (See also *Base shoe* and *Cap molding.*)

Base cap: A piece of molding that covers the top of the traditional baseboard.

Base shoe: A narrow, flexible piece of molding that covers the joint between baseboard and floor. Sometimes called shoe molding.

Bearing wall: A wall that carries a portion of the weight of the building above it.

Bedding edges: The portion of a sprung molding, such as a crown molding, that makes contact with architectural surfaces such as a wall and ceiling.

Bifold door: A door that folds in half lengthwise as it opens. Often used in pairs as closet doors.

Biscuit/biscuit joiner: The joiner, also called a plate jointer, is a tool that cuts oval-shaped slots in wood for the insertion of wood tenons (referred to as biscuits) that are glued into a pair of matching slots to join an assembly.

Blocking: Pieces of lumber that are nailed horizontally between wall studs to serve as anchor points for molding or cabinetry. Blocking also is installed between floor joists to stiffen the floor or to provide a nailing surface for the top of a partition wall.

Bookmatched: A pattern of veneer produced by laying down the individual sheets sliced from the log, a procedure similar to turning the pages of a book. Bookmatched veneer on plywood, for example, shows a mirror image of the grain pattern on both sides of the joint line.

Bow: A warp in a board along its length when viewed along its narrow dimension.

Butt joint: A joint where ends of two square-cut adjoining pieces are placed against each other. The pieces can be butted end to end to extend a piece of molding. Or, if turning a corner, the end of one piece can butt into the side of the other.

Bypass doors: Doors that slide past each other—often used for closets. Bypass doors need no swing room to open. However, only half of the closet is accessible at a time.

Cap molding: A molding made to top the edge of another material as a finishing treatment; for example, molding applied to the top edge of wainscoting.

Casement: A type of window that swings outward, pivoting from its top and bottom, when a crank is turned. (Also see *Awning* and *Hopper.*)

Casing: Trim that surrounds a door or window opening.

Centerline: A line that is an equal distance from two edges or ends. In biscuit joinery, for example, the slot is often cut at the centerline of a rail.

Chair rail: Trim running across a wall approximately midway between the ceiling and the floor. Although often used for decorative purposes, chair rail is designed to protect the wall from chairs, particularly in dining rooms.

Chamfer: An angled cut used as a decorative treatment along the edges of solid lumber. It is defined by the height of the cut and its angle, for example, a ¹⁄₈-inch×45-degree chamfer.

Check: A crack in a board that may be the result of damage incurred while the tree was alive or the result of improper felling techniques or drying procedures.

Circuit breaker: A protective device in a service panel that automatically shuts off power to its circuit when it senses a short or circuit overload.

Coffered: A type of ceiling construction consisting of one or more stepped surfaces.

Compound mitersaw: A tool that makes cuts that are simultaneously beveled and mitered on stock that is held flat against the worktable. A compound mitersaw with a sliding head (to increase cutting capacity) is helpful when installing crown molding.

Coped joint: A joint between two pieces of molding where the end of one piece is cut to accommodate the profile of the other. Usually used for inside corners.

Coping saw: A saw with a thin blade in a C-shape frame. It readily cuts curves and is most often used for making coped joints.

Corner bead: A plastic or metal molding that is attached to outside drywall corners to make them easier to finish and to protect them from damage.

Corner block: A piece of wood utilized between two runs of molding (at the corner of door or window casing, for example) for decorative effect or to eliminate the necessity of mitered cuts. When used at the inside corner of a run of baseboard or crown molding, a corner block can eliminate coped cuts.

Cornice: A molding treatment at the junction between walls and ceiling. Cornice also refers to a structure on top of a window treatment that conceals drapery hardware.

Cove: A type of molding that has a dished (concave) profile. Also the design of a router bit that's used to make a cut of this shape.

Cripple stud: A short stud. Most typically used above door openings in nonbearing walls and below window openings.

Crook: A warp in a board along its length when viewed along its wide dimension.

Crosscut: To cut a board to length across its width.

Cross-legged: The condition in which the walls on either side of a door opening are not in the same plane.

Crown molding: The molding, sometimes simply called crown, installed where a wall meets the ceiling.

Cup: A warp in a board across its width. In an end view, the defect has a dished appearance.

Dado: A flat-bottomed groove cut across the grain direction of a board. (See *Groove*.)

Deadman: A T-shape brace used to help hold drywall in place against ceiling joists while the drywall is fastened in place.

Dimension lumber: Lumber that is 2 to 5 inches in nominal thickness and up to 12 inches in nominal width.

Door strike: The metal hardware attached to the door frame that receives the bolt from the lockset. Also called a strike plate.

Drywall: A sheet product made for use as a wall surface, consisting of paper faces covering a core of gypsum.

Edge banding: Wood applied to the edges and ends of plywood to conceal its laminated construction. It may be as thin as iron-on veneer or a thicker section of solid wood. It is usually the same species of wood as the panel, but it may be different to achieve a decorative effect.

Fire-stop: A piece of wood nailed across a stud bay to prevent the bay from acting as a chimney and spreading a fire.

Flute: A coved cut usually made in parallel multiples. Fluting is frequently employed as a decorative element in columns and vertical casing members.

Framing: The structure of a house. It encompasses all the wooden parts of a house frame including the wall studs, headers, joists, rafters, and such.

Furring strips: Strips of wood, often made from 1×2s or 1×3s, attached to a surface as spacers/anchor points for an additional wall surface. Basement walls often have furring strips added to provide a means of attaching drywall.

Golden Section: A ratio equal to approximately 1:1.618 and often considered a pleasing proportion. A rectangle with sides that conform to this proportion is called a Golden Rectangle.

Groove: A cut, usually rectangular in section, made in a direction parallel to the grain of solid wood or parallel to the face veneer of a piece of plywood. (See *Dado*.)

Header: The part of a house frame that spans a door or window opening. Often made from two pieces of 2× lumber with a spacer of ½-inch plywood. Also, any piece of wood (such as trim) that spans the top of an opening.

Headless pinner: A pneumatic tool that drives small-gauge fasteners with a constant diameter along their length. The tool is generally employed with small moldings because the fastener leaves only a tiny hole to be filled.

Hinge mortise: A recessed area cut into the edge of a door and its frame to accommodate hinge leaves.

Hopper: A type of window that opens as its top end pivots inward. (Also see *Awning* and *Casement*.)

J-bead: A molding made to cover the edge of a drywall sheet so the raw edge does not show in the finished installation.

Jack stud: One part of the pairs of studs that make up a door or window opening. The jack studs are cut to match the height of the opening. The header for the opening rests on top of the jack studs. Sometimes called a trimmer. (Also see *King stud*.)

Jamb: The wooden frame that lines a door or window opening. In both applications, the top horizontal jamb is called the head. In door jambs, the vertical members are referred to as legs.

Joint compound: Often called mud, this thick-bodied substance fills holes and seams in drywall. It may be a premixed variety or the powdered setting-type formulation that's mixed with water.

Joist: A horizontal part of a house frame that carries floor and/or ceiling.

GLOSSARY *(continued)*

King stud: One part of the pairs of studs that make up a door or window opening. The king studs are cut to the same length as the other wall studs. Jack studs are nailed to king studs.

Lath: Thin strips of wood applied to a wall surface to serve as a substrate for plaster. More recent plasterwork often uses an expanded metal mesh as lath.

Lauan: A tropical hardwood that is often cut into veneers to cover hollow-core doors and plywood. Sometimes called Philippine mahogany, although it's not a true member of the mahogany family.

Leg: A side jamb, particularly referring to the framing of a door.

Level: Perfectly horizontal with no part higher or lower than another. Also, a tool used to measure this condition.

Light: The glass of a window or door, particularly when there are a number of small panes, referred to as a divided light.

Lockset: The hardware used for keeping a door closed, usually consisting of doorknobs, lock, bolt, and strike plate.

MDF: Medium-density fiberboard, a manufactured panel composed of fine wood fibers held together with a bonding agent. MDF panels have a smooth surface that accepts a painted finish well.

MDO: Medium-density overlay, an exterior plywood panel topped with a smooth paper face that conceals the wood grain. Because of its excellent painting surface, it is often used for signage.

Millwork: A broad category of wood items that have been cut, shaped, and sometimes assembled into specific products ranging from moldings to doors and windows.

Miter: A corner joint between two pieces of wood where the adjoining ends are cut at matching angles. Also, the process of cutting these angles.

Miter box: A device that guides a saw for the production of accurate crosscuts in lumber and molding. The cuts may be straight across or at an angle, and the device may be manual or motorized.

Molding: Strips of millwork, usually with a decorative profile. Sometimes spelled in the Anglicized form as *moulding*.

Mud: In the construction business, any of a number of wet materials that harden as they dry (such as mortar). In interior work, mud usually refers to the joint compound used to fill holes and joints in drywall.

Mullion: A vertical element in the construction of a door or window that is not one of the full-length stiles at the edges of the assembly.

Nail pops: Places in finished drywall where a nail has begun to back out of the stud (or was never completely driven home). They appear as small circular lumps on the wall surface.

Open time: The time during which pieces with applied adhesive can be easily repositioned.

PSA: Pressure-sensitive adhesive, a description of the backing utilized on some sandpapers and veneers.

Partition wall: A wall with the sole purpose of dividing a space—it does not help support the weight of the building.

Penny: Commonly used term for describing the length of nails, abbreviated as "d." The larger the penny number, the longer the nail.

Picture-hanger molding: A style of decorative millwork applied to the walls of a room near the ceiling. Designed to accept hooks for hanging framed pictures without putting nails in a wall.

Plate: A horizontal piece of lumber to which wall studs are attached. The bottom plate is anchored to the floor. The top plate is usually a double thickness to tie walls together and help carry the load from above.

Plate joiner: A biscuit joiner. (See *Biscuit/biscuit joiner*.)

Plinth: The base of a column or the bottom element in a molding construction. Pieces of wood that serve as a transition between vertical and horizontal elements are usually called plinth blocks.

Plumb: Perfectly vertical. This can be judged by using a level that's held in a vertical position or by using a plumb bob.

Plywood: A sheet product made from thin layers of wood (veneers) stacked and glued together (laminated). Generally available in 4×8 sheets. The composition of the adhesive determines whether the sheet is rated for interior or exterior application.

Pneumatic: Powered by air, usually via a compressor. Common pneumatic tools include nail and brad guns as well as headless pinners.

Precuts: Studs purchased already cut to length for an 8-foot ceiling (92⅝ inches), allowing for a single bottom plate and a double top plate.

Prehung door: A door that is purchased already hinged and hanging within a completed doorjamb.

Protractor: A device for measuring the angle between two surfaces.

Rail: A horizontal member, such as in the construction of a door or the face frame of a cabinet. The vertical members are stiles.

Relief cut: See *Back cut*.

Return: When used with regard to trim, a piece of molding which completes a run by turning into the wall.

Reveal: A narrow flat area on a molding or board left uncovered for visual effect. It may be used to create a shadow line or simply to eliminate the work required to achieve a perfectly flush edge.

Ringshank: A nail with annular ridges around the shaft designed to increase its pullout resistance. This is an effective design for drywall nails.

Rip: To cut a board along its length to achieve needed width. Rip cuts are most easily accomplished with a tablesaw.

Roughing-in: The process of installing the first stages of utilities such as plumbing and electrical wiring. This usually involves running the pipes and wiring that will be hidden inside the walls. The finish work (installing the various fixtures) is done after the walls are in place.

Rough opening: The opening in the framing made for a door or window.

Sash: The frame of a window surrounding the glass.

Scarf joint: A joint used to extend the length of a board or piece of trim. Usually the pieces are cut with mating angles to help disguise the juncture.

Scribe: The process of making an item, such as a shelf or countertop, conform to the irregularities of another surface—such as a wall—in order to achieve a fit without gaps.

Shim: A strip of wood, usually tapered, employed as a filler to create a solid surface between two elements. For example, pairs of tapered softwood shims take up the space between a doorjamb and the rough framing of an opening so that the two can be joined solidly.

Sill: The bottom horizontal member of a window assembly, it slopes outward from the house to shed water. At the interior of the house, the sill is usually capped by a trim piece called a stool.

Snapping a line: A term used to describe the process of marking a layout line with a chalk line, which is held taut between two points and plucked so it snaps against the surface. This action transfers chalk from the line to the surface.

Spirit level: A device with a nonfreezing fluid in a vial to indicate plumb and level. Most levels utilized as tools are spirit levels. Other types include the water level, which is particularly useful in large-scale construction applications, and laser levels.

Spring angle: A pair of angles that describes the placement of a piece of millwork, such as crown molding, between two surfaces, such as a ceiling and wall. Crown molding with a spring angle of 52/38 is the most common, although some varieties of crown are 45/45. The first number indicates the angle between the back of the molding and the ceiling, and the second describes the angle between the back of the molding and the wall.

Stile: A vertical member, such as in the construction of a door or the face frame of a cabinet. The horizontal members are rails.

Stool: A horizontal piece of trim installed at the bottom of a window, often mistakenly called the sill.

Stop: A narrow strip of wood installed inside a doorjamb that keeps the door from swinging too far closed.

Stop block: A piece of wood or metal utilized in conjunction with machine setups. A stop block registers a series of blanks in identical position in order to produce identical parts.

Stud: The vertical members of a house frame. Often made from 2×4s or 2×6s.

Stud bay: The space between two studs making up a wall.

Subfloor: The first decking applied on top of the floor joists and usually made from plywood. The finished floor, such as hardwood strips or carpet, is attached to the subfloor.

Tack cloth: A piece of fabric, usually of cheesecloth construction, with a tacky surface that removes dust and other contaminants from a surface prior to the application of a finish, in order to achieve a smooth result.

Toenailing: Driving a nail at an angle through one framing member into a second framing surface. Toenailing is often done with a pair of nails driven at opposing angles to achieve an interlocking effect.

Trim-head screw: A design of screw with an extremely small head, making it a useful fastener for attaching moldings while producing a minimal hole to be filled.

Twist: A warp in a board along its length, similar to that of an airplane propeller.

Veneer: A thin layer of wood sliced or sawn from a log. Veneer is used to maximize the surface area produced by valuable timber species. Hardwood plywood, for example, consists of a thin application of premium veneer on top of layers of lesser-quality material. Veneer with a backing of pressure-sensitive adhesive is used in applications such as refacing kitchen cabinets.

Wainscoting: Wooden paneling applied to a wall. Traditionally wainscoting was made up of a series of frame and panel units, although today the term is used to describe almost any wooden paneling, particularly that which reaches only partway up a wall.

Wane: A defect in lumber consisting of an irregular edge that was once the outer surface. It may or may not show bark.

Warp: A surface that is not true or flat. Warp is any combination of bow, crook, cup, and/or twist.

RESOURCE GUIDE

Andersen
9900 Jamaica Ave. S
Cottage Grove, MN 55016
877-773-6392
www.renewalbyandersen.com
Manufacturer of new and replacement windows

Bartley Collection Ltd.
65 Engerman Ave.
Denton, MD 21629
800-787-2800
www.bartleycollection.com
Manufacturer of gel stains and finishing supplies

Dixie-Pacific
800-468-5993
www.schlage.com (click on Consumer)
Manufacturer of fiberglass columns

Ferche Millwork
P.O. Box 39
Rice, MN 56367
320-393-5700
www.ferche.com
Distributor of a wide range of moldings; specializes in hardwood millwork

The Flood Company
P.O. Box 2535
Hudson, OH 44263
800-321-3444
www.floodco.com
Manufacturer of wood finishes and additives, including Floetrol and Penetrol

Focal Point Architectural Products
3006 Anaconda Dr.
Tarboro, NC 27886
800-662-5550
www.focalpointap.com
Manufacturer of plastic crown moldings and blocks, wall niches, and other architectural items

Franklin International
2020 Bruck St.
Columbus, OH 43207
800-669-4583
www.titebond.com
Manufacturer of adhesives and caulks

General Finishes
P.O. Box 510567
New Berlin, WI 53151
800-783-6050
www.generalfinishes.com
Manufacturer of wood finishing products

Macco Adhesives
925 Euclid Ave.
Cleveland, OH 44115
800-634-0015
www.liquidnails.com
Manufacturer of construction adhesives

Marvin Windows and Doors
P.O. Box 100
Warroad, MN 56763
888-537-7828
www.marvin.com
Manufacturer of new and replacement windows and doors

Maze Nails
P.O. Box 449
Peru, IL 61354
800-435-5949
www.mazenails.com
Manufacturer of a wide variety of nails

McFeely's Square Drive Screws
1620 Wythe Rd., P.O. Box 11169
Lynchburg, VA 24506
800-443-7937
www.mcfeelys.com
Manufacturer of screws, including specialty and hard-to-find varieties

Minwax Company
10 Mountainview Rd.
Upper Saddle River, NJ 07458
800-523-9299
www.minwax.com
Manufacturer of stains and wood finishes

Ornamental Mouldings
3804 Comanche Rd., P.O. Box 4068
Archdale, NC 27263
800-779-1135
www.ornamental.com
Manufacturer of solid-wood moldings, corner blocks, rosettes, and similar items

Quint Measuring Systems
P.O. Box 280
San Ramon, CA 94583
800-745-5045
www.compoundmiter.com
Manufacturer of protractors, squares, and templates to measure angles for molding installation

Renovator's Supply
800-659-2211
www.rensup.com
Distributor of a wide range of materials, including wall niches and moldings

Rockler Woodworking and Hardware
4365 Willow Dr.
Medina, MN 55340
800-279-4441
www.rockler.com
Distributor of a comprehensive line of woodworking tools and supplies, including doors, drawers, veneers, and hardware for kitchen refacing

Stanley Tools Product Group
480 Myrtle St.
New Britain, CT 06053
800-262-2161
www.stanleyworks.com
Manufacturer of a wide range of hand and power tools, including Bostitch pneumatic tools

Superior Art Glass Studios
4311 SW. Ninth St.
Des Moines, IA 50315
515-282-4106
Glass supplier and custom fabricator

Wood Moulding & Millwork Producers Association
507 First St.
Woodland, CA 95695
800-550-7889/530-661-9586
www.wmmpa.com
Trade organization for manufacturers and distributors of wood moldings

INDEX